CONNING HARVARD

CONNING HARVARD

Adam Wheeler, the Con Artist Who Faked
His Way into the Ivy League

JULIE ZAUZMER

With additional reporting by Xi Yu

LYONS PRESS
Guilford, Connecticut
An imprint of Globe Pequot Press

Dedicated to all those who uphold Harvard's standards

Lyons Press is an imprint of Globe Pequot Press.

Some of the reporting and research for this book was funded by and conducted for *The Harvard Crimson*. Such materials are used here with permission.

Project editor: Meredith Dias
Layout: Mary Ballachino

Library of Congress Cataloging-in-Publication Data

Zauzmer, Julie.
   Conning Harvard : Adam Wheeler, the con artist who faked his way into the Ivy League / Julie Zauzmer ; with additional reporting by Xi Yu.
      p. cm.
   Summary: "Conning Harvard tells the story of Adam Wheeler's lie-filled path into Harvard, his compulsive conning of grant and scholarship boards after enrolling, and the eventual discovery of his fraudulent past"— Provided by publisher.
   ISBN 978-0-7627-8002-0 (hardback)
   1. Cheating (Education)—United States. 2. Wheeler, Adam (Adam B.) 3. Harvard University—Students. 4. Harvard University—Funds and scholarships. 5. Swindlers and swindling—United States. I. Yu, Xi. II. Title.
   LB3609.Z38 2012
   378.1'98—dc23

2012018145

Printed in the United States of America

10 9 8 7 6 5 4 3 2 1

Contents

To indicate as explicitly as possible the instances where the author could not know the exact words spoken by the participants in this story, some dialogue in this book appears without quotation marks. That dialogue should be read as the author's effort, based on statements made by one or more participants in each conversation, to reconstruct actual conversations in the manner most faithful to the likely words exchanged between the speakers.

INTRODUCTION

This book chronicles an academic fraud of stunning proportions. Over a period of six years, Adam B. Wheeler tricked the smartest institutions in the country time and time again. He plagiarized application essays to get into one of the country's best liberal arts colleges. He stole a Pulitzer Prize winner's work to win a poetry prize. Then he took on Harvard University—the world's most recognized institution of higher education, whose very name has meant prestige, privilege, excellence, and exclusivity for centuries.

Adam Wheeler was an expert forger and a skillful liar with seemingly few scruples about fabricating his academic credentials whenever the occasion arose. In snagging admission to Harvard, he unfairly attained an honor that millions of students worldwide dream of. In striving to scam institutions at the pinnacle of higher education—Yale, Brown, Stanford, the Rhodes and Fulbright scholarships, and more—he astonished the nation with the story of his audacity. Many were outraged that he took a precious spot at Harvard that could have gone to an honest applicant, not to mention thousands of dollars in prizes that selection committees could have bestowed on deserving young scholars. Others were impressed by his skillful cons or even smugly amused to see Harvard outsmarted for once.

But whether one perceives him as the hero or the villain of his tale, this ultimately is not about Adam Wheeler. His fraudulent path is extraordinary, but on its own, his story is unimportant.

What is important is that high school students today face unprecedented pressure when it comes to college admissions. What is important is that as many as 14 percent of essays are plagiarized, 50 percent of transcripts are faked, and 90 percent of recommendation letters are forged among some groups of college applicants. What is important is that a generation of teenagers, raised in an educational system that emphasizes standardized testing and in an age of abundant technological options for untruthfulness, cheats on tests and homework with shocking frequency. As the pressure to win an ever-more-elusive ticket to a top-tier college ratchets higher each year, college admissions could be facing a crisis of honesty.

Far more than a victimless hoax, deception on an application is a violation of ethical and often legal precepts that affects the larger community. In the absence of integrity, a diploma is a meaningless piece of paper on the wall, a mockery of true intellectual achievement. To anyone who has ever been tempted to inflate some details on a résumé, to scribble answers on his hand or peek over her classmate's shoulder, to pass off writing downloaded from the Internet as original, or to ink in a plus next to a grade on a transcript—this book is a cautionary tale.

PROLOGUE

In the fall of 2009, life seemed to be going great for Harvard senior Adam Wheeler. His friends knew him as a lanky 21-year-old with muscles that showed his near-obsessive hours at the gym, a tall frame that made heads turn, and penetratingly blue eyes that drew women to him at parties. He was respected among his classmates as an academic all-star, working diligently for five or even six classes at a time on a campus where the norm was four. He had won awed recognition from his peers for the rare feat of winning Harvard's top writing prize as a junior.

Though quiet, he was part of a large circle of friends who threw parties and played video games in their spacious suite. He had a steady girlfriend, an attractive Wellesley undergrad whom he had met the previous spring. He could frequently be found tossing a Frisbee across the courtyard of his dorm, Kirkland House.

To all appearances, Wheeler was in an enviable position. He was not only respected and well-liked among his peers, but also in a spot that students around the world pine for. He was a Harvard student, part of the minuscule percentage of applicants accepted each year. And in that rarified world of Harvard, Wheeler had essentially reached his peak. As his senior year started, he was on top of his game.

But one fall day in 2009, Wheeler was not playing Frisbee in Kirkland courtyard. Rather, he was indoors, sitting formally in an office, and the flawless identity he had built was about to come crashing down.

He did not know why the dean of Kirkland House had called him into his office, but a summons from the resident dean typically was not a good omen.

It was about his applications for the Rhodes and Fulbright scholarships, Dean Smith said. These were two of the most prestigious awards a graduating senior could win. Based on the strength of his application materials, Wheeler had a good shot at getting Harvard's recommendation for one or both of them.

But what Dean David Smith said now was not, Congratulations. Instead, it was, You plagiarized your essay.

Wheeler froze. "I must have made a mistake," he said. "I didn't really plagiarize it."

Smith picked up two items and offered them to Wheeler. One was a copy of the essay Wheeler knew he had recently submitted to the judging committees, and the other was a crimson-colored book.

Smith had opened the book to a certain page. Centered at the top in capital letters, it said, "By STEPHEN GREENBLATT." Wheeler knew the name: Greenblatt was his English professor from sophomore year, not to mention one of the world's most famous Shakespeare experts. Then he glanced at the other piece of paper, his own essay.

The text is almost identical, Smith pointed out.

He started telling Wheeler about what would come next: a meeting with another dean. A hearing before the college's disciplinary board. Intimidating procedures. He was invited.

Wheeler had no intention of showing up.

CHAPTER ONE

It is hard to get into Harvard nowadays.

All right, fine. It has always been hard to get into Harvard. Back when the college was founded in 1636 (a good 140 years before the United States declared independence), Harvard students had to be white, male, wealthy enough to pay tuition, and able to read the Bible in Latin and Greek. Over the decades, those requirements dropped away one by one. But while Harvard became more egalitarian, it never became less exclusive.

Today's applicants are judged on a set of criteria that the colonial founders of Harvard could never have imagined: standardized test scores. High school grades. Extracurricular activities. Evaluative interviews with alumni. Letters of recommendation. Videos of students' opera performances and CDs of the concertos they wrote. Personal statements about their world travels or scientific breakthroughs or athletic feats or dramatic rises out of any number of adverse childhood circumstances. The staff of Harvard's admissions office considers all of these factors in order to select the brilliant scholars, the talented artists, the standout athletes, and the all-of-the-aboves who will make up each new class. Those who make the cut are a staggeringly lucky bunch. During the most recent cycle, just 5.9 percent of more than 30,000 applicants were admitted to the Class of 2016.

None of this is unique to Harvard, of course. Several colleges across the United States post acceptance rates of 20 percent or lower. Hundreds of them follow the same philosophy of evaluating applicants as holistically as possible—judging not just grades and test scores but also extracurricular activities, community service, family background, and character. Students who want to be admitted know that earning a 4.0 GPA or a perfect SAT score is not enough. After enthusiastically pursuing their favorite activities throughout high school, they must tell their stories of passion and perseverance in essays and interviews.

Increased federal financial aid, a shifting view of higher education as necessary rather than optional, and the removal of racial and gender barriers have brought the benefits of a college education to a vastly larger swath of the population in recent decades. Flooded by more applications than ever before, many of America's institutions of higher education have responded in venerable fashion by crafting highly personalized admissions systems. Today, these elite schools' application processes, along with the wide-reaching financial aid that backs up the egalitarian acceptances, give any student a chance at the best education the world can offer. Regardless of race, religion, nationality, hometown, school, or socioeconomic status, all teenagers receive equal consideration from the admissions committees of the nation's top institutions.

That is truly remarkable. And the communities that are formed as a result of this stunningly complicated and surprisingly compassionate process are more remarkable still. Home to such carefully selected assortments of diverse students and professors, colleges are abuzz with creative achievement in every field. Scientists on the cutting edge of lifesaving research, up-and-coming political giants, virtuoso composers and performers, and blockbuster actors all produce valuable work at these centers of learning and emerge from their educations to conquer the world at large.

Teenagers worldwide ardently desire to join these high-powered campus communities. They apply in droves, from more parts of the world and the socioeconomic spectrum every year. As the number of college-bound students continues to climb higher, though, students' anxiety intensifies too. As colleges across the country receive more applications, their acceptance rates in turn decrease. Students at all academic strata find that even their so-called safety schools have become harder to get into. And so they hedge their bets by sending out more applications to more colleges, sometimes as many as 15 or 20. Colleges, swamped with applications for a finite number of spots, then accept an even smaller portion of the students who apply. The next year's acceptance rates come out, and once again, they are lower than before. And that is how hysteria starts to mount.

Added to this rat race is the fact that some students are being groomed from childhood for the college admissions process by parents and educators who want them not just to go to college but to go to the right college. In some parts of the country, such as New York City, some parents are known to search for the select preschool that will lead their progeny to the right elementary and secondary schools in order to eventually reach the Ivy League. (Those preschools observe the pint-size applicants as they play with blocks to glean evidence of whether they are worthy of admission.) Some children are shuttled to after-school clarinet lessons and fencing practices in the hopes that they will discover a latent talent that will impress admissions officers later on. Some are offered monetary rewards for bringing home straight-A report cards in elementary school or grounded for getting a B in high school. Some parents pay college tuition prices to send their children to private secondary schools, with the expectation that they are buying them tickets to top-tier colleges down the line. Those students, certainly, are prone to feeling overwhelmed by great expectations.

Students spend their high school years taking standardized tests called by all sorts of acronyms—APs and the ACT and the dread SAT, which, after decades of terrorizing youngsters as the Scholastic Aptitude Test and then as the Scholastic Assessment Test, announced back in 1994 that the acronym did not stand for anything at all. Those three letters in and of themselves have long been enough to instill fear in students' hearts and number-two-pencil-induced cramps in their hands.

Cheating is alarmingly pervasive among high school test-takers. In a 2010 survey of more than 40,000 high school students, 80 percent said that they had copied someone else's homework, and 59 percent said that they had cheated on a test in the previous year. Moreover, 25 percent said at the end that they lied on that very survey. Another survey found that more than 90 percent of students had cheated in school in one way or another. Their methods of dishonesty on standardized exams as well as classroom quizzes and homework assignments have expanded with the explosion in technology. More than half the teenagers in yet another study said that they had used the Internet to cheat, and more than a third of those who owned cell phones said that they had used their phones to cheat, whether by looking up answers, snapping photos of test pages, or texting questions to their friends. About a fifth of the teen population did not even believe that those behaviors constituted cheating.

Concerned educators blame the increase in cheating on the intensified emphasis that schools place on test performance and educational credentials. The attention that even the legions of upright students devote to the college application process reflects this atmosphere. At high school lunch tables, students discuss their college visits and upcoming interviews ad nauseam. Rumors fly about that classmate who seemed to have it all—flawless grades, a perfect SAT score, and a performance at Carnegie Hall—and still got rejected by Columbia. With the advent of online forums for communal hand-wringing over every detail of the college admissions process, most notably the highly trafficked College Confidential, this fretting is more public nowadays than it has ever been.

As students worry over every hundredth of a point in their GPAs and every question on their practice SAT exams, the same anxious cry echoes through America's high schools: "I'm not going to get into college!"

The public school in Delaware where our story begins was no exception to this nationwide phenomenon. To be sure, Caesar Rodney High School had never been the most competitive. From time to time, graduates went on to Ivy League schools, but more often than not, they attended the University of Delaware, an hour to the north of the high school, or Delaware State University, just six miles away, or any number of fine community colleges and other schools. Many college recruiters visited the school each year to make presentations that all sounded somewhat alike. The representative would tell interested students about the dozens of majors they could pursue, the quality of the food in the dining hall, the opportunities to study abroad, the success that graduates achieve in the real world. Then the students would raise their hands to ask, inevitably, about how to get in. Do grades from senior year matter? How many SAT Subject Tests are required? Is there an early decision option?

The recruiters being peppered with questions at Caesar Rodney High School were not typically from top-tier colleges; in fact, in one recent year, not a single visitor came from a school that Caesar Rodney classified in the most competitive category (colleges that would expect an SAT score of at least 1800 out of 2400). From the tier below that, Caesar Rodney drew one—the University of Richmond.

Caesar Rodney High School enrolled almost 1,800 students in 2005. Every year, about 75 to 90 percent of the seniors graduate, though the school failed to meet the national standard for Adequate Yearly Progress for a couple of years and its students' average SAT score usually landed 70 to 90 points shy of the national average. The school offered opportunities for motivated students to enroll in Advanced Placement (or AP) courses. Available to students nationwide, AP classes follow curricula set by the College Board and culminate at the end of the school year with exams administered by the Board. Students who score well on the exams can sometimes receive college credit for their work, because those classes are meant to be equivalent to college courses. In addition to the AP programs, Caesar Rodney also listed courses such as architecture; audio, radio, and video engineering; landscape and turf management; agribusiness; and more.

And though Ivy League applications coming out of Caesar Rodney are rare, Superintendent Kevin Fitzgerald said that most students find that the preparation they received there suits them well, whatever their goals. "We just want to provide our students with different opportunities," he said. "The background that they receive allows them to compete."

One student trying to compete—in Caesar Rodney High School and in the bigger realm of college admissions—was Adam Wheeler.

Wheeler lived outside of the district in a more rural part of the state, but he chose to attend Caesar Rodney because his father worked there, as a technology education teacher. Wheeler came to school each morning with his father and usually ate lunch in his dad's classroom rather than in the cafeteria. He even took his dad's classes three times during his high school career. (His dad gave him a 97, 98, and 95.)

In his other classes, he did well too. He maintained an A average through his junior year, though just barely, making him eligible for the school's National Honor Society chapter. He had a reputation among teachers and administrators as a strong writer, and he expressed interest in great literature. He even enjoyed the chance to see the places where much of his favorite literature originated on a school trip to England.

Wheeler was not at the very top of the class, but he was in the top 10 percent. That crowd all took AP and honors classes and focused more competitively when it came to college applications, according to Fitzgerald. Serving as the high school principal at the time, Fitzgerald recognized Wheeler as part of that upper set, but he did not think Wheeler had quite the same edge. "I didn't see that competitive streak in him," Fitzgerald said. "He seemed like a more laid-back young man."

He added, "He did not appear to me to be the type of person that would have to be at the very best."

But at least one of Wheeler's teachers saw a need for perfection in the young man. In the one year that Wheeler did not take a technology class from his father, he took a drafting course in which students learned to draw technical designs. His teacher, Richard Pieshala, recalled that Wheeler was intent on making his sketches perfect.

Once, Wheeler received a 95 on a drawing because he had written his name in the corner of the page in lowercase letters instead of uppercase. He could have just erased his name and rewritten it, Pieshala said, but instead he redid the entire drawing. "He was frustrated with himself. I think he really wanted to be perfect," Pieshala said. "He was working for 100."

As this pattern of perfectionism continued, Pieshala decided to say something to Wheeler about it on one of the days when he stayed after school to fine-tune a drawing. As Pieshala told *The Boston Globe*, "He had a quiet disgust with himself when he did something wrong. Once I said, 'Adam, not everybody gets As.' He said, 'I do.'"

Pieshala noticed one more example of Wheeler's academic drive. Like other students at Caesar Rodney with high ambitions, Wheeler paid to take two mandatory courses—physical education and driver's education—over the summer one year. That way, he would have more time during the school year to fill every possible period with academics.

He came home most days and went straight to his room to study. According to his parents, he focused on schoolwork of his own volition, not at their urging. He was a serious student who had liked learning from a young age. As his mother put it, "He cared about ideas."

But he did make time for fun and games. He played in the school band. Though he was extremely quiet in the classroom, he always had a few friends willing to toss a Frisbee with him in the parking lot while he waited for his father to drive home from school.

When it came time for him to apply to college, his parents took him on a trek that has become a ritual for many American families: the college tour. The Wheelers piled into their car and headed up the highway to stop at one leafy campus after another. They learned whether the central grassy area at each institution was called the quad or the green or the yard or the lawn. They sat through information sessions led by perky students or admissions officers. They saw gleaming gyms and 24-hour libraries and that one dorm room whose occupants had been warned to keep their beer cans hidden because theirs was "the tour room."

The Wheelers were of modest means, but with financial aid from whatever college their younger son would attend, they could afford to send him to one of the private colleges they toured. On their road trip, they went as far north as Brunswick, Maine. There, they visited Bowdoin College, a tight-knit school of just 1,750 students (fewer than in Wheeler's high school). No two points on campus were more than five minutes' walking distance apart—surely a welcome fact, given the bone-chilling temperatures in the winter. Bowdoin may not have had quite the name recognition of large universities, but it was certainly well-regarded. In 2005, the year that Wheeler graduated from high school, the rankings juggernaut *U.S. News & World Report* deemed it the sixth-best liberal arts college in the country.

Bowdoin was not Wheeler's first choice, but when he saw the campus on that family road trip, he loved it. He came home ready to write his college applications.

Like many college applicants, he started the arduous process of reducing his life story to words in tiny boxes on one form: the Common Application. This form, most frequently filled out and submitted online, is the application method of choice for hundreds of colleges across the country, including many of the most selective schools. Instead of filling out a tedious application for each college, a student can send the Common Application (or Common App) to many colleges with a single click. Many people say that the Common App, alongside its less popular competitor the Universal College Application, is a major factor in the surge in the number of applications each student submits nowadays. It is just that easy, the argument goes, to add one more school to a Common App list, whereas the tedium of an entirely new application used to deter students from applying to extra schools.

Nevertheless, the process is still burdensome. The application fees—which averaged $37.64 at last count and shot as high as $90 at some colleges—keep application tallies somewhat in check. And for most highly selective schools, the Common App is only the first step. Students also complete a second school-specific form, called a supplement, which generally calls for another essay or two in addition to the writing on the Common App.

The essay, without a doubt, is the component of a college application that most students worry over more than any other part. High school grades are beyond a student's control by the time he applies. All that he can do is deliver a stack of properly addressed envelopes to his guidance counselor so that his transcript, whatever marks it contains, can be mailed off to college admissions offices. Letters of recommendation are also mostly out of the applicant's control. He will probably never see what his teachers write about him. And regardless of whether he is happy with his performance, standardized test scores are set in stone too.

Essentially, by the time a student decides how to present himself to colleges, his work over the past several years of high school has mostly determined what it is he has to present. If he has been a C student in Spanish, he cannot change that. If there is a suspension on his record, he cannot erase it. If his résumé lacks the community service hours that have become de rigueur for ambitious students, there is no time to remedy that now. The essay alone is still a blank slate.

How can one best capture 18 years of experiences, personal character, and academic goals in 500 words? Is an essay on

Grandpa's illness moving or trite? What about winning the soccer game or traveling to Peru? Is it a problem that I am just not funny? And what if my dad or my English teacher thinks my draft is terrible? Then it is back to square one.

It is enough pressure to make many students feel like they need help. Some parents shell out thousands of dollars to engage private coaches who prep students for their college interviews and help them write their application essays. Some applicants turn to the Internet. One website promises that it can accurately predict a student's chances of admission to a certain college, spewing odds like 37 percent at Northwestern and 84 percent at Duke, at a price of $16.95 per college for seniors and $13.95 for younger students. More or less clueless students spend hours on online forums trying to answer each other's anxious questions about every aspect of college admissions. Dozens of sites offer editing services at a price of up to $1,000 per essay.

Some students seek help from printed literature. Among the numerous guidebooks for students strategizing about how to get into college is a shelf of books specifically devoted to the art of writing application essays. If Wheeler wanted help drafting his, he could have opened *How to Write Your College Application Essay*, *Writing Your College Application Essay*, *The College Application Essay*, *On Writing the College Application Essay*, and *How to Write a Winning College Application Essay* (which warned ominously that since a student's competitors nationwide were already reading the book and enrolling in the author's course on essay writing, "you can hardly afford to be left behind").

Others went a step further by providing a profusion of examples—actual essays. Books like *Essays That Worked* and *100 Successful College Application Essays* contained, word for word, writing samples by real-life students who had earned entrance to competitive schools. Those essays were meant to be models, the books insisted, not to be copied wholesale. But it does not take too much imagination to realize that a book like that might provide fertile ground for plagiarism.

It is hard to measure just how many students lift essays from these books, but when it comes to websites, evidence indicates that this sort of plagiarism is widespread. In the 2006–07 school year, a computerized service called TurnItIn.com, which scans students' writing for plagiarism, ran a test on college admissions essays. Out of the 500,000 essays under inspection, 70,000 contained a significant chunk of another text—a full 14 percent of the applications.

Most of those students were cutting and pasting directly from sites with sample college application essays. The most popular choice was PersonalStatement.info, which lets students register to read hundreds of fully written application essays for free, all neatly sorted into categories like "Languages," "Graphic Design," and "Travel & Tourism." Other sites with example essays like the editing services EssayEdge.com and GetIntoUni.com also made the top 10 list of sites from which students in the 2007 study were plagiarizing.

Like so many students before and since, Wheeler decided to avoid the daunting task of writing his own college application essay. He filled out the first few pages of the Common Application. He gave his name and address, his email address, and the name of his high school. He checked off "white" when asked for his race. He said that he wanted to major in psychology and pursue a career in medicine.

Then he came to the first question that called for a written response. It asked him to describe one of his extracurricular activities in 150 words or less. He was going to write about his experience playing in his high school's symphonic band. Perhaps he tried jotting down his thoughts about after-school practices, hours spent staring at sheet music, giddy performances in front of a packed high school auditorium. But sooner or later, he picked up a paperback book called *50 Successful Harvard Application Essays*, published by the Harvard student newspaper, *The Harvard Crimson*. Even though Wheeler was not applying to Harvard or any other Ivy

League universities, he found these essays to be a good batch to imitate—or to just plain steal.

He saw an entry called "Sound of Music." Underneath the title, he read that the essay's author was named Alexander Young and he had attended a small public school in Miami. It started out, "As I fill out this application, I hear music no one else can hear."

Mr. Young from Miami was apparently a composer. According to the book, he had mailed the Harvard admissions committee a piece of music that he had written to accompany the essay. Wheeler was not a composer. But he typed the words "Symphonic Band" at the top of the waiting empty box on the Common App to indicate which of his own activities he was writing about in response to the question, then started filling in Young's words.

The book that Wheeler was using contained commentary on each essay by the staff of *The Crimson*. In Young's case, the student newspaper writer offering his critique complained that Young's conclusion was weak. He did not need to make such grandiose claims about his own artistic legacy, the undergraduate evaluator said. If he were editing the essay, he would take out every reference to "the world," like Young's assertion that by composing, he would "leave a piece of myself to the world." Even with those suggestions right there on the page, Wheeler did not edit a word except to cut one paragraph so that he would meet the Common App's length restriction.

With his short answer complete, he moved on to the longer Common App essay. This one was supposed to be up to 500 words, and there were six topics to choose from—the last of which was "Topic of your choice," so the subject matter actually was unlimited.

From all 50 essays in the Harvard book, Wheeler chose a piece called "Should I Jump?" It recounted the essayist's great enjoyment of jumping off a railroad bridge into water six stories below. It was his way, he wrote, of rebelling. He was just too rule-abiding in his everyday life. In case anyone worried, he assured the admissions committee, "I do not have a fascination with death, and I do not display suicidal tendencies."

Wheeler might never have jumped off a bridge himself, but he was comfortable telling Bowdoin that he had been "trembling with anticipation" before he "hurled" himself into the air. He did make some edits to this essay, though, to better match his own experiences and tastes. While the original writer claimed, "I have rock-climbed and rappelled extensively," Wheeler realistically took out the adverb. And instead of the original writer's picks of Jimmy Hoffa and Elvis, Wheeler plugged in Marlon Brando and John Steinbeck as celebrities he might meet if he died from his fall.

Two copied essays were not enough for Wheeler. The Common App offers a section for additional information. Some applicants use this space to explain an unusual circumstance in their lives that might be reflected in their schoolwork, like a prolonged illness. Others use it to upload a newspaper article about their achievements or a sonnet they wrote. Wheeler decided to send in three extra personal statements. And all three came from *The Crimson*'s essay book.

One was about his supposed passion for model railroading. Wheeler edited it down considerably, taking out descriptions of all the travels the original writer had taken on real trains as well as his activities—piano and yearbook—that did not match Wheeler's own. But he left the musing that he might be "a modern-day hobo" and the pun that his first toy car came into his life "full steam ahead."

Another was about playing chess with his grandfather, losing again and again but picking up lessons about concentration and patience as their games stretched into the wee hours of the night. (Wheeler made their bedtime a bit earlier: 3 a.m. rather than the 3:30 reported in the original version.) Wheeler made sure to change the name of the grandchild to Adam so that the last line of the essay no longer read, "Good game, Robby. Good game." The real Robby, who had sent this essay off to Harvard as a high school student from New York City back in the 1990s, had no way of knowing that Wheeler was pawning off his memories with his beloved grandfather as his own.

Finally, Wheeler chose an essay that sang the praises of the writer's high school physics teacher, even comparing him to Albert Einstein. In the piece, the writer exuberantly described the hands-on experiments and quirky humor that his teacher brought to the classroom. While the science teacher was a hit among students and deserved credit for instilling a love of science in the writer of the essay, he was condemned by administrators for his unusual teaching style and was fired, the essay said.

With this essay as well, Wheeler made sure to take out the real names of the players and put in names from his own life. The original subject did not measure up to "the standard notions of a teacher at St. Ignatius." In Wheeler's submission, those notions were held at Caesar Rodney. He exchanged the teacher's name for that of his own physics teacher—William Farschman.

Farschman found Wheeler to be a mediocre student in his physics class. He did not know where Wheeler was applying to college, and he certainly had no idea that Wheeler was extolling his teaching style in his application essay. The teacher in the essay that Wheeler typed into the Common App wore khaki shorts and open-neck shirts to school; Farschman wore long pants, with a tie on many days. Farschman had never assigned a creative writing assignment as the essay claimed he had. Nor did he drink coffee in class, though the essay said he always had a caffeinated beverage in hand. Most significantly, of course, he had never been fired.

But the truth did not stop Wheeler. Just as his winter break during his senior year of high school was coming to a close, he turned in his completed application packet. All five essays were attached when he reached the very last question on the application. It asked for his electronic signature under a bolded and italicized statement:

I certify that all information in my application, including my Personal Statement, is my own work, factually true, and honestly presented.

Wheeler signed the form and clicked submit.

CHAPTER TWO

On his first day at Bowdoin College, Wheeler became a part of an academic community that has been described as quirky. Eccentric. Tiny. Respected. Laid-back. Intimidating. Prestigious. Hard. Supportive. Easygoing. Charming. Close-knit. Cutting-edge. And that is all just from one professor.

Brunswick, Maine, where Bowdoin is located, boasts a population just north of 20,000 people and a healthy distance between its borders and those of Portland, the nearest city of any significant size. The college started holding classes in 1802 and graduated its most famous alumni in its early years: Civil War general Joshua Lawrence Chamberlain, author Nathaniel Hawthorne, poet Henry Wadsworth Longfellow, and United States President Franklin Pierce all called Bowdoin home. The college touts the founder of Netflix and an Olympic marathon champion among its most successful recent graduates.

More than 40 percent of the student body hails from New England and another 20 percent from the Mid-Atlantic states. There has been a surge in recent years in the number of students from the farther reaches of the United States and from 92 different foreign countries. As more and more students from a wide range of backgrounds apply to college, Bowdoin has seen a marked increase in geographic, ethnic, and socioeconomic diversity, which the college has heartily encouraged. Nowadays, more than 40 percent of students receive financial aid from Bowdoin or the government. The aid comes in the form of grants, not loans, so students never need to pay back their debts after college.

Bowdoin is a tiny place, so young men and women from all backgrounds get to know each other quickly. International students, for example, can and often do choose to stick together, but they also bump up against lifelong locals, Southern belles, and California girls in their dorms, dining halls, and classes. With under 2,000 students—a few hundred fewer than Wheeler went to high school with, in fact—all sleeping, eating, and studying in the same small area, members of the Bowdoin community soon recognize almost every one of their classmates. Come the end of the first semester, if a student brings a friend who is visiting from another college to the dining hall, most Bowdoin students know that this person is not one of them.

The campus is minutes from the ocean—surely enticing for Wheeler, who had grown up near the Delaware coastline and had long been enamored with surfing and swimming. But Bowdoin students cannot take a dip in the ocean very often. The average low temperature in Brunswick remains below freezing for almost half the year.

Moving 10 hours north of his home, Wheeler had much to get acclimated to, culturally as well as meteorologically. Living in a dorm, eating dining hall food (not all that bad, since Bowdoin routinely picks up awards for the best college food in the country), doing his laundry—like all his classmates Wheeler was learning to live on his own and to live in close proximity to hundreds of other young people. At the outset, he admitted frankly to his assigned adviser and the upperclassman supervisor who lived on his floor that he was worried about adjusting to the college environment and making new friends.

He also had to figure out what he wanted to study. In a survey for entering students, he displayed a voracious appetite for learning about nearly everything. He wrote that he was most interested in trying English, biology, theater, and music and that he also anticipated taking chemistry, math, French, philosophy, and art. Though he reported his study skills as "great" without elaborating, he also said that he might seek out extra help with writing, math, and exam preparation.

This same questionnaire asked for his academic goals for his first year. In minuscule letters, he wrote a few lines idealistic enough to suit any college brochure:

> *I hope that my perception of the world will be slightly turned on its head and that I will be made to defend my beliefs and experience the true meaning of intellectual discovery. Thus, my only real expectation for the coming year is to be challenged.*

It was a getting-to-know-you survey sent by the college to entering students. He had already been admitted, and he was not being graded on anything yet. But he still decided to steal someone else's words rather than write his own honest expectations for the academic journey he was beginning. The two lofty sentences were plucked from a student named Hilary Levey, whose work had been published in *The Crimson*'s book of successful Harvard application essays. Wheeler tweaked only the words "the coming year"—in Levey's version, that said "college" instead.

Wheeler did not borrow Levey's next few sentences. Immediately after writing about her expectations for her collegiate career, she spurned an academic experience centered solely on attaining credentials. She wrote, and Wheeler did not copy, "I look upon the next four years of my life as an opportunity; I can either seize the chance and significantly better myself through the accumulation of new knowledge or I can merely go through the paces, achieve good grades, but never really feel the excitement of the words themselves. Obviously, I am looking for the former scenario."

Wheeler did care about scores. The questionnaire asked him how important earning good grades was to his "personal satisfaction," and he checked off five out of five, the box that was labeled "of utmost importance."

He selected courses his first semester that allowed him to try out a few different departments. He took introductory poetry, introductory biology, a religion course on Theravada Buddhism, and an English course on Nathaniel Hawthorne.

Biology, he quickly realized, was not his forte. He earned a C in the class. But the other courses involved writing, the field where he decided his ambitions lay.

His teachers said he was exceptionally quiet. He came to class every day and seemed attentive to their lectures, but while others eagerly participated in discussions, Wheeler was silent. He sat in the same seat, usually in a back corner, in every single class. When other students greeted him, he would chat briefly in response, but he never initiated conversations. In courses with as few as 12 students, which are fairly common at Bowdoin, he was typically the only one who clammed up. He almost never sought attention from his professors outside of class by visiting during their office hours.

Yet despite this lack of communication, his professors managed to form the impression that he wanted to be a writer. One of his English professors recalled, "It seems to me that his plan, as is the case with so many aspiring writers, was to go to a city like New York and get a job and sit there during the day—and try to write. That seemed to be his ambition."

Unlike a lot of students in the class on Buddhism, Wheeler signed up again for the second semester. After teaching him for an entire year, the professor thought that literary aspirations rather than religious curiosity might have drawn Wheeler to the class. "He had real interest in writing," the religion professor said. "Sometimes you get students who see themselves in traditions of American writers who had an interest in Asian thought, and that's kind of how I understood Adam."

Perhaps he was fashioning himself in that course after Jack Kerouac or Allen Ginsberg, but outside of the classroom, he seemed more influenced by earlier writers. At parties in dorm rooms, he would recite snippets of Shakespeare once he had a beer or two in him. (Dogfish Head, brewed in his native Delaware, was known to be his favorite brand, even though it was hard to come by in Maine.) "Give us some poetry!" his classmates would shout at him, and he would comply.

Seeking a social outlet, he signed up for the ultimate Frisbee team. The players competed against other colleges, but their fellow students did not usually consider them athletes. For many, it was primarily a social opportunity. Teammates ate dinner together and partied together. The men's team was called Stoned Clown, and according to many observers on campus, the players did their best to live up to both halves of that name. Every Friday afternoon, they would play Frisbee golf on a course they had created that crisscrossed the entire campus. They would hit professors' windows with errant discs, then lope past in a jaunty pack, all dressed in clownish costumes.

The group boasted plenty of offbeat traditions. All of the players received nicknames. Wheeler played alongside guys called Buster, Snatch, Wonder, and Rodeo. After Wheeler dove into a puddle during one game and came out covered in mud, he was dubbed Fudge. The team chose "Bananaphone" by the children's musician Raffi as its fight song and blasted its inspired lines like "It's a phone with a peel!" and "Now you can have your phone and eat it too!" from the sidelines of its matches. An annual Bowdoin naked party, which had started with 12 nude participants two years earlier, had become a campus-wide event by Wheeler's first year. Ultimate Frisbee team members were among the most reliable and enthusiastic attendees.

His new teammates did not think that Wheeler had much talent for ultimate Frisbee, but they did not mind. "He was not athletic. He was a terrible Frisbee player," one of them said with a good-natured grin. "But he went to all the team dinners and practices. He was always practicing throwing a Frisbee. He went to the tournaments." He laughed, remembering Wheeler's earnest efforts to be part of the team. "This is what people loved about him."

He was quiet, but teammates felt that he was interesting and unfailingly kind whenever they engaged him in conversation. He sometimes sat in while two friends he had met at Frisbee practices hosted their semiweekly radio show. Occasionally he would crack a joke on the air.

But for the most part, Wheeler kept a very low profile at Bowdoin during his first year. That all changed in the spring, when he entered a poetry contest with a piece titled "Hay."

Literary critics may find it reassuring to learn that Wheeler won the poetry contest. If some poetry is better than other poetry—based on the intrinsic quality of the writing rather than what magazine prints it or the poet's name—then it follows that if someone slips a poem by a professional poet into a pool of works by undergraduates, the judges should be able to pick out that poet's piece as the best in the bunch. Even if the poet's recognizable name is taken off the poem. Even if an unremarkable college student puts his name on it instead.

When the Llewellyn Poetry Prize was judged at Bowdoin, that was exactly what happened.

Wheeler tied with one other student for first prize in the contest. His poem was printed in the school literary magazine. One of Wheeler's English professors read it and idly wondered how Wheeler knew anything about farming. But nobody noticed that the poem "Hay" was written by Paul Muldoon, a world-famous poet with more than 30 published books, an editorship at *The New Yorker*, a professorial position at Princeton, and a Pulitzer Prize to his name.

Wheeler basked in his victory. He started hanging around the students who edited the literary magazine, bringing them poems he had written. They were impressed by the wide variety of styles that he used in his writing and the prolific pace at which he turned out new work. For the first time, someone called him talkative; some of the campus literary crowd mentioned that when Wheeler chatted about his ambitions as a poet and the pieces he had just completed, "he was hard to shut up."

He could frequently be seen in the dining hall hunched over a notebook. His poetry party trick became far more popular. Instead of standing in the corner on Saturday nights, he was reciting Shakespearean sonnets for the crowd.

"Everybody knew him as the literature buff," one friend recalled. Based on Wheeler's performances and his odd vocabulary that "sounded like it was Shakespeare," his friend assumed that the tall first-year must be "very, very bright."

The year was coming to an end, and the first-years were abuzz with talk about their sophomore housing choices. Many had their eyes on a set of eight selective dorms. When the college banished its fraternities and sororities in 1997, Bowdoin repurposed eight beautiful New England mansions as coed college houses, almost always called social houses instead. A berth in a social house is widely considered the most coveted living arrangement that a student can get in his sophomore year. Bowdoin takes both the "social" and the "house" part seriously. Any student who wants to live in a house has to apply for the spot by attending an interview and filling out a lengthy form, complete with written responses and the name of a reference. In his application, he has to persuade the residential life staff that he will help plan major social events on the weekends that are hosted by his house but usually open to the entire school. Landing a room in a social house means writing up a list of ideas to become the college's next great party planner.

Each house typically receives more applications than the number of spots it has to fill. Sometimes, however, a house is undersubscribed. In the case of Howell House, it is clear why some students might be dissuaded from applying to live there. It is the only one of the social houses that is, in Bowdoin terminology, "chem free." No alcohol, marijuana, or other drugs are allowed.

When Wheeler was looking for a sophomore room, he learned that Howell House had not had enough applicants to fill all its beds when the social house assignments had been made a few weeks earlier. That meant that the remaining spots in Howell House were open to anyone, even someone who had not filled out any social house applications. The students placed in Howell now, through the regular housing lottery, would not be part of Howell's social organization. They would have no responsibility for planning events, nor any stake in the close-knit community that lived there. They would be called residents, but not members.

When Wheeler's turn to pick a room came, the upperclassmen whose seniority entitled them to pick before him had already taken the most desirable rooms on campus, like the spacious suites in the high-rise known as The Tower. But there was still a room in Howell, and he took it.

Over the course of his sophomore year, Wheeler continued to drink Dogfish Head with the Stoned Clown and did not become close with the members of Howell. He rarely ate meals at the long family-style tables in the house's dining room or joined in the cooking in its gleaming stainless steel kitchen. He did not attend the social events that the members spent hours planning and advertising. Most of them nodded hello to him in passing, but they might not even have known his name. That was understandable. He usually came in the front door, crossed the polished wood floor of the entrance hall, and went straight to his own room.

During the summer after his first year, Wheeler had acquired a hobby that did draw some attention to him on campus: weightlifting. The once-skinny teenager put on 20 pounds of muscle before he returned to Bowdoin as a sophomore. He attracted attention for the long hours he put into pumping iron at the college's gym that second year and the fastidious health food diet he kept. His imposing physique was apparent as he walked around campus in shorts, flip-flops, and muscle-hugging T-shirts despite the painfully cold temperatures.

Wheeler seemed to care a lot about impressing people with his physical fitness and his chops as a writer. But as far as at least one friend could tell, he did not seem to care all that much about grades in the classroom. "He was not the kind of kid who was ever talking about, 'I got this grade on this paper or this test.' He was not competitive in that sense," his friend said. At best, he would describe Wheeler's schoolwork as "methodical." When he sat down to write a paper, he worked steadily and efficiently until it was done.

By his second semester, he had abandoned his plans to try everything from theater to chemistry. He stuck entirely to literature and religion classes for the next several semesters. His grades improved, though they never became stellar. He started consistently scoring B-pluses and A-minuses in every class. Many of his professors noted that he started the semester with strong essays and petered out as the course went on. The decline was never drastic, maybe dropping from A-minus grades at first to B-minus grades by the last few assignments, but it was noticeable enough that they discerned a pattern.

After two semesters devoted mostly to English courses, he developed an interest in philosophy in his sophomore spring. He had never taken a class in it before, but that semester, he signed up for three. None of them were introductory classes, either. Though there were no strict prerequisites for enrolling, "Environmental Ethics," "Philosophy of Law," and "History, Freedom, and Reason" were all considered intermediate level in the course catalog. Regardless, Wheeler dove right in.

As a newcomer to philosophy, he had a lot to learn. For "Philosophy of Law," the syllabus included dense essays like "Positivism and the Separation of Law and Morals" and "On Interpretation and Objectivity," in addition to court rulings. And for every one of those readings, three assignments each week, he had to write a journal entry to prove that he understood the assignment and then submit it online to the professor.

As Scott Sehon, the professor who taught that legal philosophy course, handed out the course syllabus on the first day, he also passed out another paper: Bowdoin's academic honor code. This document

Wheeler had seen before. Like everyone else at Bowdoin, he had signed it when he first arrived on campus. It warned against all sorts of academic offenses: altering transcripts, helping someone out on a test, even "purposeful failure to return library materials on a timely basis." But the bulk of the document was a harsh reminder to never use someone else's work without proper attribution. "Plagiarism" was the key word of the document, and it was clear that it was not going to be treated lightly if the college found that it had occurred.

The instrument by which Bowdoin punishes suspected plagiarists was well known to Wheeler and all the other students in Sehon's class. Its name was most often spoken in hushed tones: the J-Board. Only a few students each year actually faced investigation by the Judicial Board—"got J-Boarded," in Bowdoin lingo. Among the rest, only speculation and rumor informed their knowledge of the shadowy board's hearings. To further obfuscate matters, those students who did enter the J-Board's chambers often did not get to stick around Bowdoin for very long.

The J-Board's 16 members were under strict orders to stay mum about the disciplinary body's proceedings. The process of punishing a student for plagiarism starts when a professor reports his suspicions. Next, a college administrator investigates the claim by searching for the text that the student supposedly presented as her own work. The student also has the opportunity to provide a defense of her actions. Then at a hearing, the accused and the accuser sit at a table in the bowels of an administrative building to plead their cases before a panel of judges who determine the student's guilt or innocence. If they find her guilty, they also decide her fate at the college. This is a fairly common model for college discipline. What is not as common is that at Bowdoin, the judges lined up to scrutinize the claims of the accused student are predominantly her fellow undergrads.

These students, 12 sophomores, juniors, and seniors picked from a competitive applicant pool each year, hold a good deal of power, and they are not afraid to use it. Several professors who have served on the board alongside students say that the younger members are often the harshest judges in the room. "They're not quite so gullible," said retired Romance languages professor John Turner, a former J-Board member. "Sometimes I've seen the committee's faculty members say, 'Maybe this story makes sense.' Students often tend to see through it." Turner summed up why students make good board members: "They do know their fellow students. Better than we do."

The J-Board hears about 10 to 20 cases per year, split between academic violations, like cheating and plagiarism, and social breaches, like sexual assault and drunken misbehavior. For those whom it convicts—and it convicts the vast majority of students who are accused—the range of penalties that the board metes out is wide. At the less serious end of the scale, a social violation might merit only a warning or a fine. The best outcome that a confirmed plagiarist could hope for would be an F on the assignment or an F in the class. More severely, she might be suspended from Bowdoin for a semester or more, or even expelled. A letter sent to all students at the beginning of the school year warns them in bold that, in plagiarism cases, "suspension is likely."

On the first day of his "Philosophy of Law" class, Professor Sehon used Bowdoin's own judicial system to kick off his lesson. He tossed out some hypothetical cases that might come before the J-Board. He knew the field fairly well: He had served on the board in the past, and he also had come before it as an accuser from time to time. In his 13 years of teaching, he had brought almost that many plagiarism cases to the J-Board—more than most professors, he acknowledged.

His purpose in discussing applications of the Honor Code that day was not to warn against cheating in his class. Rather, the discourse was intended to serve as a lesson on judicial interpretation before he delved into a real court case in the next lecture. But at the end of the discussion, Sehon threw in a note of caution to any would-be plagiarists.

"The J-Board is a very nice group of people," he told the students, "but I do not want to meet with them this semester."

Wheeler was not going to make it easy for Sehon's wish to come true.

Just like his application to Bowdoin two years earlier and his entry in the poetry contest, the three-times-a-week journal assignments for Sehon's class were tasks that he would rather complete with somebody else's words than his own. This time, he plagiarized from sources like the *Michigan Law Review* and *American Bar Foundation Research Journal.*

He had something else on his mind besides plodding through philosophy homework. His time at Bowdoin, he felt, was coming to an end. He had decided to transfer to Harvard.

CHAPTER THREE

Transferring from one college to another means going through the whole arduous college application process all over again. While Adam Wheeler continued to show up, dutifully if silently, for Scott Sehon's class and his three other courses, his attention that spring was more focused on the application slowly taking shape on his laptop.

It had to be perfect. Bowdoin was prestigious, and he had worked hard to be accepted. He had accurately reported his good high school grades, and he had been lucky that Bowdoin did not require him to submit his SAT scores. (His two attempts had resulted in scores of 1160 and 1220 out of 1600, which, while respectable, put him quite a bit below Bowdoin's median range.) And of course, as an extra boost, he had exploited other people's essays.

Those essays he had used two years earlier had been Harvard application essays. But as good as their writing might have been, none of those students had been accepted to Harvard on the strength of their essays alone. Wheeler would have to put together a much more compelling package this time around.

Harvard is accustomed to seeing students with perfect SAT scores, effusive letters of recommendation, tearjerker essays, and résumés listing laboratory research breakthroughs they made and volunteer tutoring they provided—and then rejecting them. Ivy League applicants are just too abundant and too accomplished for all the qualified students to make the cut.

The applicant pool includes Broadway and Hollywood actors, international math contest winners, spelling bee champions, published authors, and nationally ranked athletes. Some students have invented new technologies. Scores are virtuosos on one musical instrument or another. High school valedictorians, student council presidents, and yearbook editors are a dime a dozen.

Not all accepted students, to be sure, have attained recognition on a national or international level. But all have not only stellar academic records but also significant extracurricular interests that they have developed and honed successfully. And though those interests range from cooking to cartooning to competitive speaking, all Harvard students have something in common: They got really, really lucky.

The odds are against any applicant, no matter how talented. The year that Wheeler was applying to Harvard, close to 23,000 students vied for just over 2,000 freshman acceptance letters. That acceptance rate, 9 percent, was at the time the lowest in Harvard's history. Since then, the competition has only become tougher. In 2012, just five years later, applications hit 34,000, putting the acceptance rate at 5.9 percent.

To secure one of the precious few acceptances, Wheeler knew he needed to make his application stand out. First of all, the essay. No fellow student's work, no matter how compelling, was going to pass muster this time. He wanted the work of a professional. Better still, several professionals.

Wheeler's own interests had been trending more academic than literary. Instead of writing poetry or fiction, he was starting to aspire to a career in academia. He said he might want to be a literature professor and to write for academic journals instead of the popular press. So the people he picked to write his college application essay this time were shining examples of success in the academy: five Harvard professors who had written essays about the state of undergraduate education.

For the first paragraph of his essay, he stole lines from a piece by James Engell, who for decades had been publishing essays and books about Romantic poets as well as about the changing role of universities in the modern world, all while teaching at Harvard.

Words from the middle of one of his essays became the first sentence of Wheeler's statement to Harvard: "The internal orientation of knowledges has come increasingly to be characterized by more and more complex interrelationships."

After lifting a few more sentences from Engell, Wheeler switched to another Harvard English professor whose work he had reason to admire. That professor, Stephen Greenblatt, had attained one of the most prominent academic positions in the world—a special professorial designation called University Professor, conferred on only the 25 most highly acclaimed teachers at Harvard. His books were about intellectual topics such as the Renaissance and the relationship between literature and history, yet they also attracted a wide enough audience to make the *New York Times* best-seller list. On top of that, he had been tapped the year before to serve as the general editor of the *Norton Anthology of English Literature*, the massive collection of canonical works in English that holds an obligatory place on students' bookshelves worldwide. When the outgoing editor passed the scepter to Greenblatt, he said, "I don't know anybody better than him in the field of literature in his generation."

In other words, Wheeler had chosen a very impressive scholar to write the second paragraph of his college essay for him. But he felt compelled to add more. In the next paragraph, he alternated sentences written by George Whitesides, another member of the elite cadre of University Professors, with some by Jorge Domínguez, a government professor who served as a vice provost at Harvard among many other administrative posts. After that, Wheeler pasted an entire paragraph from Charles Maier, who had been teaching at Harvard since 1967. And for the big finish, he returned to Greenblatt.

The amalgamation had barely any relevance to the Common App's prompt, which asked why his first college choice had not worked out for him. Unlike the pieces he had plagiarized when he applied to Bowdoin, the pieces he borrowed from now were not meant to be personal statements but academic essays.

Every sentence might have sounded impressive on its own, if unusually intellectual for a college essay. But the end result of taking the words of five people out of context was an essay that did not make all that much sense. The hodgepodge pivoted from one thought to another without any effort at smooth transitions. For example, the four sentences below—the first from Greenblatt, the next from Whitesides, and the last two from Domínguez—were put together to read:

Departments are organized as if the division between English and, for example, French were stable and timeless, or as if the Muslim and Christian worlds had existed in hermetic isolation from one another, or as if the history of ideas were somehow entirely independent of the history of exile, migration, and economic exchange. The complexity and interest of these roles compete with undergraduate teaching. [My school] takes no explicit steps to develop communicative skills. It is at best agnostic on whether creativity would be fostered.

True, Wheeler's essay did not hang together so well. But with more than one thousand others applying as transfer students alone, he might reasonably expect that an admissions officer would be busy enough to just skim, not scrutinize, his essay. And it was full of good sentences—other people's sentences.

The next essay prompt asked what he intended to study at Harvard. He used the same composite method to put that one together. His first sentence came from Helen Vendler, a renowned poetry professor at Harvard. The rest of the paragraph used the words of Peter Galison, who taught courses in physics and the history of science, and the second paragraph plagiarized Julie Buckler, a Slavic languages professor. The final paragraph was a condensed version of another part of Vendler's essay—except for the last 21 words of a 67-word final sentence. These he culled from Buckler once more. All three of the pieces that he used as his palette for this answer, just like the five that he had chosen for the last, came from the same collection of Harvard professors' essays on undergraduate education.

After that, the application asked about his career plans after graduation. He presented himself as someone who wanted to advance to graduate school and eventually become a scholar and teacher of literature. But he did not say this outright in his essay. Instead, he used the words of Stanford professor Roland Greene. The sentences he took from Greene extolled the importance of interdisciplinary studies. All Wheeler did was insert the words "postgraduate literary scholarship" where Greene had written "new world studies," and change "us" in a phrase about the importance of such study to "me."

The application gave him still another opportunity to plagiarize. It called for a short statement about one of his extracurricular pursuits. When he had faced this question while applying to Bowdoin, he had ended up claiming to be an amateur composer, thanks to a piece in the Harvard application essays book. His choice from among other people's materials this time would again determine his purported hobby or passion. He decided to base his statement on a passage from a memoir by the much-decorated poet James Merrill—so as of that moment, Wheeler's new passion was opera.

Merrill's description of the evolution of his love of opera stretched on for several pages, but the Common App called for 150 words for this response. Wheeler's essay ended up at well over four times the requested length, even though he pruned out portions about Merrill's love affairs. He did not cut every personal detail, though. The essay, as Wheeler submitted it, began:

My operagoing self. It was born in the music room at Southampton during the summer my parents separated.

He kept in that detail, about his parents' supposed separation. Wheeler's own parents were still very much married. But in his essay, he laid claim to this memory that was actually Merrill's:

My mother called me into her room and handed me my father's brief and no doubt handsomely phrased letter saying that he was leaving her. Having read it, I was inspired (at eleven) to let it flutter from my fingers to the carpet. "Oh, don't be dramatic," said my mother with some asperity.

To back up the assertion in the essay, Wheeler checked off "separated" in the box on the Common App that asked his parents' marital status. With that lie corroborated, he turned his attention to other parts of the application.

The last time he applied to college, he had sent in his real high school transcript. He may have contemplated what he would have to offer if he used his legitimate academic record again this time. After almost two years at Bowdoin, he had a 3.27 GPA, with more B grades than As and one ugly C in biology marring his transcript. In letters of recommendation his professors were unlikely to wax poetic about his personality, since he had barely spoken to any of them. He had no leadership positions at Bowdoin to put on his résumé, which would have been even barer without the poetry prize he had deceitfully won the year before.

This time, he would have to actually submit his SAT scores—the scores he had considered barely good enough for Bowdoin, let alone Harvard. He knew that Harvard would ask to see his high school transcript too, and that would not reflect perfectly on his candidacy either. Throughout high school, he had been an A student in almost all of his classes, but he had let his grades slip during his last year. He finished up high school with a B average for his senior year and a class rank of 47 out of 348. His performance was certainly respectable, but probably not Harvard-caliber.

The truth was not good enough. Wheeler decided that the way to reach the future he wanted was to change his past. Rather than relying on his prior accomplishments to power him ahead, he chose to sculpt an imaginary past that would be worthy of a real acceptance letter from Harvard.

As long as he was planning to exercise some creativity (or criminality) on his application, he might as well dream big. SAT scores, for starters. He obviously had to make them higher. And since he was going for excellence, why not perfection? In the section of the Common App that let him type in his own scores, he gave himself flawless 800s on the verbal and math sections. Harvard was also looking for three scores from SAT Subject Tests. Wheeler doubled that number. He said he had taken six—French, Latin, literature, math, United States history, and writing—and earned perfect 800s on all but one of those. (He gave himself a 780 on the math exam.)

Less than 1 percent of the test-takers in the nation score an 800 on either the verbal or the math section of the SAT Reasoning Test. Earning a perfect score on both is even rarer. For Subject Tests, scores of 800 are also impressive feats. The difficulty of earning a perfect score varies by subject. In the year Wheeler applied to Harvard, perfect scores in literature went to less than 1 percent of students, while the Latin and writing exams gave the top score to 5 percent, and the upper-level math test that Wheeler claimed to have taken bestowed perfect marks on the top 10 percent. Even with those variances, earning multiple top-notch scores is an exceptional achievement. Of course, there are students every year who rack up a whole slate of perfect or near-perfect standardized test scores. And of course, many of those students apply to Harvard. It was not out of the question for a student to be that good. Wheeler just was not one of those students.

The easy part of making up a fantastic set of scores for himself was typing them into the Common App, where all he had to do was enter a number to make it appear. More difficult was the required official score report from the College Board, the company that administers the SAT.

Ordinarily, an applicant goes to the College Board's website when she wants her scores to be delivered to a college's admissions office. She selects the schools she wants to apply to, pays a fee, and presses a button. Then the College Board sends an official document, via snail mail, CD-ROM, or Internet transfer, telling the college what scores the student earned.

Wheeler never had the College Board deliver that official report to the Harvard admissions office. But he did make sure that Harvard received a score report from him that had all the fonts, format, and logos that the College Board uses. That piece of paper corroborated what Wheeler had indicated on the Common App— that between December 2004 and March 2005, he had taken six Subject Tests and one Reasoning Test, and all told, he had lost only 20 points, on just one of the tests.

That seemingly official document in Wheeler's application packet was not the typical score report that the College Board sends to a university. It was the version that is mailed to the applicant herself right after she takes the test to tell her how she fared. Wheeler even sent in parts of the report with advice for the student on the college application process.

The College Board never actually mailed a document with those scores to Wheeler. But somehow Harvard received a report that passed muster. The College Board had sent Wheeler real SAT score reports in the mail a few years earlier, both times that he took the SAT. All he needed at this point was to doctor his own, or perhaps someone else's, legitimate score report. A bottle of correction fluid and a carefully aligned printer, a scanner and a bit of time with image editing software . . . he knew his options for creating a credible forgery. With an acorn logo, identification numbers, and informational fine print, it looked almost exactly like his original SAT score reports. Except for the scores.

As long as he had the technical skill, he could fake additional scores. He actually had taken several AP courses in high school, but for Harvard, he wanted to say that he had taken more. And of course, he wanted to say that he had performed perfectly. He made a list of all the exams he ideally might have taken (two in French, two in Latin, two in English, two in economics, European and American history, biology, chemistry, physics, government, calculus, and art history) and gave himself 5s on all of them.

In total, his fake document said he had taken 16 AP tests, including six each year in his sophomore and junior years of high school. To fit all those in, he claimed that he had even taken the European History and English Language and Composition exams back when he was still in middle school. Again, these sorts of test-taking feats probably are not unprecedented in the elite applicant pool. But they are undoubtedly enough to raise an eyebrow. In the year Wheeler graduated from high school, 13 percent of all AP grades handed out were 5s. Lots of Harvard applicants have 5s; many have lots of 5s. But getting 5s 16 times in succession is rare indeed.

Performance aside, merely sitting for 16 exams would be a tour de force. Mastering material that the College Board considers the equivalent of a college course is no walk in the park; doing so 16 times sounds overwhelming. Just finding room in a high school schedule to take all those classes would be tough. It is an expensive proposition, too. Though low-income students can request fee waivers and some schools help defray the cost, many students have to pay what the College Board charges: more than $80 per test, far more than the fee for SAT testing. Paying full price for all 16 exams would have cost Wheeler more than $1,300.

Washington Post writer Valerie Strauss once polled college admissions offices and high school guidance counselors to ask how many AP exams were appropriate for a competitive college applicant. Of all of the respondents, the highest number reported was one school that advised taking up to eight in a high school career.

Between 2008 and 2011, more than 1.3 million students took one or two AP tests. By contrast, only 697 took more than 14. Wheeler might not have known all the statistics, but he must have had a very good idea that he was conjuring up an unusually well-qualified candidate. He typed up his long list of perfect scores and pasted it into the Additional Information section of the Common

App. Unlike the SAT requirement, sending AP scores directly from the College Board was optional, but he decided to submit official-looking documentation anyway. As he had for the SAT, he created a meticulously forged score report. Actually, he had to make two this time. The first report had room for only 14 scores.

For his high school transcript, he would give himself better grades and a more impressive course load. That much was obvious. His real high school transcript could make an easy template for a touch-up. But he decided he wanted a bigger change. He was going to switch his school entirely, from obscure Caesar Rodney to Phillips Academy, more commonly referred to by the name of the town in Massachusetts in which it is located—Andover.

Andover is not just any high school. It was founded during the Revolutionary War, making it the oldest school of its kind in the country. George Washington, Paul Revere, and John Hancock all had a hand in the school's early days. It has not relinquished its place at the forefront of outstanding secondary education for a moment since then. Today, it boasts students from 36 countries, resources that rival any fine liberal arts college, and an admissions rate of 14 percent that makes it more competitive than some of the prestigious colleges that graduates of the school reliably attend.

In many ways, it is the Harvard of high schools, and many of its graduates move on to the real Harvard and its peer institutions. Knowing that Harvard had a history of admitting Andover graduates, Wheeler decided to pretend to be one himself.

The transcript that he printed out to send in with his transfer application looked completely unlike his Caesar Rodney record. He had done his research well. He knew that Andover students change their schedules with the passing of each trimester, instead of taking one set of courses for the whole school year as he had at Caesar Rodney. Instead of typical letter grades, Andover scores its students on a scale of 1 to 6 in every class. Wheeler gave himself only 5s and 6s, with an overall average of 6 in every semester, save a 5 in the winter of his senior year.

YOUR SCORES

Test Date: MARCH 2005

APR 1 1 2007

Seq# 0000058
ADAM B. WHEELER

MILTON   DE 19968

SAT I: Reasoning Test	Score	Score Range	Percentiles College-bound Seniors National	State
Verbal	800	770-800	99	99
Math	800	770-800	99	99

Register now for next year via our website at www.collegeboard.com

WHAT DOES YOUR SCORE RANGE MEAN?
No single numerical score can exactly represent your reasoning skills. If you had taken different editions of the test within a short period of time, your performance would probably vary somewhat on the 200 to 800 scale.

HOW DO YOU COMPARE WITH COLLEGE-BOUND SENIORS?
Percentiles indicate what percentage of test takers earned a score lower than yours. The national percentile for your verbal score of 800 is 99, indicating you did better than 99 % of the national group of college-bound seniors. The national percentile for your math score of 800 is 99 , indicating you did better than 99 % of the national group of college-bound seniors.

DID YOU DO BETTER IN VERBAL OR MATH?
Your scores indicate that you performed similarly on the math test and the verbal test.

WHAT'S THE AVERAGE VERBAL OR MATH SCORE?
For college-bound seniors in the class of 2005, the average verbal score was 508 and the average math score was 520.

WILL YOUR SCORES CHANGE IF YOU TAKE THE TEST AGAIN?
If you take the test again, especially if you study between now and then, your scores may go up.

Among students with verbal scores of 800, 0% score higher on a second testing, 39% score lower, and 60% receive the same score. On average, a person with a verbal score of 800 gains 0 point(s) on a second testing.

Among students with math scores of 800, 0% score higher on a second testing, 36% score lower, and 64% receive the same score. On average, a person with a math score of 800 gains 0 point(s) on a second testing.

HOW DID YOU DO ON EACH TYPE OF QUESTION?

Type of Question	Number Right	Number Wrong	Number Omitted	Number of Questions	Raw Score	Estimated Percentile College-bound Seniors
Critical Reading	40	0	0	40	40	99
Analogies	19	0	0	19	19	99
Sentence Completion	19	0	0	19	19	99
Arithmetic and Algebraic Reasoning	43	0	0	43	43	99
Geometric Reasoning	16	1	0	17	17	99

Your responses to specific types of questions are presented as number right, number wrong, and number omitted. Raw scores are based on the specific edition of the test that you took. You cannot compare raw scores on different editions of the test or across different types of questions. For each type of question, you can compare your performance to college-bound seniors who took this test. This percentile is an estimate of the percentage of college-bound seniors who earned a raw score lower than yours on each type of question.

SUMMARY OF SCORES   *Register now for next year via our website at www.collegeboard.com*

SAT I: Reasoning Test						SAT II: Subject Tests										
Test Date	Grade Level	Verbal	Math		Test Date	Grade Level	Test 1	Score	Writing Subscores Multiple Choice	Writing Sample	Reading	Listening Subscores Reading	Listening Usage/Gram	Test 2	Score	Test 3	Score
Mar 05	11	800	800		Jan 05	11	Writing	800	80	12				Math 11C	780	Literature	800
					Dec 04	11	French	800						Latin	800	US History	800

¹Not all tests have subscores

ID INFORMATION

To take additional tests you can reregister by mail or by phone and use Visa, MasterCard, American Express or Discover. You will need the registration number below and the test date (see above). To send more score reports you will need the institution's 4-digit codes. See the back of this report for instructions on how to request these services.

Sex	Date of Birth	Social Security Number	Registration Number	Test Center Number	High School Name and Code	
M			6872700	220030	PHILLIPS ACADEMY	220030

Wheeler provided this score report, which very closely resembles reports mailed to students after they take the SAT, as part of his Harvard application. It indicates that he received perfect scores on the standardized Reasoning Test and five Subject Tests while a student at Andover.

WHEELER	ADAM	B	M			123979

12TH	FALL	06	NO

School Code and Address: 220030
PHILLIPS ACADEMY
180 MAIN STREET
ANDOVER   MA 01810

06	FRENCH LIT	5		04	ART HISTORY	5
05	BIOLOGY	5		04	CALCULUS BC	5
05	FRENCH LANG	5		04	ENG LIT/COMP	5
05	GOVT&POL COMP	5		04	LATIN: VERGIL	5
05	LATIN LIT	5		04	PHYSICS C	5
05	MACRO ECON	5		04	US HISTORY	5
05	MICRO ECON	5		03	CHEMISTRY	5

3514	06/06	ADMISSIONS OFFICE	MASS INSTITUTE TECH

In the 2003-04 school year, Java was used as the programming language for Computer Science. Prior to 2003-04, C ++ was used.

JOHN   W ANDERSON
PHILLIPS ACADEMY
180 MAIN STREET
ANDOVER   MA 01810

About .04 percent of all AP test-takers from 2008 to 2011 took more than 14 of the exams. Wheeler said he accomplished this feat; this is one of the two score reports he needed to list his full record. Moreover, he claimed perfect scores on all 16 of the tests that he said he took.

Andover grades on a scale from 1 to 6. Wheeler claimed to have an average of 6 in all but one of the trimesters he said he spent at the prestigious prep school.

PHILLIPS ACADEMY   Andover, MA 01810   Tel:(978) 749-4000   **ACADEMIC RECORD**

02061█ **Name:** Wheeler, Adam B.   **Address:** ███████ Milton, DE 19968-9479

D.O.B: ███   **Sex:** M   **S.S.#:** ████   **Entered:** 09/01/02   **Graduated:** 06/05/06

Previous School: Community Day Charter School   **Parent or Guardian:** Lee Wheeler

	TG	PG			TG	PG

GRADE 9 - FALL TRIMESTER - 2002 - 2003

	TG	PG
CHEM-580/0	Honors AP Chemistry	5
ENGL-510§	Shakespeare	6
HIST-340/0	Modern European History	6
LATN-300/0	Latin Language & Stylistics	5
FREN-420/0	French Literature	6
MATH-340	Precalculus	6

TRIMESTER AVERAGE: 6 HONOR ROLL

GRADE 10 - FALL TRIMESTER - 2003 - 2004

PHYS-550M	AP Physics C AP (M/E&M)	5
ENGL-550/1	Senior Thesis Colloquium	6
HIST-300/4	The United States	6
MATH-600/0	Honors AP Calculus BC	5
LATN-520V/0	AP Vergil	6
FREN-500/1	AP French Language	6
GREK-195/0	Accelerated Greek	6

TRIMESTER AVERAGE: 6 HONOR ROLL

GRADE 11 - FALL TRIMESTER - 2004 - 2005

BIOL-560	Cellular Biology	6
LATN-520L/1	AP: Horace and Catullus	6
FREN-520/0	AP French Literature	6
HIST-SS521	Economics II: Micro AP	6
MATH-630/1	Honors Seminar	6
GREK-300/1	Homer & The Epic Tradition	6

TRIMESTER AVERAGE: 6 HONOR ROLL

GRADE 12 - FALL TRIMESTER - 2005 - 2006

MATH-650	Linear Algebra	6
FREN-600/1	Modern Literature	6
GREK-400/1	Wisdom Sophistry Philosophy	6

TRIMESTER AVERAGE: 6 HONOR ROLL

GRADE 9 - WINTER TRIMESTER - 2002 - 2003

	TG	PG
CHEM-580/0	Honors AP Chemistry	6
ENGL-520	Old English Period	6
HIST-340/0	Modern European History	6
LATN-300/0	Latin Language & Stylistics	5
FREN-420/0	French Literature	5
MATH-350	Precalculus	6

TRIMESTER AVERAGE: 6 HONOR ROLL

GRADE 10 - WINTER TRIMESTER - 2003 - 2004

PHYS-550/4	AP Physics C AP (M/E&M)	5
ENGL-550/2	Senior Thesis Colloquium	6
HIST-300/4	The United States	6
MATH-600/0	Honors AP Calculus BC	6
LATN-520V/0	AP Vergil	5
FREN-500/2	AP French Language	6
GREK-195/0	Accelerated Greek	6

TRIMESTER AVERAGE: 6 HONOR ROLL

GRADE 11 - WINTER TRIMESTER - 2004 - 2005

BIOL-570	Human Anatomy & Physiology	5
LATN-520L/2	AP: Horace and Catullus	6
FREN-520/0	AP French Literature	6
HIST-SS521	Economics II: Micro AP	6
MATH-630/2	Honors Seminar	6
GREK-300/2	Homer & The Epic Tradition	6

TRIMESTER AVERAGE: 6 HONOR ROLL

GRADE 12 - WINTER TRIMESTER - 2005 - 2006

MATH-650/5	Vector Calculus	6
FREN-600/2	Modern Literature	6
GREK-400/2	Wisdom Sophistry Philosophy	6

TRIMESTER AVERAGE: 5 HONOR ROLL

GRADE 9 - SPRING TRIMESTER - 2002 - 2003

	TG	PG
CHEM-580/0	Honors AP Chemistry	6
ENGL-560	W.B. Yeats	6
HIST-340/0	Modern European History	6
LATN-300/0	Latin Language & Stylistics	6
FREN-420/0	French Literature	6
MATH-360	Precalculus Trigonometry	6

TRIMESTER AVERAGE: 6 HONOR ROLL

GRADE 10 - SPRING TRIMESTER - 2003 - 2004

PHYS-580/4	AP Physics C AP (E/E&M)	5
ENGL-580/3	Senior Thesis Colloquium	6
HIST-310	The United States	6
MATH-600/0	Honors AP Calculus BC	6
LATN-520V/0	AP Vergil	6
FREN-500/3	AP French Language	6
GREK-195/0	Accelerated Greek	6

TRIMESTER AVERAGE: 6 HONOR ROLL

GRADE 11 - SPRING TRIMESTER - 2004 - 2005

BIOL-580	Evolution & Ecology	5
LATN-520L/3	AP: Horace and Catullus	6
FREN-520/0	AP French Literature	6
ART-400/3	AP History of Art	6
MATH-630/3	Honors Seminar	5
GREK-300/3	Homer & The Epic Tradition	6

TRIMESTER AVERAGE: 6 HONOR ROLL

GRADE 12 - SPRING TRIMESTER - 2005 - 2006

MATH-650/5	Vector Calculus	6
FREN-600/3	Modern Literature	6
GREK-400/3	Wisdom Sophistry Philosophy	5

TRIMESTER AVERAGE: 6 HONOR ROLL

TEST SCORES

SAT	MAR 05	V.800 M.800	
SAT II	JAN 05	800 - Writing	DEC 04 800 - US History
		780 - Math IIC	800 - Latin
		800 - Literature	800 - French

Phillips Academy is accredited by the New England Association of Schools and Colleges.
Final grades(FG) are given in yearlong and two-term courses only; TG = trimester grades.

Diploma Requirement: 54 trimester credits
(modified for students who attend fewer than four years).
Classes meet 4 or 5 forty-five minute periods per week,
30 weeks per year, lab periods are 100 minutes.
TRIMESTER averages are rounded to the nearest
half-integer (e.g.,5.5,5.0,4.5).
RANK IN CLASS is not calculated.

GRADING SYSTEM

6	-	OUTSTANDING	1	-	FAILURE
5	-	SUPERIOR	0	-	SERIOUS FAILURE
4	-	SATISFACTORY	F	-	FAIL
3	-	PASS	H	-	HONORS
2	-	MINIMUM PASS	IN	-	INCOMPLETE

[signature]

JOHN ANDERSON
DIRECTOR OF COLLEGE COUNSELING
PHILLIPS ACADEMY
ANDOVER, MA 018--

He would not have been taking prosaic classes like geometry and chemistry at Andover. He filled his fake transcript with all sorts of alluring course titles: "Latin Language and Stylistics," "Accelerated Greek," "Homer and the Epic Tradition," "W. B. Yeats," "Evolution and Ecology," "Vector Calculus." He used a bit of imagination in coming up with some of the classes. (A "Senior Thesis Colloquium," which he said he had been allowed to take as a mere sophomore, did not exist for students of any grade level.) But for the most part, these were true offerings from the Andover course catalog.

He did not mimic Andover's transcript perfectly, though. He broke a few rules that a real student could not have gotten away with: He assigned himself one too many courses his sophomore year and one too few as a senior. He skipped mandatory classes like phys. ed. and introductory history. He put himself into senior English classes as a ninth grader. All of those were minor adjustments that would be highly unlikely to jump out to an admissions officer. Unfamiliar with the school himself until he decided to cast himself as an alumnus, he may well not have known he was stretching those policies. But he made one change to the transcript that was definitely intentional.

In one way, Wheeler borrowed from Caesar Rodney. Unlike Andover, his real high school printed students' SAT scores on their transcripts. In the bottom corner of the Andover transcript that he made, which otherwise closely resembled the format of a real one, he added a list of test scores. There he put his perfect SAT and his six SAT Subject Test scores. Along with his self-report on the Common App and the score report he created, this would be one more form of reinforcement to convince Harvard that those scores were legitimate even though the admissions office would never in fact receive them straight from the College Board.

To accompany that transcript, Wheeler forged a letter of recommendation from the head of college counseling at Andover. In that letter, he accidentally introduced one inconsistency to the story he was spinning. The letter stated that Wheeler came to Andover as a junior in high school. His fake transcript, however, reflected four years at the school.

He was telling too many lies to keep them all straight. Of course no one at Andover actually wrote that letter about Wheeler, but nor did Wheeler write it about himself. He found it in a book called *The Truth About Getting In*. The book, one in the abundant assortment of books about how to get into college, included a few examples of recommendation letters from guidance counselors. It advised buyers of the book, "Your college counselor may find it useful to look over the following examples of excellent college counselor recommendations."

It might be hard to imagine a legitimate applicant handing her guidance counselor a book with a sticky note marking the right page and saying, "Write a letter like that about me, please." But Wheeler did not have to involve anyone else in the process; he could just take entire portions of the letter from the book himself. Therefore, since the "Abby" praised in the book's sample letter had entered her school in her junior year, Wheeler's letter inadvertently incorporated that schedule too. Hence the inconsistency.

The letter described a teenager who was "by far, the most intellectually gifted and at the same time so incredibly unaffected, insightful, truly genuine student I have ever worked with." Of course, the young man who supposedly merited this high praise knew as he printed out his letter that he was not "truly genuine" at all.

The counselor in the book went all out in praising the exceptional Abby—just what Wheeler wanted for the exceptional Adam he was creating on paper. By changing the name and gender of the student, Wheeler's letter now read: "Each of *Adam's* teachers has come to me within weeks of knowing *him* with raves about *his* abilities. All have also stated, without knowledge of the others, that *he* is, without a doubt, the brightest student they have ever had. . . . Special, unique, one of a kind—these are words that do not come close to describing this remarkable young *man*."

Borrowing further from the guidebook's sample letter, Wheeler extolled his own "ravenous appetite for knowledge." This Abby was apparently a student whose eyes lit up upon hearing about academic opportunities, "an educator's dream" who was chomping at the bit to learn just for the sake of learning, and Wheeler used those sentences, too. He did not have the academic and personal credentials that Abby had, but he too was pursuing a chance to go to Harvard by saying that he thirsted for academia and would relish the chance to immerse himself in study there. This application suggested that he hoped Harvard would recognize him in those words about someone else.

To incorporate his specific academic interests, he added phrases from a letter about a student named Stephanie contained in another book by the same author, this one called *Rock Hard Apps*. Thanks to this letter, he suddenly possessed "the mind of a linguist and semiotician, able to parse out complex syntactical structures and determine their root rhetorical devices and grammatical principles. *He* also possesses the sensitivity and extraordinary reading skills of an advanced literary critic, able to place works of literature both in their historical and their formal context. *His* true strength lies in *his* ability to analyze literature *from the inside* [italics from original], from the perspective of a fellow writer and thinker."

Having adopted Stephanie's academic profile, he returned to Abby's letter for extracurricular achievements, co-opting them despite the fact that they did not echo his own. Abby worked as a peer counselor at her school, so Wheeler's letter said that he did as well: "As I watch *him* work with *his* counselees, *his* level of maturity amazes me. *He* treats each student as if he/she were the only student in the *freshman* class. If time were not a factor, *he* would spend hours with each student."

He borrowed a couple of sentences of praise from a third letter in the guidebook, one that was originally about a student named Amanda, before wrapping up the letter. He printed it out on what looked like Andover letterhead, scrawled a signature on the page, and the letter was done.

With his scores, transcript, and letter under his belt, he had created a profile of a student fit for Harvard. In fact, it might have been hard to believe that such an outstanding high school student had set his sights on Bowdoin rather than an even more competitive school. Bowdoin was an excellent school, of course, but this applicant bordered on extraordinary. Surely if he had wanted to go to an Ivy League school, he would have applied successfully.

And so Wheeler decided that he was no longer transferring from Bowdoin. Rather, in his scheme he was enrolled at the Massachusetts Institute of Technology, Harvard's next-door neighbor and one of the leading research institutions in the world. MIT routinely appears among Ivy League schools at the top of the *U.S. News & World Report* rankings of colleges, and its acceptance rate had dipped in recent years into the low teens, making it similarly daunting (and enticing) to applicants.

MIT's Cambridge labs draw many of the brightest scientists from around the globe not to Harvard but to the other school along the Charles River. But obviously, a student like Wheeler would be terribly out of place there. It is a place for math nerds, for aspiring computer scientists, for students who want to spend hours on end hovering over petri dishes in a lab. Close to 50 percent of the student body majors in some type of engineering alone. Many people are surprised to learn that MIT offers any humanities majors at all. All told, less than 4 percent of students choose to major in any of the 12 areas that make up the humanities, arts, and social sciences at MIT (and those include several departments with scientific leanings like economics, linguistics, and "Science, Technology, and Society"). Anecdotally, most in that small crowd are students who discovered only after they started college that they wanted to study Italian or history or theater instead of the scientific field they thought they loved when they applied, or they are students who combine a math or science major with a second one in the humanities.

Sure, he had been brilliant in high school, Wheeler could tell Harvard, and the college admissions history he dreamed up reflected that, just like his transcript did. He had been admitted to super-competitive MIT. But he was an ardent lover of literature, so he eventually realized that he was not in the right place. He was just two T stops away from a hotbed of great thinking in both the sciences and the humanities, and he needed to move. He needed to transfer to Harvard.

He did have to prepare for the possibility that Harvard might ask him why he decided to attend MIT in the first place. If the place was so obviously wrong for him, how come he did not know that earlier? The Harvard application asked him whether he had ever applied to Harvard before, and he checked off no, which was true. In high school, he had not applied to any Ivy League schools.

The application also asked what factors led him to choose the college that he currently attended, and he had no good answer. It listed a few possible reasons—"location, cost, size of student body, only option, special program offered, Early Decision plan"—so he just picked the last one. In the paragraph-size space designated for him to write his response, all he typed was "Early Decision plan." He disregarded the fact that MIT did not even have an early decision option that requires students to attend if they are accepted early. (Bowdoin does, and he had not applied early.)

Now to create a fake MIT transcript. Wheeler decided to cast himself as a college freshman rather than a sophomore as he currently was at Bowdoin. If he were accepted to Harvard, he would get to spend three years there instead of two.

But just because he was purporting to be a freshman did not mean that he listed only one semester of MIT grades. He claimed that he had been a visiting student for four semesters before he matriculated as a full-time student. According to this transcript, he had been taking two or three classes at MIT every semester of his junior and senior years of high school, even while he was shouldering an advanced course load at Andover. The classes were all about literature or philosophy, and he gave himself As in every single one of them.

Then once he started at MIT as a freshman, so his tale went, he had increased his load to six courses per semester. In picking those classes, he stuck to his well-established interests in philosophy and literature. But since this was MIT, he also threw in a math class for good measure: "Analysis I: Fourier Series." Even if math was not his true love, this transcript said that he apparently could hold his own, even among the math whizzes at one of the nation's most esteemed scientific schools. He gave himself an A in that class, and in every class he took that first semester.

A real MIT student could not have earned this transcript. First-semester students at MIT—just like at Harvard—are not allowed to take more than four classes. Some obtain special permission to enroll in extra seminars and programs just for freshmen, but nobody takes six full classes as Wheeler claimed. And no matter how many classes he took, he would not have been able to put down grades in them.

First-semester students at MIT do not receive grades. In every class, they receive either a passing mark on their transcript or, if they fail, no mark at all. Professors secretly assign letter grades for these classes, and the students learn those results in a private meeting with an adviser at the semester's end. Only in rare circumstances—when a student is applying to one of a few very selective medical schools or for certain government grants—can he submit paperwork asking MIT to include those first grades he earned on his official record. Wheeler did not have to fill out any forms, though, because he authorized himself to give himself grades.

For letters of recommendation from MIT, he created three from professors and one from a dean of students who, he said, served as his academic adviser. For Andover, he used the name of the real college counselor there. But for MIT, he used the names of professors whose classes he really had taken—at Bowdoin. If someone were to Google these four people's names, she would quickly see that

Massachusetts Institute of Technology   Office of the Registrar

Academic Transcript

Iam Butler Wheeler

Subject	Subject Name	Lvl	Cred

MIT ID: 922 376 219   Birthdate: ▓▓▓▓▓▓▓

Admitted as a Regular Student for Fall Term 2006-2007
  from PHILLIPS ACADEMY
        ANDOVER, MA

Program/Degree Objective as of Current Term:
  Undeclared

Subject	Subject Name	Lvl	Cred	Grade
FALL TERM 2004-2005	**COURSE:**		**VISITING STUDENT**	
21L721	Milton	U	12	A
24.249	The Philosophy of Aristotle	U	12	A
	* * *			
SPRING TERM 2004-2005	**COURSE:**		**VISITING STUDENT**	
21L700	Arch & 19th Cent American Lit	U	12	A
24.250	The Philosophy of Kant	U	12	A
	* * *			
FALL TERM 2005-2006	**COURSE:**		**VISITING STUDENT**	
21L704	The Bible, Criticism & Theory	U	12	A
17.504	Tocqueville & Mill on Democracy	U	12	A
24.248	Pre Kantian Rationalism	U	12	A
	* * *			
PRING TERM 2005-2006	**COURSE:**		**VISITING STUDENT**	
21L720	Between Literature & Philosophy	U	12	A
24.200	Philosophy & the Study of Rel	U	12	A
24.241	The Philosophy of Plato	U	12	A
	* * *			
FALL TERM 2006-2007	**COURSE:**		**UNDERGRADUATE STUDENT**	
21L701	Place & History in Dickens & Eli	U	12	A
24.253	Philosophy of Mathematics	U	12	A
18.502	Analysis I: Fourier Series	U	12	A
21F340	Reading Proust	U	12	A
17.821	Formal Political Analysis I	U	12	A
24.201	Philosophy & Religious Language	U	12	A
	* * *			
SPRING TERM 2006-2007	**COURSE:**		**UNDERGRADUATE STUDENT**	
.21L702	James Joyce & the Legacy of Mod	U	12	IP
24.263	The Nature of Creativity	U	12	IP
18.504	Seminar in Logic	U	12	IP
21F346	Modern French Literature	U	12	IP
24.251	Philosophy of Language	U	12	IP
21L706	Shakespeare on Film	U	12	IP
	* * *			

OFFICIAL TRANSCRIPT: ISSUED 15-MAR-2007
Order #: 000661727

Issued to

Harvard College Admissions
86 Brattle Street
Cambridge, MA 02138

****
Undergraduate Cumulative GPA: 5.0 (on a 5.0 scale)
****
          -- END OF RECORD --
  -- No Entries Valid Below This Line --

First-semester students at MIT can only take four classes with no letter grades, but Wheeler's forgery said that he took six and earned straight As.

the supposed recommenders worked at Bowdoin, not MIT. But Wheeler was willing to gamble that the admissions officers would be wowed by the praise in the letters without feeling compelled to check their sources.

Together, the letters painted a picture yet again of a phenomenal student. In a room full of college seniors, Wheeler as a high school student had displayed "the most acute critical insights, the most daring and precise intellect, and the strongest analytical and imaginative powers," according to one of the letters. He wrote papers "at a level of complexity and detail that surpassed many published articles." He was the best student in his 50-person math class and perhaps the best to have taken the class in the past four years. He had won two highly competitive fellowships even though he was only a freshman. More remarkable still, he was slated to teach his own course that spring.

In addition to praising the quality of Wheeler's work, the letters referred once more to the genuine enthusiasm with which he approached learning. As one of the recommendations poetically put it, Wheeler showed an "unembarrassed love for the power of the written word."

If he had asked any of the four Bowdoin professors whose signatures he planned to forge to write a real letter of recommendation for him, they probably would have said that he was a skilled writer. They might even have said that he performed well in their classes and that he apparently liked the subject matter. But if they had to comment on his classroom participation, all they could have said was that he was withdrawn.

That is not what Wheeler wrote about himself. He asserted that he was "brilliant, tireless, variously creative, mature, and a leader." One of his falsified recommenders allegedly worried that Wheeler was so far ahead of the rest of the class intellectually that his classmates might have trouble understanding his diction, but fortunately, "Adam articulated his rich and complicated responses to the novels with enormous clarity and rhetorical alertness, and thus kept all of us with him as his mind raced along." It all stood in stark contrast to the aloof young man often seen in the back corner of the classroom.

The letters referred to Wheeler's imaginary extracurricular activities, too. Two mentioned his volunteer work teaching elementary school children to write. One said that he was in charge of training new tutors at MIT's writing center, a role so important that "the welfare of the entire program depends" on it. Another professor had purportedly observed him as he worked as a peer counselor to two of his classmates suffering from "severe psychological difficulties." The professor's reaction to that experience read, "Adam dealt with these challenging situations with remarkable degrees of maturity, patience, and compassion—more, I suspect, than I would have been able to muster had I been confronted as directly with the problems as he was." That line, as well as some other snippets in the letter that Wheeler created, actually came from the testimonials section on the website of a meditation guru called Tracy Quantum, who had no association whatsoever with MIT.

One of the recommenders, the supposed dean of students at MIT (even though his name was actually that of the Bowdoin professor whose classes on Buddhism Wheeler had taken the year before), summed it up more grandiosely than any of the rest: Wheeler was the best freshman at MIT, bar none. It is hard to believe that among the international math contest champions and researchers who had been working on curing cancer since middle school and similar prodigies who fill the halls of MIT every year, Wheeler could be, as the letter said, "the most honored and decorated member of the class." But that was the situation that Wheeler's fake dean of students relayed in his letter to the Harvard admissions committee.

To add detail about all those honors and decorations he had supposedly won, Wheeler attached a list of accolades. His résumé did not list the sort of higher-level math and science recognition that some legitimate MIT and Harvard applicants attain. But it showed a flourishing extracurricular life at MIT: assistant stage manager and set designer for a Gilbert and Sullivan operetta, literature editor of a publication, member of the Shakespeare ensemble and Model United Nations, plus a paid teaching job at the campus writing center and other odds and ends.

He named a few high school awards that would look familiar to any college admissions officer. For one, he claimed to have snagged a National Merit Scholarship, a monetary award given every year to about 8,000 of the top scorers among the 3.5 million students who take the PSAT, a preliminary version of the SAT. Wheeler wrote in one section of his application that he had won the scholarship in 10th grade and in another place that he had won it in 11th—even though the award is only given to high school seniors, plenty of whom apply to Harvard every year. He claimed to have won a writing prize from the National Council of Teachers of English, another organization that admissions officers would certainly recognize.

He also included information about how he had spent the past several summers. When he applied to Bowdoin, he wrote that he had worked in a surf shop at the Delaware beach over the summer. Applying to Harvard, he apparently did not want to declare that he had passed his summer days enjoying sand and sun. Instead, he described academic opportunities that he had pursued over four consecutive summers. He said that in high school, he had participated in Boys State and a Telluride Association Summer Program—a leadership program and an academic camp that both carry name recognition on a national level. Following those experiences, he claimed, he spent his summers on two different research projects in MIT's humanities departments.

To round out his résumé, he listed several local publications that had allegedly printed his poetry. And as proof of his poetic brilliance, he sent nine pages of his poetry directly to Harvard. He took the poems from a book called *The Evolution of the Flightless Bird*. Its writer, Richard Kenney, was a successful yet not widely known living poet. His words were unlikely to be recognized by anyone but a contemporary poetry aficionado. And Wheeler had an extra tie to this book—its foreword was written by James Merrill, whose essay on the opera Wheeler had turned into his moving personal essay.

Kenney's poetry is distinguished by endless clauses, unusual vocabulary, and unconventional punctuation. The selections that Wheeler stole contained words like *oscilloscope*, mentions of the extinct bird species *Phororhacos* and *Diatryma*, and arcane references to a sixth-century Welsh battle poem. Those nine pages of distinctive poetry in small type, taken straight from Kenney's book, were the finishing touch on Wheeler's application.

After hours upon hours of hard work crafting the perfect application, he was ready. He sent his fraudulent package on its way to Harvard.

CHAPTER FOUR

While Adam Wheeler was crafting his Harvard application, he was still a Bowdoin student. He went to class and Frisbee practice by day and pored over fabricated transcripts and score reports by night. He was 10 days away from submitting his finished Harvard application when he received a group email from the professor of his "Philosophy of Law" class.

"A couple of questions have arisen concerning citation," Scott Sehon wrote to the class. "If you use a secondary source of any sort for your journal entries, you should cite the source and make it perfectly clear if you are quoting or paraphrasing. But, given the nature of the assignments, using a secondary source would be missing the point, so I certainly don't recommend it."

Wheeler had been on Sehon's mind when the professor typed those words. He had noticed that Wheeler was consistently submitting whole paragraphs that he had not written himself when he was supposed to be composing his own responses to the class readings. Maybe he misunderstood, Sehon thought optimistically. If so, he thought this email would send a clear message to the student: I'm on to you, and you had better clean up your act. If it is an honest mistake, he thought, Wheeler will come running to my office to explain himself.

The next day, Wheeler turned in his fifth plagiarized journal entry.

Sehon waited nearly a week before he brought the topic up with Wheeler. Then on February 26, he told Wheeler that he wanted to speak with him after class. Once the two of them were alone, Sehon handed Wheeler a piece of paper. It was his recent email about citing sources. He had printed it out especially for this encounter.

Did you receive it? he asked.

I didn't see it, Wheeler said. Maybe I deleted it by accident.

Silence ensued as Wheeler sat reading the paper. Eventually, the professor realized that he had finished reading and simply was not saying anything.

Sehon supposed he would have to talk first. He pointed out the part of the email that instructed students to identify any secondary sources that they used in their journal entries. "The question arose because I found some of the language in your journal entries very philosopher-esque," Sehon said. "Are they yours?"

"They are mine, but I did read some secondary sources," Wheeler replied. He told the professor that he had been intimidated by the assignments. After all, this was his first semester taking philosophy, and he was taking this intermediate-level class without having taken an introductory one. The readings were daunting. So he had looked at some other sources that helped him understand them before completing his journal entries.

"But the material in them is yours?" Sehon asked him.

"Right."

Wheeler came back to Sehon's office later that day of his own accord. I can show you the secondary sources that I looked at when I was writing my journal entries, he offered.

I already found them myself, Sehon said. I think I have no choice but to take this to the J-Board.

The next day, Sehon sent a thick packet to the J-Board. He compiled a meticulously organized table matching the full text of every one of Wheeler's plagiarized journal entries to the original source. He also sent full copies of all the scholarly articles Wheeler had stolen paragraphs from. The final page in the packet was Bowdoin's academic honor code, which Sehon emphasized in his cover letter he had discussed with his students. Any of the great lawyers on the syllabus of Sehon's class might have envied the professor's detailed and damning presentation of evidence.

Two days later, Wheeler clicked "submit" on his Harvard transfer application. The day after that, he received a letter from the J-Board: "You have been charged with violating the Bowdoin College Academic Honor Code."

With the Harvard application off his to-do list, Wheeler had more free time, but he had not planned on spending it in deans' offices. Now, on the very day that he learned he had been charged with an academic violation, he found himself meeting with an administrator to review his rights as an accused student. He was not too interested in exercising most of them. He did not want to write a request to remove one of the J-Board's members from hearing his case. He did not want to bring anybody from the college to support him at his upcoming hearing. Even finding out the evidence against him could not have been too intriguing. He already knew that Sehon had noticed he was plagiarizing his journal entries.

He had had his brush with administrators before. At the end of his freshman year at Bowdoin, he did not turn in any of his final papers or attend his exams. There had been a fuss about it. One dean had called his father and scribbled down notes like "anxiety high," "perfectionism," "not open to others," "reclusive," "not share feelings/thoughts." In the end, he had received a personal excuse from a dean, meaning that he could turn all his papers in more than a week late. He had gone home to Delaware, and the whole episode had blown over so quickly that two of the three professors involved did not even recall after the fact that he had ever missed any deadlines. This time, Wheeler's encounter with Bowdoin administrators was likely to leave a more lasting mark.

He showed up for his hearing on the appointed evening, less than a week after his original summons. In a stark conference room, a process unfolded not unlike the judicial procedure he had been studying in the class that had landed him in all this trouble.

The three students and two adults sitting in front of him had read Sehon's account of Wheeler's plagiarism already. They asked some questions of both Wheeler and Sehon. The accuser and the accused were both expected to be present at the hearing, but they were not allowed to talk to each other. If the student wanted to ask the professor a question, he would have to ask it to the committee instead. Then one of the J-Board members would repeat it, and the professor would direct his response to the J-Board, not the student. The same procedure would apply if the professor had a question for the student.

After the questioning, Wheeler was told to leave the room. He knew the members of the J-Board were discussing his fate at Bowdoin. In all likelihood, he would be convicted of plagiarizing his journal entries as Sehon had so thoroughly demonstrated. But he still did not know what punishment he would be handed. The discussion going on among those few students and teachers on the other side of the door would determine whether he would receive just a failing grade in Sehon's class or a ban on returning to Bowdoin for a semester or more.

Most students probably quake in their boots while awaiting a J-Board decision. But Wheeler already intended to leave the college that had been his home for two years. If he never saw his Frisbee friends again or he missed the next snowfall to hit Maine, that would be his choice, not just the J-Board's. All that he needed now was for Harvard to say yes to the application that he had worked so hard to prepare, and he would be headed out of Brunswick whether Bowdoin allowed him to stay or not. The J-Board did not have a clue how little its verdict mattered to his future.

Sometimes, J-Board members debate for an entire day on one case. This time, it did not take nearly that long. Less than four hours after the hearing began, the student who had been appointed to chair the discussion of Wheeler's case emailed the dean of students to report the board's ruling. A one-semester suspension and an F in Sehon's class, the board had decided, would be the appropriate punishment. Wheeler received a letter the next day telling him he could finish up the semester but he could not come back next fall. Even setting foot on campus during the semester could get him kicked out permanently.

It was a grim letter. But the senders did not know about Wheeler's intent to transfer to Harvard. Bowdoin administrators had no reason to suspect that just one state south of Brunswick, admissions officers in Cambridge were mulling over an intriguing transfer application from an Andover alumnus/MIT freshman/published poet who happened to share a name with one of their own Bowdoin sophomores.

Just as his semester was winding down at Bowdoin, Wheeler heard from Harvard for the first time. Since he was so close to Harvard, the admissions officer said—just down the road at MIT—they would like to invite him to come to the admissions office for an interview.

I'm actually in Maine right now, he responded. I won't be back in Cambridge for a while.

The coordinator of transfer admissions put out an urgent request for an interviewer in Maine to get in touch with Wheeler, and the very next day, he had an interview. He had not told any officials at Bowdoin about his transfer application, though he did tell his parents. They advised him to wait out his one-semester suspension and then return to his beloved Bowdoin, but when he insisted that he wanted to try transferring, they agreed to pay the application fee. And regardless of the fact that his Harvard application was a secret at Bowdoin, he brazenly planned to meet up with his Harvard interviewer, an alumnus from the Class of 1975, inside a Bowdoin library.

The first question the interviewer asked, of course, was what an MIT student was doing at Bowdoin. Wheeler said that none of the classes he was taking at MIT that semester had final exams, so he was free to depart from campus and finish writing his MIT papers wherever he found himself. An English professor at MIT put him in touch with an acquaintance at Bowdoin who happened to need some help with a chapter of a book on legal references in Shakespearean sonnets. Halfway through the semester, Wheeler said, he left Cambridge and moved up to Bowdoin, where he worked as the professor's research assistant, audited a senior seminar, and lived in an extra room in student housing.

The interviewer noticed right away that Wheeler had already proved that he could navigate the unusual experience of switching colleges midway through his education—certainly a selling point for a would-be transfer student. He asked Wheeler about the differences between urban MIT and rural Bowdoin and about his experience becoming part of a new college community in the middle of the spring semester. He was impressed by all the answers Wheeler gave. He seemed to have met many students and familiarized himself with campus culture remarkably well in just a few weeks. Wheeler also spoke warmly of his MIT friends and said he would be sorry to leave them even though he hoped to enjoy academic experiences at Harvard that were more amenable to his interests. Here is a student, the interviewer told the Harvard admissions committee in his report about the conversation, "who has 'fit in' in two places in a short time, and is not a loner (in a circumstance where it could easily happen)."

He asked Wheeler about social life on campus. "Does everyone vanish on the weekends," he wondered, since there is not much to do in Brunswick? Alternately, do they stick around for the parties? "Is there a lot of weekend drinking?"

"I hear that there is some," Wheeler replied. "But I was fortuitously placed in a 'chem free' dorm, where all the others have made a conscious choice to bypass that scene. We have individual rooms, but a lot of common areas on the ground floor where we hang out together unless we have specific plans."

Wheeler was making Bowdoin sound very agreeable in his answers. The interviewer confided that his wife had audited a class there and had not been nearly as pleased with the college as Wheeler seemed to be. As she had seen it, students showed up to class, but then they "tuned out." Had he observed the same tendency?

"Not at all in my class," Wheeler said. "It's mostly seniors, many of whom are *not* English majors, but they're all there because they want to be, and are clearly prepared for class."

He had to make himself sound a bit superior, though. "There is some 'like' and 'you know' scattered here and there, but it's not overwhelming," he said. "A friend and I were just talking about 'you know' in the context of a Joyce Carol Oates play that uses it to good effect—we finally decided we'd just have to get used to it."

He had a knack for bringing every thread of conversation back to literature. In their hour-long talk, Wheeler expounded on the social and political climate that gave birth to Elizabethan literature, the fear and uncertainty that are evident in art produced during periods of religious transition, and even Ronald Dworkin's legal philosophy (which, he did not mention, he had encountered in the class that had just led to his suspension from Bowdoin).

Wheeler's flair for bending the conversation toward academic subjects did not seem calculated to impress the interviewer. He just seemed to naturally connect everything to his favorite topics. "There is *no* doubt," his interviewer wrote, "that Adam's interest is separate from the Harvard application, rather than the 'story' to justify the transfer, and that he'll pursue it as far as he can, regardless of Harvard's decision."

When it came to that decision, the interviewer did feel that it ought to come out well for Wheeler. He predicted that if admitted, Wheeler would end up doing Harvard proud. He foresaw him graduating *summa cum laude* and going on to a career in academia. His final words to the admissions committee endorsed Wheeler: "Finding and executing on the experience he's now having at Bowdoin makes him a proven academic quantity, not only compared to this year's senior high school candidates, but, I'm guessing, against many of your current freshmen. If you have room for him, he would do well, and be indistinguishable from freshmen entrants by the end of his sophomore year."

～～

It was a busy time in the Harvard admissions office when that interview report came in. Not that that was unusual. The admissions office is nearly always busy. Even during the slight lull of the summer months, when the most recent crop has been admitted (or rejected) and the next class has yet to apply, admissions officers travel the world to give presentations about Harvard, and the phones in the office ring steadily with questions from prospective applicants and their parents. Then, once the fall hits, the applications start coming in. Every single one of them is read all the way through by at least two officers, and then each application is discussed and voted on in a committee meeting.

The Harvard admissions committee scrutinizes applicants in a manner that is remarkably personal. The review goes far beyond a cursory glance at grades and test scores. It is a finely tuned, carefully guarded machine. It is an obsessively discussed process among high school students and their parents and counselors and coaches worldwide. It is intensive, rigorous, and deeply admirable in its thoroughness and its thirst for excellence of all stripes. It gets harder every year to pull it off.

As application numbers climb dizzyingly higher, admissions officers are swamped in their quest to maintain their high standards of attention to each student. They read files seven days a week in peak season. The full committee, a group of about 40 people who have the final yay or nay vote on every student in the incoming class, meets six days a week for about three weeks to put together the list of acceptees. A single officer might read the entire file—the essays, transcripts, letters of recommendation, supplementary newspaper clippings and collages and creative writing—of 1,000 applicants in one admissions cycle.

The process starts in the basement of the pristine admissions building, found on a quiet street a bit removed from the heart of campus. It is there that the mail is delivered. And even though about 95 percent of students' Common Apps plus an increasing number of secondary school reports and teacher recommendations are submitted online nowadays, the Harvard admissions office receives unbelievable amounts of mail.

Student employees and other staffers open the deluge of envelopes that pour into the mail room and print out every page of the massive number of online submissions. Then they sort all that material into applicants' personal folders, housed in a long crimson-painted room lined with about 30 filing cabinets that together hold a mind-boggling amount of paper. (At about 30 pages for the average applicant, one admissions cycle totals almost a million sheets.)

Some submissions do not fit in the filing cabinets. An entire room across the hall is devoted to holding larger specimens of student work. Pottery, oil paintings, and papier-mâché sent by crafty applicants form an impromptu art museum in the room. Stacks of CDs and DVDs bearing applicants' musical performances or football game clips or science fair presentations keep company with the art. An entire floor-to-ceiling shelf contains the manuscripts of novels written by the current year's applicant pool alone.

One wall of this room is decorated with a poster-size blow-up of the first page of the Common App, sent years ago by an applicant hoping to impress admissions officers with his creativity or at least his ability to get large objects through the United States Postal Service. It came with a gigantic paperclip too. Though the student was not admitted, his oversize application hangs at Harvard to this day.

One closet serves as a makeshift shrine to the kookiest submissions of all time: bars of handmade soap with pictures of Harvard scenery inked onto them. Knitted clothing. Homemade hot sauce.

The first person who picks up a student's completed file (along with whatever might accompany it) is the admissions officer assigned to the part of the country or the world that the student hails from. The officer reads every page of the file and takes notes on a sheet of paper filled with codes designed for efficiently marking off any of the common accolades accrued by top high school students. With a preprinted list of abbreviated extracurricular activities, all an officer has to do is circle which of the 32 usual pursuits (from cheerleading to Key Club to mock trial to Future Farmers of America to ethnic and religious groups to Quiz Bowl) the applicant participates in. For Wheeler, the admissions officer circled tutoring and magazine, plus drama with some notes scrawled in pen next to it: "G & S [Gilbert and Sullivan], Shk [Shakespeare], design & house manager." The handwritten additions mentioned two of Wheeler's activities that did not quite fit into the 32 categories: Shakespeare club and creative writing club.

Another section of the sheet is meant for academic honors, with more abbreviations designating the national recognitions that the admissions committee most commonly sees. Officers can circle designations like National Merit status, membership in the National Honor Society, and scores on the American Invitational Mathematics Examination. The National Council of Teachers of English award that Wheeler claimed to have won was on that list, and the admissions officer not only circled it but also put an exclamation mark by it. The officer also wrote down Telluride, clearly impressed by the academic summer program that Wheeler said he had attended.

Still another section records work, study abroad, or research experience; there the officer noted Wheeler's 10-hour-a-week job in MIT's writing center. The evaluation sheet also lists all sorts of tests, including not just American standards but also exams offered in foreign countries like the A-levels and the GCSE of the United Kingdom. Each of the 33 AP exams appears with its own abbreviation. The officer marked a 5 next to each of the 16 that Wheeler said he took.

Wheeler's file was thick. Thanks to his extra letters of recommendation and his poetic submissions, it totaled 50 pages, quite a bit more than average. The packet fell to a reader who efficiently perused the obtuse personal essay that Wheeler had cobbled together from the words of five different professors. The officer did not mark the strange pivots from one thought to the next, but instead circled just two words: "multidisciplinary" and "cross-disciplinary." Wheeler's letters of recommendation likewise held up under scrutiny. The officer dashed check marks next to some laudatory lines, like testimony that Wheeler's writing was "dazzling," that his work resembled that of an advanced graduate student rather than a college freshman, and that he would be teaching a course that year that he had designed himself.

When the first reader had finished with Wheeler's application, the file was whisked down the hall to the next. A second person gave it another go-through, reading every page once again and evaluating the strength of the application's components on a numerical scale. On every aspect of the application, the second reader inked in judgments nearly identical to the first. That officer also added one more note on the summary sheet. Where the first had marked down Wheeler's AP scores test by test, the second jotted in the margin, "16 x 5's!" Wheeler had wowed someone at Harvard with his lengthy list of perfect scores.

A file that has been read by two officers might be passed on to a third and even a fourth and fifth reader if for some reason one of the first two flags it as one that ought to be examined further. For example, when a musician sends a sample of her original compositions, admissions officers might pass the CD along to a music instructor to get a professional opinion on just how good the student's work is, and scientific research might be evaluated by an expert in that field.

And then, in the ordinary freshman application cycle, the meetings begin. First, 20 separate subcommittees, each representing a different part of the country or the world, gather to consider applications. The regional officer who first read an applicant's file represents him to the rest of the subcommittee, quickly summarizing the high and low points of the application and making a recommendation about whether the student should advance to the next round of consideration. Some make it out of subcommittee. Many do not.

Then the full committee convenes. This time, students from all over the world are judged against one another. Again, regional reps advocate for the students whose applications they reviewed. Sometimes, a rep places a student's personal statement or a teacher recommendation on the visualizer machine, projecting it onto the wall for the entire committee to read. All 40-something people in the room—admissions staff as well as Harvard faculty who serve on the committee—read one student's essay. The discussion is sometimes lengthy and heated when an officer has grown passionate about making a particular student's case. And eventually, there's an up-or-down vote. Slowly, the separate lists grow longer. Reject. Wait list. Accept.

Occasionally, admissions officers come across files that seem suspicious and prompt further investigation. By far the most common cause of concern, many former admissions officers say, is a student's essay. If a student has poor grades in her high school English classes or a low score on the writing section of the SAT, yet her personal statement sparkles, officers are apt to notice. All too frequently, they know, students copy and paste their essays from the Internet or pay for a pre-written essay from an online service. Even more often, they receive help, which might range from a perfectly acceptable second look to an essay entirely composed by a parent or teacher.

Sometimes, the shaky grades and test scores are damaging enough that the student is clearly one for the reject pile—so there is no reason for the admissions officer to spend time discerning whether the statement is the student's own. In other instances, officers are intrigued enough by the candidate in front of them to look into whether she actually wrote her own essay. They might call her high school guidance counselor to get a franker perspective on her abilities. He can help the college assess whether the student could have produced such an essay on her own.

An officer might also use a new tool that has been at his disposal since 2005, when the SAT added a writing section. No longer is the standardized test an ordeal only of filling in bubbles. For 25 minutes, students also have to write an essay. That essay, graded by College Board workers, is scanned into an online system. Typically, college admissions officers just look at the student's score on the writing section, a number out of 800 just like reading and math. But if they wish, they can actually pull up the essay that the student scribbled during a timed period under a proctor's supervision. That is one way, longtime college admissions counselor Matthew Greene noted, that officers can get a more accurate idea of a student's writing ability if they suspect that her essay might not be her own work.

Even more direct than making educated guesses about the honesty of a student's essay based on her prior performance, a paid service such as TurnItIn.com can scan the application statement itself for plagiarized content. In the classroom, a teacher can feed a paper that a student has submitted into the TurnItIn system, and within moments, she receives a report that identifies any potentially problematic text. That might be content from the Internet, text from a book or journal stored in TurnItIn's database, or words from any other paper that has ever been fed through TurnItIn. That last component, employees of the company say, is what makes their service better than a simple Google search for a few phrases from a student's paper. Google does not address the fact that teens frequently plagiarize not from published work but from old assignments that their friends and siblings pass down to them, or they buy essays from online sellers who do not post their work to the Internet but do secretly peddle the same essay to many students.

In 2009 the company introduced a new version designed specifically for admissions statements. So far, more than 100 universities have bought in. Jeff Lorton, a product and business manager for TurnItIn for Admissions, said that the average school using the system discovers plagiarism in about 5 percent of the essays it receives. At some institutions, that figure is as high as 20 percent. And no type of school is spared: An organization that ordains Methodist ministers signed up for the service, Lorton said, to run checks on applicants' "sermons and letters to parishioners and other things like that to show how you work with your flock." The religious institution found that "they get a lot of plagiarism in the sermons," Lorton said.

As the example of the would-be ministers shows, Lorton added, "Pretty much anybody who receives an application that includes something that is written by the applicant may use our service." He said that TurnItIn is in talks with the Common Application right now; soon, every time a student sends an essay through the Common App, it might automatically be sent through the TurnItIn for Admissions system before reaching all the schools that the student has selected. That deal, which he characterized as "very close" to materializing in the next year or two, would greatly expand the reach of systematic technology in combating plagiarized essays—a direct attack on the type of fraud Wheeler perpetrated.

Beyond the essay, officers occasionally question the veracity of the biographical details they learn about a student through his application. Sometimes, those questions come up when they are looking at the activities a student fills in on the Common App, which asks how many hours per week a student spends on each of the pursuits he lists. Do the time commitments listed exceed the number of hours in a week? That seems suspicious. On other occasions, the life stories are more far-fetched.

"If you're going to admit somebody on the basis of extraordinary facts that they put before you, you've got to make sure that they check out," cautioned Barmak Nassirian, an associate executive director of the American Association of Collegiate Registrars and Admissions Officers. He said that when the admissions officers his organization works with make their decisions based on a student's account of incredible achievement or astounding ability to overcome adversity, the officers try to call the student's high school to confirm the truth of the claim. "There are these outliers who come in with a narrative that has a single extraordinary fact. . . . If somebody tells you that what you need to know about me is that I fell off a horse when I was in ninth grade and I spent two years in a coma and I've come back from that with a sense of purpose—from summer school and tutoring and yadayadayada—and that becomes a central fact in your decision that they belong in the incoming class, then those extraordinary facts that are determinants in admission ought to be checked out."

Investigations like that, Nassirian said, are rare. Students with such extreme stories do not come along every day. Moreover, admissions officers simply do not have time to carefully vet every story. "I suspect a lot of things that might be oversights are because these offices are so busy," Greene said, pointing to increases in the number of students prepared to attend elite universities and the number of applications each of them submits. "Staffing is difficult. There is a giant increase in the number of applications that they're seeing and the complexity."

Background checks do occur despite the pressure, though. Erinn Andrews, a former Stanford admissions officer who now works as a college admissions consultant, remembers one transfer applicant who "completely impressed" her and her fellow admissions officers. "Probably one of the top applicants of the year," Andrews recalled. "Literally everything was just amazing. She had written books."

When Andrews presented the student's case at the committee table, the dean of admissions voiced hesitation about admitting the outstanding applicant off the bat. "I smell something fishy here," he said to Andrews. "It's too good to be true."

Andrews called the people whose names were on the young woman's letters of recommendation to confirm that they had written them and that the honors the student claimed were true. Andrews's conclusion? "In fact, she was as good as she said she was." But it had not hurt to be cautious.

Not all components of students' applications are handled as skeptically as the subjective pieces, though. The piece that comes with the most built-in verification methods is rarely checked at all.

That piece is the transcript. To make transcripts difficult to forge, many colleges and even some high schools purchase high-security paper that can run anywhere from a penny to more than $5 per page. This paper can incorporate a variety of technologies meant to stop a student from touching up his grades and assure an admissions office that the record on the page is real. Paper can be made so that it stains an ugly brown or suddenly reveals the word VOID in multiple languages if a student tries to bleach a bad letter grade off his transcript or scratch a printed course name from the page. It can be treated so that anyone who tries to make a photocopy will find chaotic numbers and letters or the glaring word COPY written all over his replica. Schools can add holograms or heat-sensitive images to the page.

Those technologies are hard to foil. Formerly, the more unusual techniques were used primarily for government documents. Today, however, according to George Phillips, the CEO of International Security Products, Inc., close to 500 colleges and universities pay for that sort of protection. The companies that add these security technologies to paper work hard to keep their products out of the hands of unscrupulous students. They typically refuse to sell their wares to private individuals, including calling to verify the identity of purchasers without a .edu email address. But all those companies buy the paper that they treat—a thick stock, often with a generic watermark embedded during the printing process—from just a few paper mills. A student, some officials of those companies said, can probably get that paper directly from one of the paper mills. Moreover, a forger can purchase similar 24-pound paper at any office supply store.

Richard Isom sells high-security paper through his company, Vive Studio, Inc. He knows all about watermarks and chemically reactive paper and fibers that appear under a black light. Just by looking at a piece of paper, he can tell whether it was printed on a home printer or a professional press and whether the image on it has ever been scanned. He is confident that the technologies contained in the paper he sells are enough to foil almost any scammer. Yet all of that is meaningless if the people receiving documents are not looking for those indicators. "The human factor is always the biggest part," Isom said. "If somebody doesn't really look closely, you can get away with all sorts of stuff."

Anyone intent on forgery, Phillips said, "can do a very good job of mimicking a transcript." Nowadays, he does not even need the know-how to forge a document himself. The Internet advertises dozens of companies that will do it for him. Unsurprisingly, the companies do not tend to advertise their products as forgeries. Phony degrees, they say, make great novelty gifts. Who would not want to give his cat or his coworker a Harvard diploma for Christmas?

One site suggests that a college student who spent his time at school partying rather than studying might purchase a fake transcript so that he can show his parents good grades at the end of the semester. Another site assures the buyer that holding a glowing transcript in his name, even if he did not earn those grades, will increase his self-esteem. Getting his bona fide transcript from the school he attended, especially if his college days are long past, might just be too time-consuming or complicated, other companies suggest. A few hint more directly that a counterfeit high school transcript might boost him into college, or a phony college diploma might be just what he needs to land a new job. Almost all of them insist that their products are not meant to be used as instruments of fraud, but it is obvious that a buyer might not take that message to heart.

The companies do put policies in place to ensure that their transcripts and diplomas do not fall into dangerous hands. They refuse to send fabricated documents to countries that could pose a national security threat to the United States. Some will not manufacture degrees in law, medicine, or other sensitive disciplines in which an unqualified practitioner could obviously cause real harm. Some honor the wishes of any university that requests that they never replicate its documents.

But with all the online outlets out there, a buyer can probably find the transcript he wants, and the reproduction he purchases may come with many of the security features of the real thing, from watermarks to visible and invisible fibers embedded in the paper to, ironically, protection against photocopying. The price he pays may range from $50 to $450.

Evidence of the problem is an easy Google search away. Fake transcript companies abound online, and posts to forums like Yahoo! Answers by questioners looking for ways to convince colleges and potential employers that they hold degrees that they have not actually acquired indicate that people are using the services that are out there.

Theoretically, admissions officers could call the college or high school that the transcript comes from. They could learn what the security features are on the school's valid transcripts and could then look for them, or they could ask the school if the student whose file is sitting in the admissions office was ever enrolled. That sort of audit, however, would be excessively time-consuming. Even if admissions offices were to check the credentials of only the students they planned to accept out of the tens of thousands of applicants they see each year, the workload would be overwhelming. Instead, they employ a few carefully chosen safeguards that simply cannot plug every single gap. "A college is really not able to really closely verify every document sent from every high school in the country," said David Hawkins, director of public policy and research at the National Association for College Admission Counseling. The only option is a balanced approach between scrutiny and trust. Nevertheless, Hawkins said, "That is obviously a process that is open to malfeasance."

Nassirian, the executive of the professional organization of admissions officers, recommends that colleges check the postmarks on the envelopes that transcripts arrive in. If a University of Michigan transcript arrives in an envelope sent from Arizona, that should be an indication that something is wrong. But admissions officers at several top colleges say that their mail is opened by student employees and other staffers who are not instructed to look at the place stamped on it. As the materials are sorted into neat piles—one for letters of recommendation, one for transcripts, one for Common Apps, et cetera—the envelopes go into the trash can.

At some colleges, readers review freshman applications in groups by region and even by school. If someone has 20 applications on her desk that all come from the same high school, officers say, then she will likely notice if one student has a blue transcript in his file and all the rest are green. But if the student is the only applicant from his high school—or even more difficult, if he is home-schooled or coming from a foreign country where the secondary education system might be very different—then that sort of check is nonexistent. Even when those schools advertise on the backs of their transcripts that certain features can be used to verify the document's authenticity, officers rarely take the time to hold a paper up to the light to look for a patterned watermark, tilt it in search of a holographic image, or press a thumb to a spot or breathe over it to try to activate a message that appears when exposed to heat. Busy readers do not have time to blow on paper.

"We're moving through applications so quickly that I doubt we would pick up those subtleties," Andrews said. "I think the parts that would still raise the red flag are the other components. I don't think the forged documents are the things that would set the alarm bells off. It would be the other claims. Whether it is publishing something, filing a patent, winning a medal—there are a lot of different awards and accolades that students might claim that are, especially when all put together, seemingly too good to be true."

Andrews said that as a Stanford admissions officer, she would frequently look up the International Math Olympiad or Scripps Spelling Bee winners' names from a particular year to see whether a student who claimed to have earned one of those distinctions truly had. She did not bother to check on state or local awards. Nearly every student listed those on his résumé. Only national or international recognition, she said, would be significant enough anyway to get someone into Stanford solely on the strength of one particular award. She made many searches for those types of claims, but never once did she consider whether she was looking at a forged transcript. "I just don't think people are trained to look for those," she said.

The protection that comes from reading a whole batch of applications from the same high school, too, often disappears when it comes to transfer admissions. First of all, the transfer admissions process happens after the exhaustive freshman selection process has been completed. When *The New York Times* wrote about admissions fraud in 1995, an anonymous former Ivy League dean of admissions told the newspaper, "Transfer applicants are handled in a perfunctory way. The admissions staff is tired by the time they get around to them." Moreover, regardless of how alert officers are, the entire pool is much smaller. That means an officer might only see one application per year from nearly every college that transfer students come from. Geography aside, a Harvard reader will see far more transcripts in a year from a top L.A. prep school than from Harvard's next-door neighbor, MIT. Admissions officers become experts on high schools across the nation but have far less opportunity to get to know the ins and outs of their fellow institutions of higher education. In the context of transfer admissions, it is thus easy to imagine how Wheeler's fake MIT transcript, showing grades from a school that does not give them to freshmen, did not catch the eye of Harvard's admissions workers.

In addition to the relative shelter that Wheeler might have profited from as a transfer student, he also might have escaped notice, surprisingly, in part because Harvard does see applications from Andover. The school's very familiarity to the admissions office might oddly have made it the perfect choice for sneaking in right under Harvard's nose. Admissions officers are quicker to suspect fraud from students applying from abroad, they say. Not only is it tough for them to know how to hold up foreign GPAs and test scores against American standards, but many applicants from foreign countries do cheat, and admissions officers know that. "We're on high alert for falsified documents coming in from China," Andrews said.

She and her coworkers at Stanford had good reason to keep their eyes open. Chinese families pay thousands or tens of thousands of dollars to people who promise to get their children into top American universities, and often, those counselors achieve that goal through outright fraud. A 2010 survey of 250 students from top Chinese high schools who sent applications to foreign universities revealed that about 90 percent of their applications included recommendation letters signed by teachers who never penned them. One student quoted in a 2011 study of 257 Chinese students enrolled in American universities (57 percent of whom had contracted agents in China to help them get in) confided to the researchers, "My agent wrote the recommendation letters for me. I just need to provide three names of my high school teachers or college instructors, and he took care of the rest."

School administrators in China have attested to the prevalence of fraudulent transcripts and recommendations, and American admissions officers complain of frequent too-good-to-be-true essays and test scores—anecdotes also backed up by the 2010 survey, which found that 70 percent of the Chinese applications used plagiarized essays and 50 percent included fake transcripts. Another 30 percent of the students admitted to lying on their financial aid applications, a problem that Hawkins said pops up as well among students and parents in the United States, where it can be a federal crime.

The fraud can be even more creative. One company employed by families in both Asia and the United States to get their children into top-notch colleges has gone so far as to build a website to provide "media coverage" of one student's accomplishment and founded a Model United Nations group so that another applicant could participate in it, according to *The New York Times*.

College admissions frenzy certainly is not limited to students in Asia or to those applying to American schools. In a tragic incident in January 2012, a woman was trampled to death in South Africa as a crowd of about 11,000 applicants rushed forward to seek only 800 freshman spots on an in-person application day at the University of Johannesburg.

Among American students, standardized test cheating scandals cause alarm from time to time. Most recently, a 2011 crackdown on SAT and ACT cheating in Long Island, New York, found about 40 students who either had paid anywhere from $500 to $3,600 to have someone else take one of the exams for them or had repeatedly used fake IDs to take the exams on behalf of others. Fifteen of those students at five schools who paid their peers to take the SAT for them, earning them scores between 2170 and 2220 out of 2400, were compelled to sit for the test themselves and were barred from attending prom—and were charged with misdemeanors in criminal court. Five students who created fake IDs in order to take the tests for others were charged with felonies. As soon as the scandal became public, other high school students poured out tales of similar behavior that they had witnessed. Test-takers share answers in the bathroom during breaks, surreptitiously look up vocabulary words on their cell phones, and even pass their answer sheets to each other during the test.

But even in light of proof that the same anxieties that drive foreign students to cheat can give rise to dishonesty in some of America's most educationally driven communities, admissions officers say that they reserve most of their suspicion for questionable applications from international students as well as homeschoolers and students from little-known high schools.

Admissions officers are aware that they do not know much about a small rural high school's transcript, that it is easy for an unscrupulous homeschooled student to fudge achievements, and that they have a tough time verifying foreign credentials. If a student were to craft a phony past, why would he possibly claim to come from a place that officers knew well? No one at Harvard thought to call MIT or Andover to check Wheeler's background—because why would a pretender be daring or thoughtless enough to say that he attends those schools if he does not? By fabricating the best résumé he could, Wheeler may have cooked up the best path right through Harvard's front door.

"Who would claim to be from the school one metro stop away?" Nassirian put it. "Surely if they were going to lie, they would lie from some exotic, faraway place."

That logic is commonplace in the admissions office. "With homeschooled students, we often would call," Andrews said. "When it is coming from an established institution that we're used to seeing and familiar ... we would not notice." Andrews adds, "I can certainly say for myself that I may have seen thousands of transcripts from a particular high school, and I still would not be able to pick up a forgery." This mix of trusted schools and tough-to-discern fabrication worked flawlessly for Wheeler. His file made its way through two readers and on to the full committee.

Harvard had protections in place, surely enough to catch many fakers who try and fail to get in each year. But no system can catch every con artist. "There are very few protections to stop people from making up an entire universe of their own," Hawkins said. Despite the precautions that admissions experts take, he added, "The process overall is anything but foolproof." A few of the cleverest or luckiest liars can and do manage to slip through, taking advantage of admissions officers' trust.

It is a festive day at the very end of March when freshman admissions decisions have been made and the fateful letters are ready to be mailed. Even though most students will read their admissions decisions in their email inboxes that very night, every Harvard decision goes out in hard copy as well. A specially ordered mail truck pulls up at the back door of the admissions office's building.

The admissions staff forms a human chain that winds from the truck down a ramp into the basement of the building, where the mailings have been painstakingly assembled, coating the floor of the file room in Postal Service–issued bins. It is a fitting outpouring of paper to match the million or so pages that flowed into the mailroom a few months earlier.

First the bins of acceptance letters, thick envelopes full of glossy "Welcome to Harvard" pamphlets that each cost upwards of $4 to mail (and that is just domestically), are passed from one person to the next until they are all in the truck, ready to be delivered to overjoyed teenagers around the world. That does not take very long. There are only about 2,000 of those precious envelopes. Then come the rejection letters. They are thin, as everyone knows. Far more of them fit into one postal tray. Still, it takes a long time to pass all the trays out of the office. They keep coming and coming, no after no after no.

One year, one officer commented, "That's 28,000 broken hearts!" as she slung a tray to the next person in line. Her coworker responded, "There's always grad school," to which she nodded, "Now I'll sleep better!" Afterward the staff headed inside to celebrate, toasting the newly selected class with champagne before the students even knew they had been chosen. An alum, still grateful to the admissions staff for that acceptance letter, had donated the bubbly.

Though that day turned out to be gloomy for thousands when they opened their email from Harvard after 5 p.m., it was exhilarating for a lucky 2,000 or so. It was jubilant as well for the admissions staff, fresh off a solid three weeks of round-the-clock committee meetings, but their work was not done. A few weeks down the road, once the first group of admitted students had declared whether they would attend, the full committee would meet once more to reconsider the case of every student on the wait list. Depending on that year's yield, anywhere from none to more than 100 of them would be admitted. And the committee still had to make decisions about transfer students too.

Transfer admission is even more competitive than the race for entry into the freshman class. Recently, Harvard has offered spots to only one to two dozen transfer students a year. For two years shortly after Wheeler entered, the college suspended transfer admissions altogether. The acceptance rate can be as low as a mere 1 percent. That was the pool in which Wheeler's application was competing when his application went to committee in the spring. The odds were overwhelmingly against even the most impressive of applicants. But of course, even the most impressive of applicants did not ordinarily have the opportunity to re-create their grades, test scores, and recommendation letters.

In late spring, Wheeler received his letter. He was in.

CHAPTER FIVE

That glorious acceptance letter was just the first piece of correspondence that Adam Wheeler received from Harvard. Over the next few weeks, he repeatedly found letters with crimson seals in his mailbox and inbox.

One of the most significant messages over that summer told him he would be living in a dorm called Kirkland House with four roommates.

All Harvard freshmen—including the four young men he would be living with as sophomores—face a daunting task just before spring break rolls around. They have to choose up to seven of their best friends with whom they want to live for the rest of their time in college.

Tears are shed. Friendships dissolve over who wants to invite whom to be one of the eight members of what is called a blocking group. Students jockey for spots in their friends' groups and maneuver to keep certain people out. Someone breaks up with a boyfriend or girlfriend on the night before group decisions are due and wants to reshuffle everything to get away from the erstwhile partner. Some cannot find a group at all and are relegated to the position of singletons, known in the blocking world as floaters.

To make the whole ordeal even more trying, once a student pins down her seven best friends, she also has the option of picking eight second-best friends. If students find a group that they like and if that group likes them back, then the two groups can sign up jointly in a process termed linking. Of course, every member of an eight-person blocking group probably has a different group he wants to link with, and each group is allowed to pair up with only one other.

By hook or by crook, every single freshman does make it into a blocking group or resign himself to entering the housing lottery on his own. And then some mysterious wizard behind a curtain pushes a button, and a computer system magically sorts out where those newly formed groups of freshmen will live for the next three years.

Harvard has 12 houses, and barring unusual circumstances, a student lives in the same one throughout his sophomore, junior, and senior years. Harvard students do not just sleep in their houses. Every house offers its own dining hall, library, laundry machines, exercise equipment, richly decorated common rooms, computer lab, and student mailboxes. All of the houses come with their own extra amenities, too. Late-night greasy eateries, dance spaces, and art rooms can be found in a few, while others feature a theater, a rock climbing wall, or a studio for woodturning.

Each house is home to about 400 undergraduates, and for many students, that subset of the student body becomes their Harvard community. They eat meals together, study late into the night together, and party together, all within the walls of their huge homey dormitory. A student body derided for its lack of school spirit at athletic events suddenly cranks up the enthusiasm when it comes to contests between neighboring dorms. While Harvard College does not even have a mascot, most of the houses have adopted one, ranging from Pforzheimer House's polar bear to Winthrop's lion to Currier's inanimate emblem, a tree.

Each house boasts its own crest, throws its own formal dances twice a year, and hosts its own graduation ceremony for seniors. At the helm of each of these large communities of undergraduates is a hardy professor who bravely chooses to live—often along with his or her spouse, children, and pets—among hundreds of 19- to 22-year-olds. For some reason, the job is a coveted position reserved for some of the most respected professors at Harvard. These professors, called house masters, are usually beloved figureheads among the student population. They are backed by a staff of resident tutors, mostly graduate students, who live in the dorms and help undergrads with all sorts of issues, from academic questions to grad school applications to mental health concerns. The tutors run social and educational events and cover the less popular duty of breaking up any out-of-hand parties.

When alumni meet each other in the real world long after Harvard, their first question is often, "What house were you in?" Almost every student insists, of course, that he or she lives in the very best house. Each one offers its own unique traditions, from Lowell's crack-of-dawn May Day festivities to Adams's black-tie reading of *Winnie-the-Pooh* to Dunster's annual goat roast.

Beyond those colorful distinctions, some real differences exist. The most important is location. Visitors to Harvard typically tour only Harvard Yard, the grassy, gated area that contains dormitories so old that John Adams and John Hancock once lived in them, a grandiose columned library, a picturesque church that wakes grumbling freshmen each morning with its bells, and some red brick classroom buildings. Having seen the Yard, most people think that they have seen Harvard. But the university is far larger than its historic center. Many of its academic buildings dot Cambridge's streets outside the Yard. All of the graduate schools have homes beyond the Yard as well—the law school just to the north, the Kennedy School of Government to the south, the business school across the Charles River in Boston, the medical school in another pocket of Boston a bus ride away, and so on. And though most undergraduates do take some classes in the Yard, they spend more of their time elsewhere.

Only freshmen live in the dormitories in the Yard. All 12 upperclassmen houses are a distance away. Nine of the 12 are clustered along the Charles River, with a swath of fast food restaurants and several Starbucks stores and independent bookstores cutting a path between them and the Yard. The remaining three are much farther from academic life, a mile to the north. That isolated group of houses in a residential area of Cambridge is collectively known as the Quad. Quadlings, as they call themselves in homage to the Southern folk of the original *Wizard of Oz* novel, are mocked by their River friends for their bad fortune of living so far away. In return, Quad residents insist that their accommodations are far better. While their River-bound compatriots often suffer room configurations that force one student to walk through another's bedroom in order to get to a bathroom or to his own room, Quadlings enjoy spacious singles and suites with their blockmates.

When residents of one River house, Mather, brag that all students, even lowly sophomores, get single bedrooms there (as well as access to the house that reputedly hosts the most parties on campus), neighbors jeer at Mather's hideous concrete architecture. Any Winthrop resident who tries to glory in his house's expansive riverfront property will inevitably be reminded that Winthrop, also known for the number of rodents in its rooms, once suffered the indignity of seeing its dining hall flooded with sewage.

In other words, while most students end up embracing their houses once they land there—very few move off campus or go through the application process to switch houses—a lot rides on the random housing assignments made during freshman year.

~

When four particular freshmen woke up on Housing Day in 2007, they were greeted by upperclassmen spilling into the room where they had gathered to await their fateful letter. The older students, clad in matching house T-shirts, shouted out this song:

> *Oh Kirkland, oh Kirkland, you are so good to me!*
> *Oh Kirkland, oh Kirkland, you are the place to be!*
> *Oh Kirkland, oh Kirkland, damn, you are so fine!*
> *Oh Kirkland, oh Kirkland, thank God that you are mine!*

Hearing those words—composed by one of that year's seniors and fast becoming tradition—the freshmen did not have to read their letter. They knew exactly what house they would be living in, and by most Harvard students' reckoning, they had just won the housing lottery.

Kirkland is the smallest of the 12 houses, so the community is considered to be especially intimate. It is so intimate, in fact, that the house's winter formal is known as Incest Fest. The exterior, a stately square of Neo-Georgian brick buildings surrounding a verdant courtyard, provides a breathtaking view of classic Old Harvard. Inside, in its luxurious dark wood common room, Kirkland hosts a lecture series that draws some of the hottest big-name speakers who come to campus each year. Its location is among the very closest to the Yard, and it is within shouting distance of both the college's gym and the campus's most storied late-night pizza joint.

By every account, Kirkland is a fantastic draw in the housing lottery. On that spring morning in 2007, the four young men who learned that they would be spending the next three years there had every reason to be thrilled.

They had become friends during their freshman year and chosen to room together as sophomores. Then over the summer, they received an email from the Kirkland House administrator that said they could have a better room if they accepted a fifth person into their rooming group—a floater, they thought. Kirkland's housing for sophomores is often cramped, and the chance at a nicer suite was appealing, even if it did mean taking in some unknown student with no blocking group.

As it turned out, they soon learned, their roommate-to-be was not a floater. He was a transfer student. He had not been at Harvard at all when the whole blocking process took place during freshman spring. His name was Adam Wheeler, and to introduce himself, he sent his four new roommates an email.

He started out:

Goodfellae:

He had used the title of the hit 1990 gangster movie *Goodfellas* to refer to the four young men, but he modified it based on the rule that a word in Latin ending in "a" usually ends its plural form with "ae." Not that the Martin Scorsese title was in Latin.

Then just in case that greeting was too odd, he put another one under it:

Hey,

He continued:

I'm Adam, sophomore transfer student. I'm interested in analytic philosophy, literary and cultural theory, and similarly romantic subjects. I am most often blasé, friendly, and have a somewhat sardonic sense of humor.

I will bring to the room, for communal delectation and unless otherwise desired by the relevant quorum:

   speakers
   uniquely ill-smelling hand sanitizer
   frisbee

Having introduced himself and his material possessions, he offered a forecast of activities that would take place in their Kirkland suite that year:

I'm looking forward to this fall. Roughly speaking, it's going to be a wild rumpus, which is an event similar in every but the unisexual

*respect to the Orphic Bacchanaliae of antiquity. Or, for those with
saucier cognitia, a veritable Tityas as manifest in shangrai-la.*

If his new roommates happened to be classics majors, they
might have known that the mythical Greek musician Orpheus,
who got permission to retrieve his dead wife from the underworld
but then glanced back at the wrong moment and lost her again, was
also the central figure of an ancient religious cult called Orphism.
Adherents of the sect worshipped others who had descended to the
underworld and returned—notably Bacchus, the god of wine. Bacchanaliae (again Wheeler used the "ae" form, disregarding the fact
that "bacchanalia" is actually plural in and of itself) refer to drunken
parties where that god's gifts are liberally consumed.

Rather than some figure of dissipated luxury in Shangri-La,
the paradise introduced in a 1933 novel, Tityas's name should have
meant anything but pleasure. He was, according to myth, a giant
who tried to rape Leto, one of the many paramours of his father
Zeus. For that crime, he was killed by Leto's immortal twin children, the god of the sun and goddess of the moon, then sentenced to
one of the worst postmortem punishments in all of Greek mythol-
ogy. Every day, two vultures ate his liver. Every night, it grew back
to be pecked out all over again. That surely does not sound like the
fun and games Wheeler was expecting in his dorm room.

Wheeler wrote in parentheses:

*I'm joking, of course, though I AM really excited and am sure to
enjoy living with the group.*

Then he ended his letter with this:

*To end triumphantly, I will bring a kick-ass electronic pencil-
sharpener (Panasonic KP-310). It's [sic] hole is ready for our
communal attention.*

Adam

His new roommates read his bizarre introductory message and worried among themselves that he might be "off-putting" or "a tool." But before they all met in person to find out whether that impression was correct, Wheeler had some Harvard customs to learn about.

The small group of students admitted to Harvard as sophomores or juniors comes to campus several days early for a crash course on all the social and educational conventions they have missed out on. They learn that at Harvard, a student's academic specialty is his "concentration," not his "major." They are told that during the first week of classes, known as shopping week, students can wander into any lectures they please before officially signing up for their courses for the semester. They are handed the numbers for the police and emergency medical services on campus. They get to know each other by going to a karaoke night, a bowling alley, and some of Boston's historic sites.

For Wheeler, like his fellow transfer students, Harvard was a new world. It had its own vocabulary. It had 13 undergraduate dining halls, whereas Bowdoin had two. It had 10 graduate schools with a total of nearly 15,000 students among them, while Bowdoin housed only undergraduates (and a much smaller number of them).

One of his professors from Bowdoin, Raymond Miller, had been a graduate student at Harvard. He mused about the change his student must have faced upon leaving isolated Brunswick for bustling Harvard Square and the next-door city of Boston. "To go from here, not only to a big university but to a big university in a big city—and on top of that, the reputation of Harvard—it would be jarring," Miller said. "I could see that that could be difficult, for someone who had gotten acclimated to here to suddenly be transported to that other environment."

During the preliminary week, Wheeler attended most of the social events for transfer students, but the one time he really made a splash was on paper, not in person. The transfer students were encouraged to introduce themselves to each other in writing before they arrived on campus, and Wheeler's email to the group was a knockout. The leader of the program noticed it right away for its "utter, ridiculous pretentiousness." It was similar to the one he sent his roommates, even using some of the same phrases, like "relevant quorum," but the transfer students were much more struck by its oddity than the guys he was going to be living with were. Among the recipients of this second email, Wheeler's words quickly became, as one of them put it, "legendary."

Hi,

I'm Adam, sophomore transfer. I'm interested in Shakespeare, analytic philosophy, literary and cultural theory, and similarly romantic subjects. Most recently I've aided in research at Bowdoin, though I'm originally from MIT. There, I was, to put it poorly, suckled upon the teat of disdain. That being said (fortified by a reflexive snort), I was inspired therby [sic] to apply to Harvard, where the humanities, in short, are not, simpliciter, a source of opprobrium.

I do not follow organized sports, which, to the relevant quorum, seems a neighborhood faux-pas of epic proportions.

My own, brief, assessment of my character is that I am sententious, crypto-tendentious, slightly pedantic with a streak of contrarianism, a fascination with any pedagogical approach to Shakespeare, and a decent sense of humor.

Looking forward,

Adam

As others sent straightforward descriptions of their hometowns, hobbies, and hopes for Harvard, people could not help but marvel at Wheeler's message. One student recalled, "It was kind of hilarious. No one was really quite sure if he was completely joking or half-joking." Regardless, it was the only way that he made himself noticeable during those opening days. "If it weren't for his unbelievable introductory email, all of us thought of him as a really, really quiet guy and very, very nice," one transfer student said.

There was one more group Wheeler met as he transitioned into life at Harvard. Incoming Harvard students—freshmen and transfers—have the option of participating in a social program for a few days before the official orientation starts, and Wheeler chose one called FOP.

FOP, short for First-Year Outdoor Program, takes participants on a five-day hiking trip through the woods with their new classmates. They carry heavy loads containing their tents, sleeping bags, cooking supplies, and food up and down mountains—without access to a shower and with a ban on deodorant. While arguably not the most attractive way to present oneself for the first time to new classmates, almost a quarter of the entering freshmen sign up to participate.

Wheeler picked the most advanced hike, for very athletically fit students, and according to others on the trip, he was up to the task, with his muscular body and his allusions to prior hiking experience. Within his group of six hikers and two upperclass leaders, he quickly made a name for himself. But that name was not his own. It was Brian.

For some reason, one of the two trip leaders just could not remember Adam's name. Over and over, she called him Brian, and after a few repetitions, the name stuck. For the rest of the trip, the whole group called him that, and he gamely responded to it.

He was not talkative, but some of his fellow hikers engaged him in conversation, asking friendly questions about his background. "Why did you go to MIT if you're a literature major?" one hiker asked him once. As she recalls, he responded, "I didn't think

I wanted to do literature until I got there." But she noticed that he had a lot more to say about Bowdoin, where he supposedly had spent only a few weeks as a research assistant. When she asked about life at MIT, he clammed up. She sensed that he might not want to talk about the topic for some reason, so she changed the subject. "If I felt I was making him uncomfortable, I'd bop onto another question," she recalled.

One night, the group played Mafia, a party game in which players try to deceive their opponents. One of the players did not enjoy the game. She had been friends with a compulsive liar before, and by the end of a tense round, she was close to tears.

When it was her turn to guess who was being truthful, she picked Wheeler. "He always had some kind of smile, [like] I'm amused at life and I'm amused at all of you," she remembered. With that endearing puppy-dog smile, she said, she could not believe that he could be lying to her. "I think he was better at the game than the rest of us."

He was lying, and she lost. That night, she poured out her story to one of the trip leaders as Wheeler fell asleep under the same tarp.

Back at Harvard, the hikers all settled into daily life at school, but they did get together for reunions from time to time. They met for meals in a dining hall and went out to celebrate each other's birthdays. (In an email chain planning one of those get-togethers, Wheeler's use of the word "pellucid" annoyed one of his new friends, who had to consult a dictionary.) For a while, Wheeler also lifted weights with one of the students from his FOP trip at the athletic facility across from Kirkland House.

Once the semester began, he spent time with his new roommates, too. Before the Cambridge winter set in, they played Frisbee together on the open green just outside of Kirkland House, called the MAC quad.

"It was nice having a guy that I could toss a Frisbee with that could actually get it halfway across the MAC quad without looking like a kid that had never done athletic activities in his life," one of his roommates said. He was surprised that as much as Wheeler enjoyed the game, he never went out for Kirkland's Frisbee team that competed in inter-house competitions or the Harvard club team that played against other schools. But then again, Wheeler made it clear early on that he was not one for group activities. He scoffed in particular at sports teams and at Harvard's eight all-male social clubs called final clubs.

He did join the Harvard College Law Society. Professing an interest in becoming a lawyer after college, he started attending meetings and quickly found himself running for editor of the club's occasional journal. One club member, Joe Resnek, remembered Wheeler's ambitious plan to up the magazine's frequency and quality. "He was going to sort of reform the meaningless *Harvard College Law Society Journal*," Resnek recalled. "His speech was very businesslike. . . . It was very structured. He came off as a very polished speaker." When the candidates left the room, the president of the organization told the deliberators, "Adam's really good." He won the vote.

Many of the students around him dove into the more than 400 student organizations at Harvard, often spending more time on their clubs than on their classwork. Several of his roommates were involved in *The Crimson*, the daily student newspaper that consumes vast amounts of its members' time and energy. But aside from the low-commitment law society, Wheeler mostly stayed out of the extracurricular scene. His roommates noticed that he had not shown the same attitude toward student activities during his brief stint at Bowdoin. They saw that he wore a few shirts from Bowdoin extracurricular organizations—groups that it seemed peculiar to join during just a few weeks on campus as a research assistant. By contrast, nothing in his wardrobe suggested that he had spent almost a full school year at MIT.

In his room, he came to be appreciated for a trait wholly unrelated to his clothing or his club choices: his services as an alcohol provider. When the five of them were sophomores, they were mostly, at 20, below the legal drinking age—including Wheeler, they thought. But somehow, he could get away with buying alcohol when they could not.

"He showed us his driver's license proudly," one of his roommates recalled. "He had said that he knew someone at the DMV who had moved his age up by a year so that he could buy alcohol."

That Delaware driver's license was legitimate, of course. Wheeler actually turned 21 right after he came to Harvard. But since he had taken a year off his age when he applied—to make it seem like he had spent one year in college, at MIT, rather than two years at Bowdoin—his Harvard ID gave his birth date as one year later, and that was the birthday he told his friends was his real one.

At this stage, Wheeler said that he preferred hard liquor—whiskey and bourbon were his drinks of choice, as one roommate remembers. He almost never touched the beer that his friends drank. But if they pestered him enough, he would always pick up beer for them when he went to C'est Bon, the convenience store in Harvard Square where many students buy their alcohol.

Wheeler's ID was from out of state, but when the cashier asked him whether he was a Harvard student, he said no. He could not say he was, or the clerk might ask him for that ID as confirmation and it would show a different birth date. After enough trips to the narrow, fluorescent-lit shop, the staff there grew suspicious. They started asking him why, if he was a resident of Delaware and not a college student, he was spending so much time in Cambridge. Wheeler stopped going to the store.

Most of the time, Wheeler was lying about his past. When he told the staff at C'est Bon that he was 21, he was actually telling the truth. He told his friends he was lying then.

His birthday rolled around, and according to his Harvard ID, he was turning 21. He went out to a bar with some friends to celebrate, and as he ordered a drink, supposedly marking his entrance into legality, one friend crooned, Let me see your ID!

She glanced at it, just expecting to smile at the date and hand it right back. But this was a Harvard student, after all, and in that momentary glimpse, she knew the numbers did not add up. If his driver's license was right, he was not turning 21 that day; he was turning 22.

"I didn't question it. It is his birthday," she said. "And I was impressed by how he could put back a few shots of scotch and not even show it."

Wheeler's most frequent interactions with his roommates were over food, not alcohol. He spent a lot of time studying in his bedroom, but he would reliably poke his head out into the common room, where the others were often playing video games, to ask them if they wanted to grab dinner.

Walking through the pretty yellow-walled Kirkland dining hall, he attracted attention for his tall, muscular frame and his tray loaded with low-fat foods. (At almost every meal, he ate spinach salads heaped with proteins like chicken and tuna.) A small group of students, pointing to his hunched posture and his reluctance to talk to most of the people in the room, snickered and called him The Sad Man. Many more, though, were impressed by the discipline he showed in his diet and his physique. A few house residents asked Wheeler if they could tag along during his sessions at the gym, and they joined him for meals in Kirkland afterward.

"A lot of times I would see them at the [dining] hall right after a workout," recalled Abel Acuña, a fellow Kirkland resident. "They'd just come from the gym in their gym clothes, and they'd get a close-to-identical meal together because they're trying to replicate the Adam Wheeler workout and diet. . . . He was obviously doing something right that they wanted to emulate."

And athletic friends were not the only ones who took note. Before they moved into Kirkland as sophomores, the blocking group that Wheeler lived with had become close friends with another group assigned to the same house. One member of that group, an attractive computer science whiz, asked her friends right away to tell her more about their new roommate whom she kept seeing in the dining hall. After hanging out in their room occasionally and eating some dinners with Wheeler and his roommates, she grew more interested still. At a party in their room one night, she asked his roommates to set her up with him, and within about a month of Wheeler's arrival at Harvard, the two of them were an item.

Only once in the early phase of their relationship did she voice a concern, as far as one of Wheeler's roommates remembered. She had been dating Wheeler for about five months, he recalled, when she said to him, "Adam has trouble telling the truth."

"Even about simple things," she complained, as he recollected. "I'll say, 'Did you wash my clothes?' You know, 'Oh yeah, I took care of it,' even though the clothes are still in the hamper. 'Are you coming to this social event?' 'Oh yeah, I'll be there,' and then he doesn't show up."

She would ask him where he had been the night before, and if he told her he had been studying in his room, she would almost always learn from a roommate that he had actually been working in the library. "Very simple things," Wheeler's roommate remembered her saying in exasperation. "He had nothing to hide but insisted on lying anyway."

But "it wasn't anything that was a deal breaker," his girlfriend concluded herself. "If I had the general impression that he was a dishonest person, I wouldn't have stayed with him."

So the couple stuck together. His roommates, too, chose to include him again for junior year. They even extended an invitation to a sophomore named Matt, another transfer student who had become Wheeler's favorite workout and Frisbee buddy. They also found two more friends to bring on board so that they could fill a sprawling eight-man suite affectionately known as The Swamp.

The time-worn architecture of Harvard's dorms creates many a headache for present-day residents. "Walk-throughs" force a student to awkwardly cut through someone else's bedroom to get to a bathroom or an exit. Bedrooms built for one student now house two, with another sleeping in the suite's common room. Wheelchair accessibility is a nightmare.

But occasionally, history confers gifts as well as inconveniences on modern inhabitants. Almost every house has at least one room that, due to the quirks of the architecture plus a reputation that carries over from year to year, seems especially conducive to partying.

The Swamp was one of those party suites. It was actually three separate rooms, each with a spacious common room. When the fire doors connecting the three were opened, the full suite offered plenty of party space in addition to five bedrooms for the eight residents.

Explanations for the origin of the room's name vary, but it dates back at least 10 years before Wheeler lived there. The most commonly accepted story is that those three rooms in Kirkland House have been a party spot for decades, leaving the wooden floors permanently sticky and smelly, as students living in the room in the late 1990s told *The Crimson*. In the year Wheeler lived there, *The Crimson* was still listing The Swamp as one of the best party rooms on campus, putting it on the circuit that students roaming the River in search of a party might visit on a Saturday night. Wheeler and the other Swamp residents of 2008–09 appeased that demand, throwing bashes that they called smash-up/mash-up parties for the blended popular songs that they blasted over their speakers.

On a typical day, several of the eight Swamp residents could be found in one of their connecting common rooms playing Nintendo 64 and often drinking. "It was always kind of an open invite for anyone who wanted to come over and just hang out in that space and play games there or whatever," recalled Acuña, who took to hanging around in The Swamp a lot.

Wheeler did not join in for the video games too often. Most of the time, he stayed in his bedroom in front of his computer. He had purchased a brand-new Macbook Pro, a state-of-the-art laptop that many of his friends eyed jealously.

He was not normally fussy about his stuff. Unencumbered by the video games and similar entertainment equipment that many of the guys brought with them, Wheeler had packed the lightest when he arrived on move-in day. As students were moving out for the summer, he groaned to a roommate about the fact that Kirkland residents who never talked to him most of the year suddenly wheedled him into using his obvious muscles to cart their heavy boxes down Kirkland's winding stairs.

But when it came to his computer, Wheeler cared. He made it known that he did not want anyone to lay a finger on his laptop. He let his new roommate Matt take a look at the screen for one purpose. The two of them shared a hobby of manipulating images on Photoshop. They could work wonders with the photos their friends posted on Facebook—the social networking site that had been invented in Kirkland House just a few years before.

Wheeler found out one day that one of his roommates had the newest version of Photoshop on his laptop. That roommate, who was a writer for *The Crimson*, was friendly with a student on the newspaper's IT staff. *The Crimson* had purchased the expensive software so that its student editors could prepare photographs to run in the daily newspaper, and when his friend offered to load it onto his personal laptop for free, he was more than happy to say yes. "To be honest, we were not very good about intellectual property laws," he chuckled in retrospect.

Wheeler walked into his roommate's bedroom one night and glanced over his shoulder. "Oh, is that the newest Photoshop?" he asked.

"Yeah." He gave no explanation about where it had come from. He did not see why Wheeler needed to know.

"Can you get that for me?"

His roommate resisted at first, but Wheeler was insistent. "It was the only time I'd ever seen him excited about anything, really," he said.

Eventually, he snatched the installation CD for the Mac version of the software and brought it home to Wheeler one night. "It took me about a month," he said, and during that time, Wheeler asked him repeatedly when he could get it for him. "I had to basically sneak it out of the building."

When Wheeler's girlfriend heard much later that he wanted *The Crimson*'s software, she was perplexed. If he had asked her about it, she would have told him that Harvard students could download a version of Photoshop for free at that time. But he did not ask her. Lately, he had been talking to her less and less frequently about any topic.

They had been dating for about a year and a half, and one friend had even suggested that Wheeler and his girlfriend were headed for marriage. As Wheeler's girlfriend put it, "I didn't think we would break up." But then Wheeler started to seem more distant to her, even though, as far as she knew, nothing had gone wrong between them. But he grew less and less communicative, and finally, they decided to part ways.

Wheeler dated some other women after that. Acuña met a lot of women at the all-female college Wellesley through Model United Nations conferences and was happy to introduce them to his Harvard friends. He brought four of those women over for Mather Lather, one of the most noteworthy annual parties at Harvard. For the Lather, Mather House fills the dance floor with six feet of foam bubbles, and students attend in swimsuits. The party has been shut down by the police, has set off the fire alarm, has sent students home with mysterious rashes spread through bubble-on-skin contact, and has garnered mention in *The New York Times*.

None of that deterred Acuña's friends, who arrived at Harvard and headed to The Swamp before the party. One woman noticed Wheeler and drew him into conversation. After the Mather party that night, they went on a few dinner dates. She eventually decided that he was not outgoing enough for her. By the time Acuña came up with the next opportunity to meet Wellesley women, Wheeler was once again, as his roommate put it, "on the prowl." That opportunity was an annual end-of-year fest at Wellesley called Block Party. The main attraction that year was an act named Super Mash Bros. The Swamp guys were avid players of *Super Smash Bros.*, the video game that lent the musical group its name. And at their mash-up parties in their room, they often played Super Mash Bros.' musical creations. As soon as Acuña told them about the event, they thought it was a must-go.

Four of them went to the party, and to show their enthusiasm, they dressed as characters from the *Super Smash Bros.* video game. Once the party started, they separated from each other in the crowd. But The Swamp heard the next day from Wheeler that he had met an attractive young woman named Sua there. Soon afterward, she was his girlfriend. She frequently came to Harvard, where she attended parties in The Swamp.

Settled in socially at Harvard after two years, Wheeler finally officially resigned from Bowdoin rather than continuing to ignore the letters he had been receiving every semester about how to return from his one-semester suspension. On the resignation form, he wrote, "I am conducting independent research before finishing my degree." In the space that asked whether he had transferred to another college, he claimed he had not. At the very end of his time at Bowdoin, once he knew he had been accepted to Harvard, he had told his friends that he would be spending the next semester studying Shakespeare at the University of Chicago before returning to Maine. Most of them never heard from him again after that.

But he had new friends at Harvard, and academically, Wheeler appeared to be faring well also. One admiring classmate said he respected Wheeler not just because he was "an extremely nice guy" but also because he seemed more well-rounded than other men who took humanities classes. "Here's somebody who really could lift weights next to me but also could really go the distance on Germanic philosophy," he thought.

Wheeler had not been noted for academic excellence at Harvard at the start. Despite the fact that his most recent experience with philosophy had landed him a suspension from Bowdoin, in his first semester at Harvard, he had signed up for courses that looked like the selections of a philosophy student, not an English concentrator as he ended up declaring himself. He took two philosophy classes and earned Bs in both of them, plus a government course in which he also earned a B. For his fourth course, he picked a class in deductive logic.

That class met the college's quantitative reasoning requirement, but Harvard declared Wheeler exempt from that requirement because his MIT transcript offered proof that he had already fulfilled it there. However, the course was required of all philosophy concentrators.

If intent to major in philosophy was what brought Wheeler to the class, that was not apparent, at least not to his teaching fellow Craig Nishimoto. Many Harvard courses are taught by professors in large lecture halls that can hold a few hundred people. For more personalized instruction, students gather each week for an additional assigned hour taught by teaching fellows, mostly graduate students.

Professors who stand behind podiums looking out at half-attentive faces (and a sea of laptop screens) do not always get to know students very well, but teaching fellows usually do. To Nishimoto, Wheeler seemed uninterested in putting in much work or learning about logic—and it showed in his grades. They were abysmal.

When he was confronted by administrators about his performance in the course later on, Wheeler told them that he had not thought to ask for help until the semester was in its final weeks. When he did, he said, his grades went up dramatically, but it was too late to make much of a difference. Overall, he earned a D-plus in the class.

Max Storto, a friend who had met Wheeler on the orientation hiking trip in the earliest days of their Harvard experience, thought philosophy would be Wheeler's focus. "He was really into philosophy at first. He kept on talking about Descartes after we got back to school," he remembered. "Then he decided to change to an English concentrator, which I was somewhat surprised about. . . . I know it's very different from any of the classes he had taken before, and he seemed to be really interested in the philosophy stuff."

Had Wheeler been a philosophy concentrator, he would have had to retake that same deductive logic class, which could not have been a pleasant prospect for him. The course was tough for someone with such a bent toward the humanities. True, it did not have many numbers in it. But it also did not have many words. A problem on the final exam one year started like this:

2 (45 pts total) The following questions refer to these schemata:

  (i) $(\forall x)(\exists y)(Qxy)$

  (ii) $(\exists x)(\neg Qxx)$

  (iii) $(\exists x)(\exists y)(x \neq y)$

  (iv) $(\forall x)(\neg Qxc)$

  (v) $(\exists z)(\exists x)(\exists y)(z \neq y \,.\, x \neq z \,.\, y \neq x)$

 a. (9 pts) Show by deduction that (i) and (ii) imply (iii).

"He was quite clearly interested in English from the day he showed up," a student who met Wheeler during transfer orientation opined. So a low grade in a class geared toward left-brained tasks could have caused Wheeler to sign up for the sort of courses he selected the next semester and the rest of his time at Harvard: English, English, and English, with very little else thrown in. Out of the 21 more classes he enrolled in, only five came from outside of the English department, and a few of those five still centered on the topic of literature. Those choices could have just been a decisive reaction to a bad experience in a math-oriented course.

Or he might have been making a more conniving calculation. Nishimoto maintains that quantitative courses are harder to cheat in and easier to tank. It is more difficult to tell a student that her writing or her ideas are bad than that her answer to a math problem is wrong. More passing grades get stamped onto poor papers than poor problem sets, Nishimoto thinks.

And if one wants to cheat, the methods are very different in a math or science class. Of course, it is doable. Students copy others' answers on problem sets and write formulas on their hands before they walk into exam rooms. But they cannot plagiarize essays—Wheeler's preferred form of academic dishonesty as evidenced by his Bowdoin application, his Bowdoin classwork, and his bid for Harvard admission. While he had branched out into some other forms of cheating—forged signatures, faked transcripts—plagiarism was his bread and butter.

His first semester at Harvard ended with a D-plus on his record. In a routine hearing, the administrative board placed him on academic probation until he got his grades up, meaning that a second bad semester would spell suspension from Harvard. And in the spring, he signed up for English classes, the kind of classes that would let him do what he did best.

One of those classes he took in the spring of his sophomore year was an upper-level English seminar taught by one of the world's foremost authorities on Shakespeare, Stephen Greenblatt. It was Greenblatt's work that Wheeler had plagiarized to get into Harvard. It must have been a treat for a Shakespeare enthusiast like Wheeler to sit in while Greenblatt enthusiastically expounded on *Hamlet* in a cozy seminar room in Cambridge that Wheeler had only made it into because of Greenblatt's words. Wheeler usually came to class looking "a little exhausted and disheveled," Greenblatt recalled. He was not the best student in the class or even in the top half. But just qualifying for a seat at the table in this class, usually limited to junior and senior English concentrators, was a mark of some distinction for a sophomore. He participated in the discussion from time to time. And he turned in the short papers that were due every week—though unbeknownst to his professor, he was plagiarizing even some of those brief ungraded assignments.

In another class he took that also had weekly response papers, students were asked to send their writings to the entire class. One graduate student in the class, reading Wheeler's work, noticed an odd tendency. Every sentence, he said, was sound. But they did not connect to each other. Wheeler was submitting papers made up of many good thesis statements strung together in a row, arguing many different thoughts. "He knew what is supposed to be there," the student said. "He knew what a graduate-level or professional-level sentence is supposed to sound like. And so what you would have, often, is a somewhat incoherent assembly of 25 really decent sentences."

Given the disconnect between one thought and the next, it is easy to imagine that Wheeler could have been pulling each bit of the paper from a different source as he had in his application essays. If that was his habit, then he picked his sources so well that even though he spent most of class with his gaze fixed downward, his classmate simply considered him a "contemplative figure" with his head bowed by the "immense amount of thought" swirling through his brain.

In a similar class, Wheeler rarely spoke. When he was called on by the professor one day, he gave an answer about epistemology in *Hamlet* that was so convoluted that his classmates cringed. The room sat in a memorable silence for several moments before the professor, a renowned critic named Marc Shell, finally felt the need to restart the conversation. In a forced rescue attempt, Shell said, "All right, let's all go around and say one response that we had to the reading."

The other students in the class felt bad for Wheeler. It was a graduate seminar, and he had asked the professor's permission to enroll even though he was only a junior in college. Clearly, they thought, he must be really brilliant to have been granted a seat in the course at all. So that terrible incident at the seminar table simply reflected his bad fortune in being put on the spot. Shell invited all the students to his home for dinner one night, and a classmate made a point of talking to Wheeler. She reassured him, "This may seem like a lot for you, but we're all intimidated." Another student noticed that he seemed touched by the attention.

Nobody read his work and said it was not his own or met him in a classroom and said he did not belong there. As a student who took a few classes with him put it, "He was a master of semblance."

It is impossible to know whether he was plagiarizing his schoolwork in every class, though a student who cheats even on ungraded assignments is not one to be trusted too far. What is clear, though, is that whatever he was doing was working for him. In his second semester, he scored two As and two A-minuses, and he earned his way off the academic probation list.

In his junior fall, he ramped up his game. He signed up for a whopping six courses, two more than the four-course average that most students find draining enough. Only about 20 students out of the 6,000 in the college dare take six classes in any given semester. It is such a daunting idea that anyone who wants to attempt it has to gain special permission from the resident dean of his house. Wheeler secured approval, and he received As in five of those classes and an A-minus in the sixth that semester. Five of the six were English courses, including two honors seminars and one course intended for graduate students (the one in which Shell had to brush over Wheeler's incompetence—and ended up giving Wheeler an A).

The semester after that, he notched down a level, to five classes, just one above the norm. But three of those were meant for graduate students in English and a fourth was an honors seminar. The fifth, a biology class, was the only one in which he scored an A-minus instead of an A.

He seemed to be feeling at home in the English department that he had thrown himself into. In class, Wheeler was prone to "swooping transcendent meditations on what it means to be an artist or a genius or a reader," one student said. He was not as open about his writerly ambitions as he had been with his friends at Bowdoin. But in Kirkland House, he was usually seen poring over a book whenever he was not with his girlfriend or on his laptop.

For a while, an acquaintance said, he carried a Vladimir Nabo-kov book around campus with him. A number of people had heard from Wheeler that Nabokov, best known for his novel *Lolita* about a middle-aged man's passion for his 12-year-old stepdaughter, was his favorite author. He took a seminar devoted exclusively to Nabo-kov's work. He started talking about *Lolita* constantly, his room-mate recalled.

He brought up the idea of a new course on Nabokov at a meeting of the Student Advisory Board for Arts and Humanities, an eight-person committee that he had joined. That was one of his only contributions, while other students on the committee voiced a number of complaints. Too many faculty members were on leave at one time, some said. The English department lacked introductory course options, others chimed in. Yet the committee members felt that their suggestions were falling on deaf ears. "We all thought it was going to be something that it was not," one of the committee members recalled of the group's frustration at the outcome of the recommendations. "But it hit him a little bit harder." He stopped attending the meetings after only two or three sessions.

He stuck around longer on a similar panel, the Student Advi-sory Committee that the English department creates by choos-ing up to three concentrators who live in each house. It met two or three times each semester to discuss special events hosted by English professors, ways to promote the concentration to unde-cided freshmen, and the big changes in the department's curricular requirements that debuted in 2009. Wheeler was always quiet at the meetings, but he was consistently present.

He made another decision that indicated much less interest in engaging with the English department. When he was asked for his input on who should serve as his concentration adviser, he responded by saying that he did not want an adviser at all. Per his wishes, he was never paired with someone to supervise his academic work.

Students generally complain that they do not receive enough advising, not that they are offered too much. But Wheeler did not seem hindered by the lack of guidance. Not only was he putting high marks on his transcript, but he was also winning some impressive accolades for his work.

The summer after his junior year, he earned admission to a prestigious English program at Oxford University in England. Hosted by Bread Loaf, the English graduate school of Middlebury College, the Oxford program was normally meant for English teachers looking to beef up their credentials and for a few graduate students. Enrolling as an undergrad was quite an honor. To pay for the summer abroad, Wheeler sought an award called the David Rockefeller International Experience Grant that helps about 400 Harvard undergraduates travel to foreign countries every summer. His application contained several elements that did not make sense.

First, the budget that he submitted to the grant evaluation committee was patchy. He asked for $500 for airfare from the United States "round trip, to Oxford"—presumably a very low estimate. Then he asked for $6,400 to pay for "groceries and flat." He did not list any charges at all in the "program fees/tuition" category, even though the Middlebury program cost $8,760 for the summer. It was possible, yes, to seek financial aid from Middlebury—but in that case, he would not have had to pay for a flat either, since the program guaranteed every student a room in Oxford housing.

The program ran from July 1 to August 7. On his grant application, Wheeler wrote that he would be staying in England until August 29. The Rockefeller grants only cover international journeys that are eight weeks or longer, and Wheeler would not have been the first student to pad his foreign coursework with a few weeks of travel to fill up enough time to make him eligible for the money. But if that was his plan, he did not indicate where he would be going. All he said in his application, actually, was that he would be studying in England. He did not mention the Bread Loaf program that he had been admitted to at all. He listed his purpose as research for a senior thesis called "England and Nowhere: The Situation of Poetry and the Turning of T.S. Eliot."

The grant application asked for the same sort of credentials he had turned in elsewhere: a résumé, a transcript, a letter of recommendation. Once again, Wheeler's submissions looked excellent. And once again, fakery and forgery deserved the credit.

On top of a résumé (inflated to include a couple of Harvard Law School classes he never took, a book citation he never received, and other unearned honors) and a transcript (altered to look like that of a Harvard student who started as a freshman and earned great grades all along), the application called for a statement about why he needed the grant. Wheeler turned in a dense essay, more than two single-spaced pages long. It did not mention Middlebury or Bread Loaf or even Oxford once. Instead, in sentence after sentence, it put forth literary theories that all more or less related to T.S. Eliot's poetry. To study that poetry, he obliquely claimed every so often, he needed to go to England. There was not much mention of what he would do once he was there. But he did say his aim was "to read the collected poems of T.S. Eliot for the ways that they obtain diachronically and diachorically," and he made even more perplexing statements like:

> Despite Eliot's sense of the hollowing out of prior signifying systems and the annihilatory vectors of Modernism, it is sometimes a fact, or a sensation perhaps, that there is something regressive/reposeful in his ultimate recourse to religiously founded symbols of purgatorial action and meaning, mostly via Dante via Eliot's notion of metaphysical uses of "figura" as a legitimating pre-script.

Almost every sentence was just as lofty, winding, and complex. Just as a classmate had observed earlier, his sentences were grammatically sound, even if they did employ esoteric vocabulary and syntax. But taken together, their meaning fell apart.

Just like his college application essay and pieces he had been submitting in his Harvard courses, Wheeler's grant application statement was riddled with plagiarism. A random Google search of phrases reveals at least six different writers whose words make an appearance in the conglomerate. Some works, like an essay by Professor James Engell (whose course on Romanticism Wheeler was taking that semester) and the same Greenblatt piece he had used in his Harvard application, accounted for entire paragraphs in Wheeler's essay. Others, like a book that his house master Tom Conley had written more than 10 years earlier and several other works of literary theory, lent only a couple of sentences or even a single well-worded clause to the essay. None of the many texts that Wheeler used to compose his essay had anything to do with T.S. Eliot. Wheeler sometimes inserted Eliot's name into thoughts about Shakespeare, conferring lines written about one writer onto another one centuries his junior.

It was a complex weaving of many threads that reflected, if not much writing ability or moral fiber, at least a hearty interest in literary criticism. By contrast, his fellow applicants probably wrote about a desire to see the world or outlined matter-of-fact plans to study at a foreign university or volunteer for an international charity over the summer.

The committee had enough money to award grants to about half of the people who sought them. When the judges reached Wheeler's file, they were impressed but also confused. "Unclear what he is applying for," one evaluator scribbled in his notes about Wheeler's packet. "Essay is not for the grant. Otherwise, amazing candidate."

Somehow or other, a committee member's notes indicate that the group did find out that Wheeler's plan was to enroll in the Bread Loaf program. They decided to give him the money. And more unusually still, they sent him a letter saying he would get $8,000—which was $1,000 more than he had asked for. The decision to hand out more funds than a student requests in his budget, college fellowships director Paul Bohlmann acknowledged, is "uncommon."

"There are some situations where we think students are under budget, and if need be, we will try to correct for that," Bohlmann said. But those situations rarely arise. Wheeler, charming his way into it with an erudite essay and a naively low estimate for transoceanic airfare, managed to be one of those cases. With $8,000 from Harvard in his bank account, he was headed off to a summer in England. Before the semester wrapped up and he jetted across the Atlantic, though, he scooped up a few more checks from Harvard.

Like many departments at Harvard, especially in the humanities, the English department requires all of its concentrators who wish to be on the honors track to enroll in a small, rigorous class called a tutorial in their junior year. The tutorials, taught by graduate students in English, each have a different theme, but the outcome is the same: a 20-page paper written as preparation for the longer thesis that they might write as seniors. Wheeler's junior tutorial was called "Renaissance Theatricality." In other words, Shakespeare—right up his alley, from the sound of it.

To Suparna Roychoudhury, the graduate student who taught his tutorial, it seemed like Wheeler was grappling earnestly with his junior paper. He turned in a first draft, and she told him that his writing was "needlessly ponderous." She had "strong reservations" about how his wordy, weighty paper was going to turn out. When he received those comments, he emailed to say that he agreed that he was "pushing the matter too hard" for a 20-page paper. His thesis might apply only "cursorily" to *The Tempest*, but he thought he could still handle "a chronotopic analysis of time and space" in a Shakespearean text. He just had to change plays. He said he would write about *The Winter's Tale* instead. That way, he could take "a more formal structuralist approach" without making the resulting paper "unavoidably tendentious."

Six days later, he decided either that it was not so bad to be tendentious (meaning to show an intentional bias or purpose in his writing) or that it was actually not so unavoidable. He wrote to say that he had traveled home to Delaware, where the Atlantic Ocean had given him the inspiration he needed to keep going with his original paper. It would be about *The Tempest* after all.

"He needs to edit himself more aggressively," Roychoudhury wrote in her critique of his work. Nevertheless, she thought that the paper he handed in was in terrific shape. She said in Wheeler's end-of-semester evaluation that she was impressed by his "intellectually rich and ornate prose" and that his paper was "bold, substantive, and exhaustively researched."

It was so good, in fact, that Roychoudhury nominated it for a prize that the English department gives out for the best junior paper of the semester. Wheeler won. For several years, the department's prize for the best tutorial teacher has gone almost every semester to the graduate student who taught the winner of the student writing prize—and that semester, Roychoudhury won the prize for teaching, too.

The tutorial met during the fall semester, and even after the course ended, Wheeler did not want to be done with the paper. He spent the early spring tinkering with it and expanding it. By the time he was done, it was 146 pages long. He showed his new draft to Roychoudhury, who agreed to nominate his work for another award.

This one was the Hoopes Prize, Harvard's top undergraduate writing award. Conferred annually on roughly 80 to 90 students, mostly culled from the 1,600-person senior class, it is one of the most widely recognized marks of academic excellence at Harvard. Even among Harvard students, who all had to have top grades and test scores to get in once upon a time, some kids are thought of as the smart kids. And "Hoopes winner," everyone knows, means smart. Really smart.

The prize almost always goes to senior theses, but other pieces of undergraduate academic writing are technically eligible, and once in a while, one wins. Roychoudhury wanted Wheeler's expanded junior paper to garner one of those rare early awards. She wrote up an eloquent summary of Wheeler's project and his efforts to draft it, telling the prize committee, "The subtle, elegant, and profound thesis of this essay is nothing short of a genuine contribution to the field."

The committee agreed with her praise. Wheeler won a $4,000 prize, and Roychoudhury received $1,000 for sponsoring him. To top that off, he also won the Winthrop Sargent Prize for that same piece of writing. That prize, given out by the English department, honors the best essay produced each year about Shakespeare—by any student, undergraduate or graduate.

Wheeler's essay gained so much acclaim that it came up for discussion among the judges who were awarding the Captain Jonathan Fay Prize. This award is even more prestigious than the Hoopes—because it is picked from the ultra-talented Hoopes-winning pool. It is given to the best senior thesis out of all Harvard senior theses. Wheeler's essay was crossed off the ballot only when an English professor on the Fay committee noticed that Wheeler was not eligible because he was not yet a senior.

But ample accolades were pouring in for Wheeler. As a Hoopes winner, his paper was bound and stored in the undergraduate library. For two years, it would be displayed along with the other Hoopes winners right at the entrance to the library. Thousands of students would trudge past it on their way to long nights of hitting the books. The freshmen might think dimly that perhaps someday they would climb to such heights. Upperclassmen might sometimes glare at the shelf, with the bitter hunch that their own academic work would never merit a place on it. After that, his paper would be whisked to the library's basement, home of the Harvard University Archives, where it would stay enshrined forever. It would even be added to the online card catalog system of the Harvard University Library. Now, if he typed his name into the bar where he had so often searched for the professional writers and critics he admired, he would find his own entry.

There were more financial boons, too. For the Sargent Prize, he received a $2,000 check in addition to the $4,000 he had won for the Hoopes. A pretty impressive haul for an essay on Shakespeare.

But the $6,000, the spot on the library shelf, the admiration of friends who heard he had managed to snag a Hoopes Prize as a junior—all this was not rightfully his. The essay was not his own work. Instead, the junior paper was actually a chapter of a doctoral dissertation completed eight years earlier by a Cornell student named Daniel Brayton. Wheeler had used just chapter two of the dissertation's four chapters as his junior paper, and for his Hoopes submission, he added two more of the chapters. He made edits (changing "this dissertation" to "this essay," for example), but they were minimal. He reused all nine of the illustrations that Brayton had included in his work.

He even plagiarized from Brayton's acknowledgments page. Brayton appreciated the "intellectual generosity and indefatigable spirit" of one person and the "constant support" and "comments on my work" of another. He named one woman "without whose wit and wisdom these pages would be blank" as the person to whom "I owe whatever of good lies between the covers." Wheeler took all those words and applied them to one person, his adviser, to form his acknowledgments page.

Brayton had finished his PhD long ago and become a professor of literature at Middlebury College in Vermont. Unlike Wheeler, he was not such a big fan of his dissertation. But he liked the chapter that Wheeler picked for his junior paper. Brayton had rewritten it so many times that he knew every sentence almost by heart. "That piece of work that this Wheeler character decided to steal from me," he said, "was the best work I had ever done."

That chapter, three more rewrites after the version that went into his dissertation, made its way to publication in a book more than a decade later. But as for the rest, Brayton did not expect anyone besides a few graduate students working on similar projects to set eyes on it. He did not even know that his dissertation was available digitally to be stolen by an unscrupulous undergraduate.

"I just thought this sucker will go in a stack somewhere," Brayton said. "It's just another dissertation in English language and literature."

The most likely way to trace the path of Brayton's dissertation out of the musty Cornell stacks onto Wheeler's laptop is through Peter Coviello, an English professor who had taught Wheeler at Bowdoin. Coviello and Brayton had become friends back in graduate school. In fact, Coviello is mentioned by name in the acknowledgments of Brayton's dissertation. In addition to the parties and sports games that the two shared, "we had an intellectual relationship," Brayton said. "Pete Coviello definitely would have seen my work as well as have heard about my work for years. And you know, Pete's very likely to champion and celebrate his friends' work."

Brayton studied Shakespeare and the sea—two of Wheeler's favorite topics. If Wheeler had ever mentioned those interests around Coviello while he was at Bowdoin, Brayton mused, then his friend might well have told Wheeler about Brayton. In fact, Brayton said, "It would be surprising if he *didn't*."

In any case, Wheeler somehow found that particular piece in the online research service ProQuest that he, like all Harvard students, had access to through the university's subscription. And some impulse, a familiar one by now, led him not just to draw inspiration from it but to pilfer it outright.

Wheeler's path of plagiarism might be traceable one step further. That one chapter of Brayton's work that Wheeler plucked out first had started as a stand-alone term paper for a class Brayton had taken at Cornell. The course had been taught by a man who had just written a book called *The Self-Made Map* about cartography in Renaissance French literature. That book inspired Brayton to turn to Renaissance maps as a lens for viewing *The Tempest*.

Of course, Brayton cited the concept of "cartographic latency," put forward by his professor in *The Self-Made Map*, in the bibliography of his dissertation. And that professor happened to be none other than Tom Conley, who had moved on to Harvard and was the master at Kirkland House, the very house where Wheeler was living. Flipping through the footnotes of Brayton's dissertation, Wheeler would have noticed his house master's name. Perhaps that is how he found Conley's book to plagiarize from later that year in his Rockefeller grant application.

In Brayton's opinion, Wheeler should have been caught before he ever arrived at that coincidental juncture. There's "not a snowball's chance in hell," he says, that any qualified reader could look at the piece Wheeler's adviser nominated for the Hoopes Prize and believe that an undergraduate had written it. "The vocabulary, the conceptual apparatus, the theory, the theorization of literature," Brayton said, "this was a really highly evolved piece of graduate work. There's no way an undergraduate ever anywhere writes like that." He added, "I find it hilarious that a prize committee, a committee of readers would read it and give it that big prize believing that an undergraduate was capable of that." The acclaim was actually for Brayton's writing, but the prize went to Wheeler. Long before Brayton ever knew that the award existed, Harvard circulated the 2009 list of Hoopes Prize winners, with Wheeler's name inscribed on it.

A Kirkland student forwarded the announcement of the winners to the house email list with a note congratulating by name the Kirkland seniors who had won the prize. One of Wheeler's roommates quickly replied to the list with an addendum: "Adam Wheeler '10!" Another Swamp resident replied to the list one minute later, "ADAM WHEELER FOR THE WIN. YEAH 2010."

"Just out of curiosity," one house resident replied, "did Adam write a thesis a year early?"

His roommate, the one who had first broadcast the news of Wheeler's win, was quick to jump in again. "Adam wrote a 150-page paper," he said, still copying the entire house community on the chain, "in his spare time, for fun, when he was not doing work for his six classes. I wish I were making this up."

And the other roommate replied again too, even more exuberantly: "He also got paid to write it. And then got paid more once he won the award. Ladies, make your move—this man is now intelligent, rich, AND famous."

It is hard to imagine how Wheeler must have felt, reading these heartfelt expressions of pride from his closest friends but knowing that he did not deserve the praise. But if he felt any compunction, it did not show in his demeanor.

To his roommates, the awkward young man they had welcomed into their suite nearly two years before had finally come into his own at Harvard. As one of them recalled, "Our junior spring when he won the Hoopes, when he broke up with [his former girlfriend], when he started dating Sua, when . . . he started hosting room parties and having a drink—it really seemed like he'd put things together."

Wheeler had reached his peak indeed. His next audacious gamble, after his summer in England, would bring his carefully constructed academic identity crashing down.

CHAPTER SIX

Fresh from a summer at Oxford, Adam Wheeler returned to Harvard his senior year ready to push his luck once more. This time, he decided to apply for the Rhodes and Fulbright Scholarships.

The Rhodes has routinely been called the world's most prestigious scholarship. With a brutal 2 percent acceptance rate (just 32 American students per year), it puts even Harvard to shame in selectivity. The lucky few win an all-expenses-paid graduate education at Oxford University in England. Winners of this glamorous opportunity to study at one of the world's leading academic powerhouses have gone on to become luminaries in a variety of fields, from science to journalism to sports to the Supreme Court.

One of the many distinguished recipients was United States Senator James William Fulbright, who later founded a similar program that grants free upper-level education to exceptionally bright students. Today, Fulbright's program is nearly as renowned as the Rhodes. The Fulbright grant sponsors a variety of trips, including some that send American teachers and other professionals abroad and some that whisk foreign students to the United States for cultural education. What interested Wheeler was the award that pays for American students to study, research, or teach abroad for a year.

It is a recognized mark of academic excellence for a student to walk away from college with one of these cushy fellowships. Wheeler, who had already sought so hungrily to establish his credentials as an academic, would make an eager candidate.

Through his skill as a forger and plagiarist, he had already earned $6,000 in prizes, a summer in England, and admission to Harvard. He was out to get himself a Rhodes or Fulbright, too.

The applications were rigorous, but they looked a lot like the applications he had seen when applying to college (the first and second times). Both scholarships demanded a transcript, letters of recommendation, and a personal essay. The Fulbright also required a written proposal for the research project that the money would fund. The Rhodes wanted a list of his activities and a photograph.

The photo could be real. All the rest was going to take some doctoring.

With the experience of faking transcripts from Andover and MIT under his belt, he turned in a forged Harvard transcript this time. It depicted him as a student at Harvard since freshman year. Recalling the one semester he took six classes, he decided that the version of him that would merit a Rhodes or Fulbright would have taken six classes in each semester of his sophomore and junior years, including a few at Harvard Law School in addition to his graduate coursework in English. His freshman year, when by Harvard rules he would have been allowed to take just four classes in his first semester (if he had actually been at Harvard at all), he put himself down as having taken five each semester anyway. He gave himself As in every single class except for an A-minus in one biology course. Altogether, it added up to a distinctly untrue GPA of 3.99.

Writing about what he would study with the grant money, Wheeler declared in a dense two-page essay that his chosen path of scholarship was something he called mobility studies. His stated desire to study mobility from a literary and cultural perspective— the movements of people, objects, and traditions, not mobility in a physics sense—fit well with Daniel Brayton's paper on literary mappings for which Wheeler had won prizes the year before and with the book on "Geographies of English Eloquence" that Wheeler claimed on his résumé to be writing. Furthermore, "cultural

Wheeler, Adam Butler   607-056■   Kirkland House

HARVARD COLLEGE
Cambridge, Massachusetts 02138

Admitted in 2006 from St. Andrew's School
Status: Good Standing

Date of issue: September 1, 2009

Field: English

Barry Kane, Registrar
Not valid unless signed and sealed

COURSE TITLES		GRADE full half	COURSE TITLES		GRADE full half
2006-2007			**2008-2009**		
ENGLISH 90QH	Exotica in Renaissance Drama	A	ENGLISH 227	Fictions of Kin and Kind	A
HISTSCI 295R	Scientific and Legal Doubt	A	ENGLISH 98R	Renaissance Theatricality	A
ENGLISH 255	European Romantic & Post-Roma	A	LAW-40410A	Jurisprudence: Legal Ideals	A
RELIGION 2480	Karl Barth	A	PHIL 263	Metaontology	A
ENGLISH 90HW	Wordsworth and Coleridge	A	COMP LIT 286	Metaphor	A
PHIL 278	Nonsequentialist Ethical T	A	PHIL 278X	Virtue Ethics	A
EXPOS 20	The Art of the Essay	A	OEB 52	Biology of Plants	A-
QUANT-REAS 22	Deductive Logic	A	ENGLISH 251	Comparative Romantic Theory	A
HISTSCI 231V	Expertise in the History of N	A	ENGLISH 257	Joyce: Graduate Seminar	A
GOV 90MI	Plato's Political Thought	A	ENGLISH 270	American Civil War (GSGE)	A
			ENGLISH 281	Studies in Modern Poetry	A
			ENGLISH 304HF	The Extended 18th Century: Doc	A
ANNUAL GPA: 4.000		COURSES PASSED: 10.00	ANNUAL GPA: 3.972		COURSES PASSED: 12.00
			CUMULATIVE GPA: 3.990		SATISFACTORY LETTER GRADES: 17.00
2007-2008					
ENGLISH 90IC	Coetzee and Ishiguro	A			
ENGLISH 295	Marxism & Postcolonial Studies	A			
COMP LIT 276	Renaissance Poetics and Rheto	A			
HISTORY 2332	Early Modern England	A			
PHIL 268X	Topics in Kant's Moral Philoso	A			
LAW 97351A	Freud and Nietzsche	A			
ENGLISH 97	Sophomore Seminar	A			
ENGLISH 290P	Theater and Philosophy	A			
LAW 40410A	Legal Skepticism	A			
HISTSCI 232V	The Cell in Theory and History	A			
COMP LIT 241	Reading Spinoza and Leibniz wi	A			
PHIL 204	Language and Reality in Plato	A			
ANNUAL GPA: 4.000		COURSES PASSED: 12.00			

Wheeler made himself this fake Harvard transcript to change the courses he had taken, the grades he had received, and the
record of his time before coming to Harvard. He gave himself a GPA of 3.99 in a schedule of many high-level classes.

mobility" was a buzzword borrowed from one of Wheeler's former professors, Stephen Greenblatt. In fact, the professor had edited a book with that title—*Cultural Mobility: A Manifesto*—that was set to be published that winter by Cambridge University Press.

Wheeler did not just imitate Greenblatt's focus field. Rather, he lifted his entire essay from a published Greenblatt piece. He cut two paragraphs so that his submission would stay within the required page limit; he substituted "I hope to" in place of Greenblatt's prescriptive "mobility studies should" so that his version read like a student's statement of intent; he varied the syntax and punctuation in a few tiny ways. But largely, the piece that Wheeler turned in to the scholarship judges remained unchanged from one written by Greenblatt.

Next was the résumé that Wheeler submitted in his Rhodes application packet. It was lengthy: three full pages, more like the curriculum vitae of an academic with a decent career under his belt than the résumé of someone who had not even finished his undergraduate degree yet. The formatting was polished: In a sophisticated font, he used small caps—the oft-forgotten typesetting between lowercase and uppercase—which lent the headings in his résumé the clarity and boldness of capital letters without the abrasiveness of an email typed with the caps lock key on. The clean use of lines and artful amount of white space were enough to earn any graphic designer's nod of approval.

But it was the contents of the résumé that truly stood out. The résumé first corroborated the untruths on his transcript by listing him as a Harvard student since 2006 instead of 2007, ignoring his pre-Harvard collegiate education, declaring his boosted GPA, and claiming that he had cross-registered for courses at Harvard Law School. From there, it went further.

Wheeler listed the Hoopes Prize (which he had indeed won, albeit under false pretenses) but described himself as "the first under-classman [*sic*] prize winner in the history of the college," which certainly was not true. He worded his descriptions of a few other educational particulars, like the Rockefeller grant he had received to study abroad and even his Harvard financial aid, to make them sound more impressive.

After inflating his real credentials—as, unfortunately, a number of students and jobseekers of all stripes do when they compose their résumés—Wheeler started writing pure fiction. He claimed to be the sole author of two books, a coauthor of four more, a lecturer at prestigious forums, a creator of new Harvard courses, and a member of committees that he had never served on or that had never even existed.

One of the two books that he claimed to have written single-handedly was titled *The Mapping of an Ideological Demesne*—the name of his Hoopes-winning thesis that he had plagiarized. This résumé stated that he had signed a contract with Harvard University Press to publish the book; the publishing company denies that ever happened. His assertion about his other supposed manuscript was more modest. For that book, whose description he lifted from a dissertation written by a University of Pennsylvania graduate student, Wheeler refrained from saying that he had a publisher. He demurred that his work about "the desire to transcend the vernacular's limited and insular character" was only "in progress."

Then he listed four more books, all of which he said he was coauthoring with his former professor Marc Shell and were under contract to be published soon by various academic publishers. Wisely, he did not make any claims to having a book already published, so that section of his résumé looked extremely impressive without giving his evaluators much opportunity to verify its truthfulness.

Two of the titles really were books in progress. Shell was writing them. The other two never existed at all, at least according to the printing presses to which Wheeler accredited them.

He said he had given six academic lectures as well. He gave them names like "Not Penshurst: Enclosure, Arcadia, and the Panegyric of Place" and "The Body in the Garden: The Metapoetics of

Husbandry from More to Marvell," both of which were chapter titles from Brayton's dissertation. And he claimed that he had been invited to deliver these talks at Yale, Princeton, Duke, Columbia, Cornell, and even Britain's Cambridge.

At least one of these fancifully titled speeches was real, in a sense. There was a lecture called "The Rime of the Book of the Dove: From Zoroastrian Cosmology and Armenian Heresiology to the Russian Novel." But that talk was not given by Wheeler. James Russell, another one of Wheeler's former professors, had delivered it.

Wheeler did not give Russell any of the credit for teaching about "Zoroastrian cosmology" and "Armenian heresiology." (In lay speak, these terms translate roughly to *perspectives on the universe in the ancient Persian religion that follows the prophet Zoroaster* and *the study of nonstandard religious belief in Armenia*.) But Russell did get his name elsewhere on the résumé that Wheeler crafted. According to the résumé, Professor Russell had worked with Wheeler to create two new seminars at Harvard. Both were actual classes that Wheeler had taken from Russell, but Wheeler had not had any hand in creating them.

In addition to Russell's, Wheeler listed two more courses that he said he had founded alongside a Harvard professor. One, called "The History of Cartography," he claimed to have designed in conjunction with Tom Conley, his house master, who had written a book on the subject. The other was on the American Civil War. In another case of drastic credential inflation, he listed himself as Professor John Stauffer's coauthor of that course. Wheeler did enroll in Stauffer's seminar on the Civil War in his junior year. One of Stauffer's express purposes in teaching the class, made up mostly of graduate students, was to test out material for an upcoming general-audience undergraduate class he would be teaching on the same topic. Stauffer made a point of sometimes asking the seminar students whether they thought he should use a certain reading or whether a particular topic would go over well in the big lecture version of the class. In that respect, though Wheeler was nearly always silent in those class discussions, he could have detected a faint hint of his role in shaping the future class, a role that he magnified into the title of coauthor. Stauffer certainly did not see it that way. Not only would he not have characterized his students as coauthors, but about Wheeler in particular, he said, "Adam was the weakest student in the class."

A page-long list of positions at Harvard, MIT, Duke, and Georgetown plus panelist slots at two Harvard doctoral conferences rounded out the hefty résumé. Positions from writing tutor at Harvard's school of continuing education to summer literature researcher at Duke were spots he never held. Some of the positions did not even exist. The Center for Electronic Projects in American Culture Studies at Georgetown University, where he said he had received a grant to perform research over a summer, had not been active for a decade. Nor does Harvard's East Asian Languages and Civilizations department hire any writing tutors, despite Wheeler's claim to that job, too.

A large portion of the activities Wheeler listed on that part of his résumé purportedly happened at MIT, all in the years 2006 and 2007. By the time he was filling out scholarship applications in his senior year at Harvard, however, his backstory had evolved from a humanities-hungry transplant from MIT to a four-year Harvard student. Accordingly, he erased any mention of collegiate enrollment before Harvard. But he apparently forgot to scrub the MIT pursuits from his résumé, leaving a slightly strange record of service to the school down the river while supposedly enrolled at Harvard.

It would have been hard to notice that discrepancy on this résumé, which was longer and filled with more false claims than any Wheeler had crafted so far. Book deals, international lecturing—he had put himself in a whole new league, regardless of minor slips in location. Any reader could have been awed by this student's ostensible achievements, or bored senseless, by the time he hit the MIT activities on page three. It helped that the vocabulary he used to describe his accomplishments included words like *panegyric* (definition: *elaborate praise*) and *metapoetics* (that one has no Dictionary.com definition, Wikipedia page, or even entry in the *Oxford English Dictionary*, the gold standard of lexical comprehensiveness; one must turn to the blogosphere to learn that the term means *poetry about poetry*).

Once again, the application called for letters of recommendation. The old ones that he had written for himself were outdated; he needed letters from his Harvard professors. In the past, when he had put professors' names on recommendations, he never told them. But this time, he tried asking them for letters up front before he resorted to forgery.

With one professor, it worked. This professor had been impressed by Wheeler when he taught him in two small seminars and was further wowed by his résumé. Wheeler did not need to alter a word of the three-page letter that professor wrote for him. No student, practiced forger or not, could wish for a better letter. It started:

> *I have never, in thirty years of teaching, at Yale, Oxford, Johns Hopkins, and Harvard, encountered a student with Adam Wheeler's scope of selfless intellectual ambition, coupled with the gifts and stamina to fulfill them. Nor have I known a student who has already demonstrated such a dazzling combination of acknowledged achievement and of near-horizonless potential. This would be high recommendation already, but I need to add that the particular vectors and the attributes of Wheeler's work will certainly influence his profession in a number of disciplines, and the future of the academy and culture at large. These seem almost absurdly high claims, but I shall try to sketch out various lines of substantiation.*

Indeed, they were "absurdly high claims." The reason that the letter was so effusive lay in what Wheeler's résumé had led his professor to believe: that he had been the first underclassman ever to win the Hoopes Prize. That he was an author or coauthor of six scholarly books, which the professor called "unprecedented" for an undergraduate, even at Harvard. That he chaired task forces on the arts and on curricular requirements, even though, the professor acknowledged, it sounded "impossibly ambitious."

Wheeler won this professor's esteem not just with his fictitious résumé but also with his likeable demeanor in the classroom. "What staggered me was his utter modesty, his patience with other students, his scrupulous avoidance of any opportunity to eclipse his fellows," the professor wrote. "His contributions to discussion tended to be philosophical and analytical, but were always to the point, and he opened up large perspectives to the seminar as a whole." Based also on his excellent writing for the course, "I thought at the time that he had unlimited potential."

He had found the student to be "deeply congenial" and "very appealing" outside of the classroom as well. He wrote:

> He is an all-rounder, too, having been involved in community initiatives, and having a very close and athletic relation to the natural world. He is a competitive swimmer and an active surfer—not in some trite "California" mode, but as it involves a deep love and understanding of the sea (as an ex-surfer I have learned the distinction, and I can see how Wheeler's recreational and creative lives are seriously integrated).

He recommended Wheeler wholeheartedly for the scholarships. "Having been a Rhodes Scholar myself, I can assure you that I was nowhere nearly as qualified as Wheeler, nor did I have anything approximating his vision, his focus, and his carefully established intellectual and cultural purpose," he wrote. Not only did he find Wheeler richly deserving of the chance to spend time studying in England, but, he added, "He would be a splendid ambassador for his country."

This was a letter that would be tough to beat, but Wheeler needed two more professorial recommendations to submit to the scholarship committees. For these, he turned to his old habit of forgery.

Wheeler asked the second professor to send him a recommendation by email. He received a complimentary letter from James Russell, the instructor who had given the Armenian lecture whose title Wheeler had stolen for his résumé. With the file sitting there on his own laptop, sent straight to him by the writer, it was only too easy for Wheeler to touch up the letter to make it exceptional.

While Russell said that Wheeler had taken two of his classes, Wheeler changed this to "developed two courses with me" to match his résumé. He also had Russell affirm that he had lectured at Columbia and developed other Harvard courses that formed "perhaps even a new hybrid field." He inserted a description of himself as "a specialist in an ancient Transcaucasian civilization," one of the most outlandish phrases he ever applied to himself in his prolific career as an academic fraudster. He added only one full sentence to Russell's letter, but it was a zinger: "I am profoundly, profoundly grateful, moved, and impressed by Adam's fluent, masterful, and publishable exploration of Bible and Patristics, Zoroastrian myth and Sufi Persian imagery, Turkish balladry, and so on."

Wheeler exercised that same kind of creativity with the third letter. He asked Christine Gerrard, his professor from his summer at Oxford, to email the letter to him, and the version he received in his inbox was flattering. It cited Wheeler's pleasant demeanor, his obvious enthusiasm for academics, and his strong writing. But apparently it did not meet Wheeler's standards. He scrapped it entirely and wrote a completely new version to submit under Gerrard's signature.

When the two meticulously crafted packets—one for the Fulbright, one for the Rhodes—were ready at last, Wheeler turned them in for the first round of judging.

For both programs, applicants are supposed to secure their own schools' endorsement before they seek the scholarship on a national level. So Wheeler's bid would first have to go head to head with the applications of his fellow Harvard students. In the Rhodes pool, Wheeler fared well—so well, in fact, that one of the judges wanted to shower him with even more accolades than the lofty ones he was pursuing.

All 12 houses at Harvard assign a few of the live-in graduate students to the role of fellowship advising. This pool of fellowship tutors initially reads and evaluates the Rhodes applications. When one tutor from Lowell House, right down the road from Wheeler's Kirkland home, read the applicants' materials, she was so struck by Wheeler's packet that she wrote a special message to the college's fellowships director:

> *With regards to one unbelievably amazing candidate, Rhodes-applicant* ***Adam Wheeler*** *(Kirkland) should also be offered an endorsement for the Marshall. The merit of his application speaks for itself and it would be an embarrassment for Harvard not to endorse him for both. . . . It would be a shame that the best student the English department has seen in 30 years (whose c.v. reads like junior faculty) not be endorsed for the Marshall.*

That tutor was certainly sold on Wheeler. The fellowships director, Paul Bohlmann, later said that only "once in a blue moon" does the committee think to recommend someone for an award he is not even seeking. Soon the full evaluating committee would meet to consider Wheeler's shot at the Rhodes at the very least and perhaps the Marshall scholarship, another prestigious fellowship for study in England, as well. From the sound of that glowing email, he was probably a shoo-in for the Rhodes endorsement, which goes to about half of the cream-of-the-crop Harvard students who apply for it. From there, Harvard's candidates compete with the rest of the nation.

For the Fulbright, students must have an interview with a member of Harvard's judging committee. One faculty member, James Simpson, was assigned to interview Wheeler. Simpson, a prominent English professor who focused on medieval literature, was a logical choice to serve as the first-round evaluator for Wheeler since his area of expertise aligned well with the subject Wheeler was petitioning to study with his Fulbright money.

Before the interview, Simpson sat down with Wheeler's application file. He was the first on the Fulbright committee to look it over. He was surprised by what he saw. As far as he knew, he had never met Wheeler before nor seen him in one of his classes. But this record told him that Wheeler was a highly enthusiastic student in his department and, from the look of his résumé, a talented one, too. Professors had written effusive praise of this student's work in their letters of recommendation. His transcript listed perfect marks in a long string of high-level English classes. And, most astonishing of all, his colleagues were writing books with Wheeler.

Simpson knew plenty of professors who hired undergraduates as research assistants. Normally, those students tracked down information in the library or acted as copyeditors. But putting their names on the covers of faculty members' books was an entirely different matter, and Simpson did not approve. "I don't care how clever this person is," he thought, looking down at the application packet. "It's inappropriate for an undergraduate, one, to be writing books with faculty at Harvard and, two, to have a book contract. This is too much burden to place on shoulders so young."

He may have made a mental note to speak to his colleagues about it afterward. Simpson was known for his thoughtfulness to students. When he became chair of the English department the following year, he organized personal exit chats with graduating seniors and small-group lunches with students and faculty members, where his distinguished presence—marked by his tall frame and lofty Australian accent—meant he could hold court with ease. His natural reaction to Wheeler's résumé was neither respect for this seemingly extraordinary student nor skepticism at his grand claims. It was instead heartfelt concern.

"This person must be a genius," he thought, turning to Wheeler's personal statement. "But still, I don't think he's being well advised."

He read the first sentence of Wheeler's essay: "It is a truth universally acknowledged that we live in an intensely mobile society." *A truth universally acknowledged* . . . borrowed from Jane Austen. Common English major fare, the clever or not-so-clever reworking of beloved words until they almost become everyone's and no one's. He read on.

As he proceeded, he was surprised to find that the essay still felt familiar. It was, as the opening line implied, about mobility. The writer quickly connected the frenetic pace of global movement to life at his own college, stating that "the simple phenomenon of an undergraduate education at an institution such as mine assumes and indeed requires mobility." Then in the next paragraph, he discussed the lack of opportunities for studying mobility at Harvard. This paragraph gently criticized academia for assuming that the blending and swapping that take place between civilizations represent outlying cases rather than the core of all cultural development.

"It's funny the way an idea comes of age," Simpson mused as he read, "the way an idea all of a sudden is being expressed by different people in independent moments." He was fairly sure he had come across this idea in particular before. It sounded just like something his colleague Stephen Greenblatt had written a few years earlier. After a few sentences more, he was overcome by the nagging feeling that he had already read these thoughts. He put Wheeler's essay down and walked across his office to one of his several ceiling-high bookshelves. He spotted the volume he was looking for and pulled it from the shelf: *Essays on General Education in Harvard College.*

The crimson-covered paperback had been printed four years earlier when the college was considering revamping its decades-old Core Curriculum. The byzantine set of requirements mandated that every undergraduate pass one class in each of seven out of 11 groups with names like "Social Analysis," "Moral Reasoning," "Foreign Cultures," and "Literature and Arts A, B, and C." To make matters more confusing, the four categories from which students were exempted were not up to them; they were determined based on a student's concentration. Figuring out which course groups one did or did not need to pass in order to graduate meant opening a 28-page booklet and following a long chain of fine-print asterisks and plus signs.

Back in 2002, the college had started talking about overhauling this system. At a place like Harvard, though, even a move to simplify things gets complicated. When the Core Curriculum itself was instituted back in 1978, the then-new framework of required classes was actually called "radical" by *The New York Times* and was hotly debated on campus and even nationwide. Derek Bok, who was president of Harvard at the time, wryly told *The Washington Post* that "changing undergraduate education is like trying to move a graveyard."

But change they did, under Bok, and in the early years of the new millennium, the powers that be decided that it was time to dig up those bones all over again now that they had settled back into the ground. In order to start that change in the most Harvardian way possible, it was decided that they should write a book mulling over the idea.

A number of notable professors were solicited to write down their thoughts about what the new required course groups— termed General Education rather than Core—should look like. Those essays, paperbound and circulated among the faculty as well as posted on a Harvard website, made up the book that Simpson now held in his hands.

It was a book Wheeler was more familiar with than most people. He had been stealing pieces from it even before he came to

Harvard. It was the collection from which he had amalgamated five different professors' words for his Harvard application essay. He had used other pieces from it for his Rockefeller grant application. Greenblatt's was clearly his favorite. It was the only essay that he had used in both of those applications, and for the Fulbright and Rhodes, he had not even mixed it with other pieces from the same book. In the past, he had drawn from pieces that said that a Harvard education should include more environmental studies, that it should emphasize creativity and communication skills, and that it should teach students about capitalism and terrorism. Greenblatt said in his entry that he wanted an undergraduate curriculum that focused on cultural mobility.

Simpson flipped through that book until he reached Greenblatt's piece. There he read, "It is a truth universally acknowledged. . . . " He sat down, placing the student's essay and the professor's side by side. Word for word, they were almost identical. Once in a while, the copy in the bound booklet used the pronoun "one" and the copy Simpson was holding next to it said "I." Simpson was completely convinced that he was looking at the most blatant plagiarism he had ever seen in his years as an educator.

Just three minutes after locating Greenblatt's essay, Simpson picked up his office phone. He dialed Adonica Lui, the chair of both the Fulbright and the Rhodes nominating committees at Harvard. Someone answered, but it was not Lui. She was in a meeting, Simpson was told.

"I think you should go get Adonica," Simpson said firmly. It took a moment of convincing. Finally, he was put on hold.

In University Hall, the stately administrative building just a short walk from Simpson's office, Lui was indeed in a meeting. It was the final meeting of the Rhodes and Marshall judging committee. At the close of the session, the group assembled around that table would distribute a list of students who had and had not received Harvard's endorsement for each scholarship. One by one, the committee members were passing judgment on each application.

The process was winding down. All the applications had been reviewed, and they had a tentative list of candidates to endorse that they were getting ready to finalize. Then someone knocked on the door. "Call for you," the staffer said to Lui.

Lui spoke to Simpson for a moment. She had to come over to his office right now, he insisted. It was urgent, more urgent than wrapping up the Rhodes and Marshall deliberations.

Minutes after she picked up Wheeler's writing sample and the Gen Ed book herself, Lui too was persuaded that they had a plagiarist on their hands. "It was lucky you called me," she said, turning to Simpson. "Wheeler had just been put on the short list for the Rhodes Scholarship."

It might not seem prudent of Wheeler to have plagiarized the work of a Harvard English professor, and one of the most famous Harvard English professors at that, when his essay would be read by a member of the Harvard English faculty. But Wheeler's choice was actually quite keen. If he had enjoyed slightly better luck, then his selection might have been just the ticket to getting away with a Rhodes or Fulbright Scholarship.

In this day and age, many a professor has bemoaned, plagiarism is easy. No more treks through the snow to the library. No more wandering the musty miles of underground stacks. No more copying text out of a book and typing it, word by word, into the cheater's own paper draft. Want some pre-written words about Descartes or domino theory or Dubai? Just turn to a search engine. Open up whatever webpage it suggests, drag a cursor over the words, and hold down CTRL+C. Voilà. Plagiarism in the Internet age is incredibly simple, indeed so simple that some students commit the crime without ever meaning to, just by assembling information they have gathered on the Internet and forgetting to properly put quotation marks around it or rework it into their own words.

Yet if the Internet is exceptionally good at facilitating plagiarism, it is nearly as good at vanquishing it, too. Crooked students do not have to set foot in the library anymore, but neither do suspicious professors. In the past, even if a teacher had a hunch that a student's writing was not his own, it was difficult to prove. The theft could be from any of the millions of books in the library. Unless the teacher happened to have read the text from which the student had borrowed and was able to locate the offending passage, it was almost impossible to convict a plagiarist.

Today, the guesswork can be done by machines, in a fraction of a second. Type any phrase from a plagiarized paper into Google, and chances are high that the entire original work will pop right up on the computer screen. Internet-based services designed specifically to detect plagiarism can take an entire essay and mark all instances of theft from other sources.

Choosing to plagiarize a big-name professor, instead of some little-known graduate student, was a risky move for Wheeler. But if he wanted Greenblatt to be his voice when he spoke to the Fulbright and Rhodes judging committees, he picked the safest text to make that happen. Most works by Greenblatt—his *New York Times* best-selling biography of Shakespeare, for instance—stood a chance of being recognized by someone on the national Rhodes or Fulbright judging committees. The Gen Ed book, on the other hand, was printed in a limited edition for distribution to Harvard faculty members. Five years later, when Wheeler was completing his scholarship applications, he could easily have believed that the only place the booklet could still be found was in Lamont Library, where a few copies had been deposited for the historical record. It is unclear how Wheeler himself found it. It had been posted online at one point, but by this time it was hard to find. A Google search for the first sentence resulted in hundreds of Jane Austen hits, and even without her famous words included in the search, Greenblatt's essay did not readily appear.

If he had made it past Simpson, Wheeler probably would have won Harvard's nomination for one or both scholarships.

And the judges in the next round most likely never would have seen the document Harvard had created for its curricular review. They might not have recognized the essay as plagiarized, and they could easily have decided to give the scholarship to a young man who performed at the top of his class in high-level academic work at Harvard—and who gave lectures on Armenian religion and wrote books on the side. And penned eloquent sentences about the interesting concept of cultural mobility.

If it had not been for Simpson, Wheeler could have snagged a Rhodes or Fulbright on top of all his other ill-earned achievements thus far. He probably would have made it through the remaining months until his Harvard graduation uncaught and then walked away with a diploma, too.

Wheeler's plan for stealing the Rhodes or Fulbright, just like his earlier plans for stealing Harvard admission and a Hoopes Prize, was supposed to be airtight. What he did not know was that Simpson was going to be his first-round evaluator. And Simpson worked closely with Greenblatt, whose office was just a few doors away. He had read Greenblatt's General Education essay, had kept the words in mind, and had a copy of it right there on his bookshelf.

Lui headed back to University Hall. The faculty and administrators on the committee were still gathered in the conference room where she had left them. We're not endorsing Adam Wheeler, she told them. Then she spread out copies of Greenblatt's essay for all the judges to see. As the evaluators realized that a student had violated their trust, "the sadness in the committee room," Lui said, "was palpable."

One of the judges in the room, Jay Ellison, examined the two nearly identical essays—Wheeler's and Greenblatt's. He asked, This was his Fulbright application that James Simpson was reading?

We have this same essay for the Rhodes here, Ellison pointed out. He submitted plagiarized essays not once but twice.

Ellison was the secretary of the Administrative Board, the college's disciplinary body that is responsible for investigating and punishing all sorts of student misbehavior, from plagiarism and cheating to theft and rape. His job was to dig into documents and witness statements in order to root out students' wrongdoings. And his background was in law enforcement: He had patrolled the streets in Georgia as a police officer.

To Ellison, it was clear that the committees should not just cross Wheeler off the shortlist for the Rhodes and wash their hands of the plagiarist. This sort of behavior merited further scrutiny, he thought. His first order of business would be a call to David Smith, the Kirkland resident dean. Then the two of them would see if there was anything more they should know about this Adam Wheeler.

For the time being, Wheeler did not yet know that he had been detected, and his interview with Simpson was scheduled for that afternoon. Simpson's first thought was that he should go ahead with the interview. He knew what his main question would be. He would show the student the evidence of plagiarism and ask, "What's going on here?"

But he asked Lui's opinion. After all, Wheeler seemed to be trying to tamper with one of the most prestigious post-graduate scholarships around. This might be out of an English professor's league. Lui agreed. She did not want Simpson to meet with Wheeler at all.

Soon enough, the interview time rolled around, and Simpson saw a well-dressed student waiting outside his office door, just as expected. He looked "cool as a cucumber," Simpson noted, and he felt as though he had seen him before, probably walking around the English department to get paperwork signed or turn in assignments or meet with his professors during office hours. "Sort of an interesting face," Simpson mused. "Rather beautiful face. Dreamy. Deep, deep, deep blue eyes."

He turned to those deep blue eyes and gave an excuse. "I've been to the dentist today." He was not feeling up to the interview, he said. "We'll make another time."

It was a Friday afternoon, he thought, justifying the decision to postpone the conversation. There was a whole weekend ahead in which Wheeler would not be able to get in touch with anyone in the college to talk about what he had been accused of. "He might do something dangerous to himself. . . . Friday afternoons are tricky for telling students bad things." True to form, Simpson phrased his decision in the framework of his great care for his students. The confrontation with Wheeler would wait, then, and it would not be Simpson who would initiate it. He never saw the student again.

Instead, on Sunday night, Dean Smith of Kirkland House sent a two-sentence email asking Wheeler to meet him in his office the next morning. The encounter was brief. Smith handed him a copy of his essay and a copy of Greenblatt's. "I must have made a mistake," was Wheeler's immediate reaction. I meant to turn in an essay I wrote about cosmopolitanism. I had Professor Greenblatt's essay on my computer. I must have just mixed up the files.

Smith was not moved. There would be a formal Ad Board hearing on the matter soon, he said, and Wheeler was invited to attend.

There was no way he was going to stick around and let the Ad Board poke into his business. If he went to the hearing, he would have to defend himself in front of a room full of the college's top administrators (because at Harvard, unlike Bowdoin, the judiciary board included only deans), and he certainly did not want them to look any further than that Greenblatt essay. He knew they could find a lot more—the fake grades, the false résumé, the forged recommendations—within his scholarship applications alone. And if the Ad Board opened up anything else in his file . . . well, he just was not going to let them.

I want to take a leave of absence, he told Smith. Right away. I'll go home tomorrow. And minutes after his half-hour meeting with Smith ended, he sent him a brief email:

Dear Dean Smith, I am writing to let you know that I choose not to appear at the Ad Board hearings, and to request immediate withdrawal from the College. Thank you.

Yours, Adam

He packed his belongings, and his parents picked him up at Harvard the next day. Driving away from Harvard for good, when he was less than one year away from making it to graduation, must have been a devastating blow—yet he knew his bid for scholarships could have turned out even worse. That had been a close shave. But he could still escape without being found out entirely.

CHAPTER SEVEN

It was the fall of his senior year, in 2009, when Adam Wheeler left Harvard. He had just settled into his new dorm room and chosen his classes a few weeks before. Then one day, he told his roommates that he was going home.

One of his roommates sent around a group text message to all the former Swamp residents and the blocking group of women with whom they most often socialized in Kirkland. He wanted to make sure that everyone had a chance to drop by their room to say goodbye to Wheeler. As his friends popped in, Wheeler told them only that he was leaving to deal with an issue at home. None of them wanted to pry further than that. And so rumors started to spread.

One friend picked up hints from what Wheeler said that there was financial trouble at home. Abel Acuña heard from another Kirkland resident that Wheeler was studying abroad for the semester at Oxford or Cambridge. One roommate told another that Wheeler had a brother whom he had never mentioned up until now who had run away from home and then returned very ill.

Matt, the roommate who had been closest to Wheeler, called him from time to time. When January rolled around and Wheeler did not return for the spring semester, Matt asked what was going on. "Oh, my brother's just still ill," he told Matt, according to another one of the former Swamp residents. "And I'm not sure I'm really ready to come back. I feel like I want college to last a little longer."

His disappearance did not cause much of a stir. One young woman who lived nearby recalled, "I vaguely remembered a good-looking guy talking about Shakespeare at the beginning of the year, and then wondered where he had gone, and then convinced myself that I had made him up." Another friend, unaware that Wheeler had left Harvard at all, continued to send him Facebook invitations whenever he threw parties.

His Swamp rooming group had split into two separate rooms for senior year. One of the men who was now living one floor above Wheeler's room walked downstairs months later and said, "It's great to see everyone, but where's Adam?" His friends did not know why Wheeler had jumped ship, and they thought he would come back eventually. But Wheeler knew his days at Harvard were over.

A few short weeks earlier, he had been a Harvard senior, only about nine months away from walking out with one of the world's most prestigious college diplomas in hand and probably some sweet post-grad opportunities to boot. Now he was sitting day after day in front of his computer in his parents' house in Delaware.

But Wheeler apparently did not wallow in resentment toward Harvard or remorse for his own actions that brought him to this moment. Instead, he looked to the future—and that meant borrowing a few strategies from the past.

He would apply to college yet again—third time's the charm. Maybe this time Wheeler would actually end up with a degree from some highly regarded institution. After all, he already had the résumé, transcripts, and score reports lined up on his computer. With a few touch-ups, he could have a ready-made application for any occasion.

First, he changed his backstory again. He was now looking to transfer out of Harvard, where he had been enrolled for two years before taking the year off to work on his two book manuscripts. He listed his real high school, Caesar Rodney, which had not appeared on his résumé since his long collegiate career began.

But what he created on paper did not much resemble the Caesar Rodney he had attended or the record he had charted there. He claimed he had been the only student out of 433 in his class to earn a 4.0 GPA, even while taking the toughest courses available. He modeled his new Caesar Rodney transcript on his old fake Andover transcript that listed his courses by the trimester, a practice that CRHS does not follow. Since the transcript was copied from an Andover document, it said that the school does not calculate class rank—even though Wheeler had already professed to be first in his high school class.

He also adjusted his high school graduation date from 2005 to 2007. Now he was trying to knock not one but two years off his real history—the one he had lost by leaving Bowdoin and a second for the same at Harvard. He said that at Harvard, he had earned all As in classes ranging from honors math to advanced German, classical Armenian, and Old Persian, although English was still his focus. He said that he had taken higher-level English courses as early as his freshman year and been promoted to a junior year tutorial as a sophomore.

His résumé listed many of the old lies (writing two books and cowriting four more), familiar puffery (inflated titles like "chair" and "head tutor" on a long list of committees), and new obfuscations (the poetry prize from Bowdoin was reincarnated as a supposed Harvard award).

He made up a new set of extraordinary standardized test scores to list on the Common App. He said he had scored 5s on 13 different AP exams this time, adjusting the dates to fit a high school graduation year of 2007. For good measure, he gave himself perfect 800s on three SAT Subject Tests. His only blemish was a 790 on the math SAT Subject Test, 10 points that he humbly docked from his self-made record.

This latest incarnation of Adam Wheeler—public school standout, Harvard English superstar, book-writing prodigy— looked excellent on paper. The real Adam Wheeler was ready to present his newest alter ego to a fresh set of admissions committees at Yale, Stanford, and Brown.

By the time Wheeler was getting his application packets ready, it was after New Year's. Aside from one letter he received from Harvard in October, he had not heard anything from the college. He probably thought he had fled at just the right moment. He was free to fire off another salvo of applications, and given his track record and the strength of his fake materials, he had a good chance of hitting the mark. Back at Harvard, he must be off their hands and out of their thoughts forever.

If that was Wheeler's calculation, then it was much too optimistic. He did not know it, but since the very day that he packed his things and drove away from Kirkland House, Wheeler had been anything but forgotten in the halls of Harvard.

David Smith, Wheeler's resident dean, grew worried when his student said he wanted to go home rather than sit through a disciplinary hearing. He contacted Wheeler several times during the day of their morning meeting to check in with him. He was concerned enough about Wheeler's mental state that he called the young man's parents too. They had already planned to come up from Delaware the following day to take their son home.

Even after that, Smith did not put the student's abrupt departure out of his mind. Something seemed wrong here. The Ad Board proceedings would not move forward until the suspect came back, if he did at all. Nevertheless, Smith talked to Jay Ellison, the head of the Ad Board, on the day the Wheeler family drove away.

On the phone in their offices a few blocks apart—Ellison in the Yard, Smith in Kirkland by the River—the two men rehashed the events of the past few days, from the time Simpson spotted the plagiarism on Friday to now, only Tuesday afternoon, when the student was suddenly gone.

Smith pulled up Wheeler's record while he talked to Ellison. He really turned his grades around after that first semester, he remarked.

Ellison flipped through Wheeler's Rhodes application folder that he still had on his desk. His grades are great, he said. Amazing. But his first semester was great too.

What are you talking about? Smith replied.

Ellison scanned the transcript in front of him. Wheeler earned all As freshman year. And every year after that. Just one A-minus ever, nothing worse.

Right, after his first semester, it was all As and A-minuses, Smith agreed. But he got a D-plus that first fall. And two B-pluses and a B. Then after that something happened and he got his act together.

Ellison was perplexed. I'm not seeing that semester here, he said. On the transcript in front of me, he got all As all the way.

It dawned on both of them. They were looking at two different transcripts, even though the same student's name was at the top. One was genuine, and one was counterfeit. This kid's misbehavior went way beyond his plagiarized essay.

They kicked into investigative high gear, quickly comparing notes on the two records they were viewing. Smith had the one that a Harvard official, such as a student's academic adviser or a resident dean, could pull up through an online system. That record started with Wheeler's sophomore year, when he received poor grades at first. Then it showed a heavy junior year in which he took a staggering number of classes and racked up brownie points in graduate-level English courses. It said he had been a transfer student from MIT. Given his rocky start, plus the influence of the A-minuses in the semesters when he was consistently earning good grades, his GPA was just over 3.6.

On the paper in Ellison's office, Wheeler's GPA was 3.99, reflecting three full years of five or six classes every semester with As in all but one of them. Those courses were much more varied than the nearly all-English lineup in Smith's real document; they included religion, government, history of science, and three courses at Harvard Law School. He had come straight from a private high school in Delaware called St. Andrew's School and started as a freshman rather than a transfer student.

The transcript on Ellison's desk was, of course, the fake one. That was the one with the better grades in more classes, the one that Wheeler had handed in to the Rhodes and Fulbright committees. What Smith was seeing had not been altered by Wheeler. Moreover, Ellison realized that the one Wheeler had provided did not have the right background image, the drawing of Harvard Yard used on all authentic Harvard transcripts. The two deans also checked Wheeler's file and saw that he had attended MIT and Andover, so the transcript from his Rhodes and Fulbright applications that did not mention either of those schools could not be correct.

Since Wheeler had left that very day, they would not get a chance to confront him with this newly uncovered information at an Ad Board hearing. But that did not mean they could not do a little fact-checking.

◦—◦

Wheeler, meanwhile, was not done with the Stephen Greenblatt piece that had landed him in trouble at Harvard. He was plugging in the very same essay on all of his transfer applications. That may seem gutsy or even foolhardy. But even though a professor at Harvard had somehow found the piece in the General Education book, that was Harvard. With a new array of schools in front of him, he could use it again.

For the second essay on his applications, he lifted from an entry in the Gen Ed book by his former professor James Engell. Even for a question that asked him to write 150 words about one of his extracurricular activities, he turned to that book. He borrowed his opening words from Harvard dean William Kirby's preface and much of the body from Slavic languages professor Julie Buckler. He also reached beyond Harvard for some of the words in that 150-word response, grabbing phrases about "the unity of intellectual frameworks" from an essay by a professor at Wheeling Jesuit University in West Virginia. In total, only a handful of words in the one-paragraph statement (the assertive ones, like "I chaired a University-wide task force") were not plagiarized. Just filling that little box with pieces from so many sources must have required considerable effort. It might have been substantially easier to just write it himself.

On his application to Brown, Wheeler was supposed to write about why he wanted to go there. For that one, he borrowed more words from Buckler about what an ideal interdisciplinary course might cover (touching on everything from Foucault to "cognitive theory" to "Mannheim's sociology of knowledge"). And then instead of saying that these would all be found in the perfect Harvard Gen Ed class, which is what Buckler had written, Wheeler posited that they would all fit in comparative literature—the major he declared he would pursue if Brown admitted him. Then he praised comparative literature classes as "manifestly topical, thematic, idiosyncratic, and intended to provoke rather than to instantiate a canon"—words taken from yet another entry in the Gen Ed book, by English professor Marjorie Garber. Wheeler's copy of the crimson paperback must have been getting well-worn at this point.

He had to write one more essay about what he had been doing during his time off from college. For this, he again went to a document circulated at Harvard, presumably hoping that the outside world would not catch him. This time, he went to the highest source at the university.

Drew Gilpin Faust, the university president, had sent a letter to everyone in the university community in November 2008 on the subject of the global financial crisis. Now, a year later, Wheeler grabbed some of her opening lines:

We all know of the extraordinary turbulence still roiling the world's financial markets and the broader economy. The downturn is widely seen as the most serious in decades, and each day's headlines remind us that heightened volatility and persisting uncertainty have become our new economic reality.

While Faust's letter went on to address the university's sinking endowment, its need to reevaluate its grand plan of building a major extension of the campus across the river from Cambridge, and its continued commitment to financial aid, Wheeler took a totally different tack. He wrote about his job as a research assistant in an education program at McLean Hospital, a psychiatric treatment facility affiliated with Harvard. True, he had applied for the position and received some emails that made it sound as if he were likely to get it. But he never started working there. He had not created and led conferences at eight public high schools, as he claimed. And he had not, more grandiosely still, "founded a center at Harvard for the study of community improvement efforts . . . across a wide range of fields of scientific and humanistic inquiry." (That bit, from "wide range of fields" on, came from Faust's letter, too.)

To hear him tell it, his time off from Harvard had not been an ignominious escape. It was instead "an almost unprecedented opportunity to contribute both to public service and to public solutions in a time of global crisis"—and it was going to help him perform a "deeper analysis of financial parameters" once he was back in a classroom at whatever university took the bait.

— ᵔ —

Back at Harvard, Ellison and Smith felt they had a better understanding of why Wheeler had been in such a hurry to get out. He had forged his transcript. He had good reason to want to avoid a detailed examination into his record. But even though Wheeler was no longer in Cambridge, that detective work was exactly what they were going to do.

First they picked through the three-page résumé that Wheeler had submitted with his scholarship applications. He had lied about his GPA there, too. Within a week they ascertained that he was not writing any books with Marc Shell, had not given the lectures he said he had, and was not a member of most of the committees on his list.

They looked over the letters of recommendation that had so impressed the Rhodes committee. In light of what they knew now, those pages brimming with praise seemed too good to be true. Email correspondence with some of the authors revealed within days that the letters were indeed part of the ruse.

When Smith contacted James Russell, Russell said that the letter Wheeler had submitted to the committee was "baffling." He said he had emailed his letter to Wheeler, and as he optimistically put it, "it is possible the text was somehow mixed upon reception with other files Adam had." The letter Smith showed him did contain many sentences Russell had written. But interspersed among them were some fabrications that were unfathomable to Russell. "In particular," Russell wrote to Smith, "I don't recall Adam's having given a lecture on Jakobson at Columbia and cannot imagine why they would have asked him, an undergrad without Russian, to give such a lecture."

Russell was especially bothered by the assertion in the letter that Wheeler had given a talk on the Russian ballad "The Rime of the Book of the Dove." Russell had actually given that lecture himself, after an intensive study of the poem in question. Moreover, Wheeler did not have any of the requisite background in Armenian and Middle Persian. A lecture on the subject by Wheeler, Russell said, "can only have taken place in a parallel universe."

Russell criticized some of the text inserted in his letter for poor writing style. But he said that Wheeler's own writing was "beyond anything one might expect in an undergraduate essay," so to him it did not make sense to conclude that Wheeler might have tampered with the letter himself. Russell had not been fully informed of the other allegations against Wheeler. He had no reason to suspect that the essays he had seen Wheeler writing for his classes might not have been the student's own work. Only Ellison and Smith, who already knew full well that Wheeler had it in him to submit plagiarized work, suspected that Russell might not have read Wheeler's true writing before—and that this letter might be evidence of what that writing actually looked like.

So even having seen his letter corrupted and exaggerated, Russell insisted on believing the best of his former pupil. "Adam has been a superb student—an extraordinary one," he told Smith. "I've known him to be an exceptionally reliable and considerate person as well. It is hard to imagine that he would intentionally deceive anyone."

One round of emails later, Russell was asking more questions about what was going on. "How could parts of my letter have been faked . . . in such a crude, transparent, and unconvincing manner?" he asked. "Certainly not by anyone in his right mind. That is, it looks insane."

And Russell, who was already positing insanity, had not even seen the half of it. At least what the deans had seen so far was reasonable, in theory. If someone wanted to get ahead and he did not have any qualms about lying or cheating to do it, Wheeler's way made sense. Wheeler scrubbed his transcript to make his grades better. He used an essay by a man recognized as one of the best writers in the academic field he wanted to study. He stuffed sentences into Russell's recommendation to turn it from a flattering letter about a very good student to a description of an extraordinary one. Ethical, no, but logical, yes.

But then Ellison and Smith contacted Christine Gerrard, the professor at Oxford whose class Wheeler had taken over the summer and whose recommendation he had also submitted for the Fulbright and Rhodes. She looked at the letter Wheeler had handed in, and she too told the pair of sleuthing deans that it was not what she had written. She sent them the actual letter she had penned on Wheeler's behalf. And there the trail took a bizarre turn.

Gerrard's original letter read in its entirety:

Although I have only known Adam Wheeler for the past six weeks as a student on my Early Romanticism course in Bread-loaf [sic] at Oxford, I am convinced that he is going to be a famous literary scholar with a distinguished career ahead of him. It is not my style to write euphoric references, so I will register my sense that Adam is a really exceptional individual who will bring distinction to any graduate programme that takes him. The Breadloaf school of English [sic] is a programme designed mainly for high school teachers of English working towards a master's degree over the course of several summers. In recent years I have also had one or two graduate students attending the course as a way of intensively enhancing their knowledge of specific areas. Adam is the first undergraduate I have taught on the programme, but I understand that he is already taking graduate courses in English and philosophy at Harvard. Adam engaged with literary texts at a level far above that of his fellow students on this course. His reading in philosophy and political theory (Seneca, Freud, Adam Smith, and Walter Benjamin were but a few of the points of reference) is really remarkable for someone of his age. Adam is bent on asking large questions about texts—how does Wordsworth balance sympathy and 'apatheia' in his economy of feeling? This morning I marked his final, thirty page paper on Wordsworth's The Excursion *and its its [sic] use of georgic economy and thought that parts of it could be published.*

At times Adam has been perceived as a daunting figure by some of his classmates (three new students on the Breadloaf programme) but he became less shy as the weeks went on. He gave a wonderfully illuminating presentation this week on the role of the monstrous and grotesque in Frankenstein, *and in his communication of great thoughts to an audience I saw at once the makings of the charismatic lecturer. I do not know Adam very well, not having known him for very long, but I volunteered to write on his behalf before he had a chance to ask me (he might not have done so) as I am convinced that he should be considered for a graduate scholarship. He would flourish in a research environment.*

A student could not dream of a letter much better than that. Indeed, amidst all the letters that Wheeler faked, it is hard to believe that this one was not his handiwork as well. Here was a professor at Oxford predicting that Wheeler would become "a famous literary scholar." She said he had "great thoughts" and "really remarkable" knowledge. She dwelt on some of the same attributes that Wheeler usually emphasized when drafting over-the-top recommendations for himself: the publishable quality of his work, his exceptional achievement given his age, his specialized erudition, and his pleasant personality. Gerrard even used the same sort of academic language that Wheeler liked to plagiarize. She made the claim, which sounds similar to some boasts Wheeler was wont to make, that he was the first undergrad ever in her class.

And yet despite all that, Wheeler went to great lengths to improve on Gerrard's letter. Though the version that he submitted to the Fulbright and Rhodes committees was similar to Gerrard's in its introduction, it was about twice as long. Wheeler reworked her phrasing to express most of the same very positive thoughts. He embellished the language even further, making himself the best student she had seen in 20 years and a writer of "masterpieces" that were "genuinely groundbreaking." His biggest change was a huge paragraph full of academese far more noticeable than Gerrard's brief forays into literary territory.

The version of Gerrard's letter that Wheeler came up with himself had sentences like "The beautiful can thus deceive judgment of its freedom, as the *sensus communis* can yield an illusion of objectivity" and "'Reality' or noumena is unpresentable because we are always already adjoined to other consciousnesses through heteroglossia." It is hard to imagine how Wheeler thought that swapping out Gerrard's to-the-point and, more importantly, legitimate recommendation in favor of a text full of ponderous words unrelated to his own candidacy could possibly help him win a scholarship.

Smith forwarded Gerrard's original recommendation to Ellison as proof that the one they had seen in Wheeler's application was a fake. All he wrote in the forwarding email was: "As expected. . . ." It had only been three days since they discovered the altered transcript, but it had not taken them very long to see a pattern of deceit.

They followed that trail to Wheeler's prize-winning junior paper next. They pulled the copy that had been stored in the Harvard Archives and flipped through it. The first clue they spotted was the bibliography. Of all of Wheeler's sources, none were published later than 2000, even though he had turned in his project in 2009. Eventually, they turned up the source, Brayton's 2001 Cornell dissertation. After that, some searching of the terms on Wheeler's résumé pointed them toward the Penn dissertation he had used as his source for the description of the second book he was supposedly writing.

Finding those two dissertations led Smith to a theory to explain how Wheeler had improved so dramatically after his first semester at Harvard and why his professors genuinely considered him an advanced writer. Smith had a hunch that Wheeler had made a habit of grabbing chapters of doctoral dissertations through the online ProQuest system that Harvard subscribes to and submitting them as his class assignments.

Then there was one more find, one that made this seem like a case of outright identity fraud, not solely academic dishonesty. A copy of Wheeler's passport in his student file said that he was born in 1986; his Harvard forms read 1987. This was not only a student who cheated in his classes and on his applications. This was a person who in many respects simply was not who he said he was.

Leaving Harvard was not going to stop Wheeler from changing facts or co-opting professors' names for the new batch of applications he was cooking up. Though he had prepared falsified letters of recommendation for his scholarship applications just a few months before, he would not use those for his transfer applications.

He did reuse the one genuine recommendation that he had submitted with his Rhodes application. This one not only gushed for pages about academic work that "shattered any mould" but also celebrated the student's surfing hobby as evidence of his creative soul. It was definitely a keeper—and as an added bonus, it happened to be legitimate.

The others, glowing as they were, were not quite right, Wheeler must have decided. He included letters from two new professors—Peter Nohrnberg, from whom he had taken two challenging English courses about James Joyce, and Marc Shell, with whom he said he was writing four different scholarly books.

For the Nohrnberg letter, he borrowed bits and pieces from the Gen Ed book once more. He took from Dean Kirby's preface to the book and also from English professor Helen Vendler's entry. Much of it was also his own invention. The first paragraph alone conveys a sense of the lavish praise that the two-page letter heaps upon Wheeler:

> *I write this letter in complete and unwavering support of Adam Wheeler, who is quite simply the most intellectually talented literary scholar I have encountered in my six years teaching at Harvard and teaching in graduate school at Yale. Even among the best and brightest at Harvard, Adam's unparalleled talent and productivity . . . set him apart from his peers. Indeed, his accomplishments set him apart from most of Harvard's graduate students in English. He is a wildly ambitious and dedicated student, as even the most cursory look at his astonishing CV will suggest.*

The letter goes on to say that in class, Wheeler's contributions to discussion "were so intelligent and theoretically sophisticated that I did not quite know how to respond. I realized immediately, and then with deepening admiration, that he has both an extraordinary mind and a rarely authentic relation to literature, philosophy, and the work of being alive."

Yes: the work of being alive. Wheeler was even the best at that.

Wheeler also sent a letter from Smith, his resident dean, who had been the one to tell him months ago that he had been caught plagiarizing at Harvard. Wheeler had no idea that Smith was still actively investigating his misdeeds even after his departure. And Smith had no idea that Wheeler was now signing his name to a fabricated letter.

The letter gave no indication that Smith had ever sat Wheeler down in his office to tell him he had committed an academic offense. Instead, according to the recommendation form, Smith chose "accomplished" and "remarkable" as the first two words that came to mind to describe Wheeler and ranked him in the top 1 percent of students he had ever met, academically, extracurricularly, and personally.

The letter from Smith was an amalgamation of leftovers from the other fictitious recommendations. The opening paragraph of Nohrnberg's letter, which Wheeler was not sending to the same schools as Smith's, made another appearance here. Some nice words that Russell had actually written about Wheeler, as well as his own insert about Patristics and Turkish balladry from the Russell letter, were all mixed together and attributed to Smith.

Wheeler sent in a purported recommendation from his high school guidance counselor too. It offered sentence after sentence singing the praises of this "*exceptionally* gifted student." It used some of Wheeler's classic vocabulary: "He loves to banter—at times hilariously—about the quirks of academic potentates and the foibles of the world-be [*sic*] great." But much of the one-paragraph recommendation seemed odd coming from a high school employee rather than a college one. For example, the letter said that at Caesar Rodney, "Adam has chaired numerous committees involved in improving undergraduate education," even though high school students are not ordinarily called undergraduates. And it took a jab at the Harvard student body: "Unlike many of Harvard's undergraduates," the letter said about Wheeler, "he has no innate sense of entitlement."

～

Once Ellison and Smith knew about Wheeler's false essays, transcript, résumé entries, and even birth date, everything he had ever said became suspect. They contacted MIT and learned that he had never been a student there. Ditto at Andover.

Those discoveries thrust the tangle of lies into a whole different realm. Now they knew that Wheeler had not merely tried to steal two of the world's most prestigious scholarships nor just flubbed his way through Harvard coursework with plagiarized papers. Lying about where he went to school before Harvard brought this investigation into the court of the Harvard admissions office. And over there, they played hardball.

First, they did their homework. They marshaled several employees to look into every part of Wheeler's application for admission from more than two years earlier. For example, the director of transfer admissions found the Harvard alum in Maine who had interviewed Wheeler back in 2007 and called him to discuss his impression of the applicant back then. They checked with the College Board and verified that Wheeler had not taken the SAT on the date his score report said he had, let alone earned a perfect score. They checked their archive of all the scores they had ever received electronically from the College Board and found none of Wheeler's there at all.

Harvard's inquiry into Wheeler's lies was no longer about gathering evidence for an eventual Ad Board hearing. Once Ellison and Smith realized that this scam touched Wheeler's admission application, the whole game changed. It all came down to one line in the thick Harvard student handbook:

> *Occasionally candidates for admission make inaccurate or incomplete statements or submit false materials in connection with their applications. . . . If a misrepresentation or omission is discovered after a student has registered, or registered and completed courses, the offer of admission ordinarily will be rescinded, the course credit and grades will be revoked, and the student will be required to leave the College.*

A college could say that a student who cheats his way in will be expelled if he is caught after matriculating. But Harvard goes a step further. Rather than just kicking the student out of the gates, Harvard declares that anyone who faked his way into the college will be considered never to have been there at all.

Today, there is no official testament to the fact that Wheeler spent more than two years at Harvard. The classes he took, the grades he received, the house he lived in, the prizes he won—these have all been erased. According to the institutional record, those years just did not happen. That bed was not filled. Those marks were never earned. That admission decision itself was never made.

The Committee on Admissions and Financial Aid, the same body that met around a table a few years earlier and voted to welcome Wheeler to Harvard, convened in October 2009 and officially decided to rescind Wheeler's acceptance. The director of admissions sent him a letter notifying him of the decision. She wrote, "To be very clear: you are no longer a student at Harvard College, nor may you represent yourself as ever having been a student at Harvard College." Ellison sent a note to Wheeler's parents the next day that was nearly as blunt.

A few short weeks into his self-imposed distancing from Harvard, Wheeler had been banished for real. Now, with Harvard quietly expunging his name from its records, Wheeler could not come back. Not that he was planning to return anyway.

～～

Wheeler sent off applications to his new college picks and some other positions, like an internship at the magazine *The New Republic,* which turned him away. Stanford, however, let him in. This acceptance was a tremendous coup for Wheeler. Once he received that fat envelope, he had an invitation to start all over again at one of the country's top universities. And this time he would even get to enjoy California sunshine instead of Cambridge snow.

He considered spending his spring, before he could matriculate in Palo Alto in the fall, in the Maritime Studies Program run by Williams College. Based in Mystic, Connecticut, the program is open to students from any university who want to spend a semester there. Participants study all sorts of subjects, from literature to marine biology, while living by the sea and even intermittently on it. (The semester includes three long cruises with courses conducted on deck.)

Wheeler's application to this outdoorsy program puzzled the people at Williams. They took a close look at his materials and felt, in the words of the program's director James Carlton, that it was "as strange an application as I've ever seen."

Wheeler had submitted three letters of recommendation rather than simply the names of three references as requested by Williams. He said that his professors wanted to keep their contact information private. Of course, Wheeler would not want anyone calling his former Harvard professors right now. Carlton picked up on the fact that something was odd. Private? he wondered. Isn't their contact information easily searchable online anyway?

Those letters themselves seemed amiss. "No one writes a three-page single-space, let alone a two-page single-space, letter of rec for a one-semester undergrad program," Carlton emailed a colleague, perplexed. "It appears that all three letters were written to gain young Adam access to graduate school at Yale, after only two years of college at Harvard . . . . He's clearly gifted, and it may have occurred to him (and his advisors) that another two years of undergraduate work at Harvard would pretty much be a waste of time . . . . I've no doubt he's perfectly ready for a Ph.D. program."

Carlton acknowledged that a busy professor just might not have had the time to write a new recommendation tailored specifically to the Williams program. But he thought that Wheeler's own essay did not line up with what he was applying for either. He pointed out that Wheeler said he wanted to "study in a cross-disciplinary program in mobility studies at Williams-Mystic"—definitely not a course offering there.

Some of the admissions personnel at Williams-Mystic corresponded with Wheeler by email about the program. At one point, Wheeler asked a question that probably indicates what attracted him to the Mystic program in the first place, though the Williams folks could not have known it.

Is Daniel Brayton teaching there? Wheeler asked. Brayton, who wrote the dissertation that Wheeler had plagiarized to win his Hoopes Prize, had previously taught at Williams-Mystic, and it was probably Brayton's CV that brought the program to Wheeler's attention. Brayton had melded Shakespeare and the sea in ways Wheeler must have found very appealing. Brayton had taught literature courses on board ships and written pieces about the sea's role in literature. The chance to study with that person, with whose work he was intimately (and illegitimately) familiar, could have drawn Wheeler to Williams's hands-on sea semester. But that was not what he told anyone at Williams-Mystic, and even when he was informed that Brayton would not be teaching that year, he wrote back to say that he would mail in his $45 application fee right away.

Carlton was impressed by Wheeler and did not suspect foul play. His best guess was that Wheeler had decided he was through with college and might want to bide his time by spending the spring fiddling around with boats before heading to grad school the next

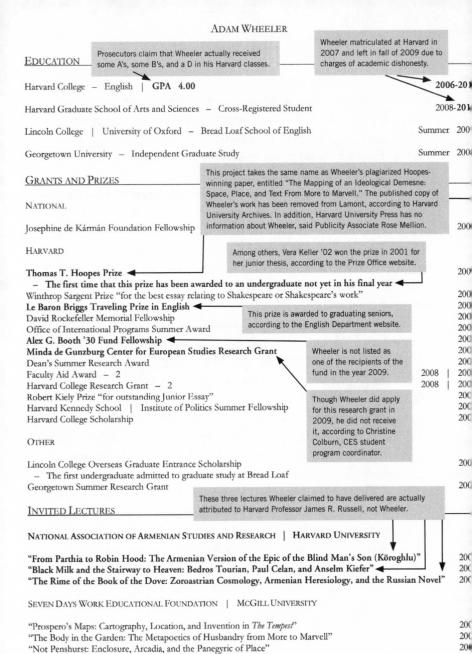

ADAM WHEELER

<u>EDUCATION</u>

Prosecutors claim that Wheeler actually received some A's, some B's, and a D in his Harvard classes.

Wheeler matriculated at Harvard in 2007 and left in fall of 2009 due to charges of academic dishonesty.

Harvard College – English | **GPA 4.00**   **2006-20**

Harvard Graduate School of Arts and Sciences – Cross-Registered Student   2008-20**

Lincoln College | University of Oxford – Bread Loaf School of English   Summer 200**

Georgetown University – Independent Graduate Study   Summer 200**

<u>GRANTS AND PRIZES</u>

This project takes the same name as Wheeler's plagiarized Hoopes-winning paper, entitled "The Mapping of an Ideological Demesne: Space, Place, and Text From More to Marvell." The published copy of Wheeler's work has been removed from Lamont, according to Harvard University Archives. In addition, Harvard University Press has no information about Wheeler, said Publicity Associate Rose Mellion.

NATIONAL

Josephine de Kármán Foundation Fellowship   200**

HARVARD

Among others, Vera Keller '02 won the prize in 2001 for her junior thesis, according to the Prize Office website.

Thomas T. Hoopes Prize ◄   200**
– **The first time that this prize has been awarded to an undergraduate not yet in his final year** ◄
Winthrop Sargent Prize "for the best essay relating to Shakespeare or Shakespeare's work"   200**
Le Baron Briggs Traveling Prize in English ◄   200**
David Rockefeller Memorial Fellowship   This prize is awarded to graduating seniors,   200**
Office of International Programs Summer Award   according to the English Department website.   200**
Alex G. Booth '30 Fund Fellowship   200**
Minda de Gunzburg Center for European Studies Research Grant   200**
Dean's Summer Research Award   Wheeler is not listed as   200**
Faculty Aid Award – 2   one of the recipients of the   2008 | 200**
Harvard College Research Grant – 2   fund in the year 2009.   2008 | 200**
Robert Kiely Prize "for outstanding Junior Essay"   200**
Harvard Kennedy School | Institute of Politics Summer Fellowship   Though Wheeler did apply   200**
Harvard College Scholarship   for this research grant in   200**
                                                                   2009, he did not receive
OTHER   it, according to Christine
                                                                   Colburn, CES student
Lincoln College Overseas Graduate Entrance Scholarship   program coordinator.   200**
– The first undergraduate admitted to graduate study at Bread Loaf
Georgetown Summer Research Grant   200**

<u>INVITED LECTURES</u>

These three lectures Wheeler claimed to have delivered are actually attributed to Harvard Professor James R. Russell, not Wheeler.

NATIONAL ASSOCIATION OF ARMENIAN STUDIES AND RESEARCH | HARVARD UNIVERSITY

"From Parthia to Robin Hood: The Armenian Version of the Epic of the Blind Man's Son (Köroghlu)"   200**
"Black Milk and the Stairway to Heaven: Bedros Tourian, Paul Celan, and Anselm Kiefer" ◄   200**
"The Rime of the Book of the Dove: Zoroastrian Cosmology, Armenian Heresiology, and the Russian Novel"   200**

SEVEN DAYS WORK EDUCATIONAL FOUNDATION | MCGILL UNIVERSITY

"Prospero's Maps: Cartography, Location, and Invention in *The Tempest*"   200**
"The Body in the Garden: The Metapoetics of Husbandry from More to Marvell" 200**
"Not Penshurst: Enclosure, Arcadia, and the Panegyric of Place"   200**

When news of Wheeler's frauds came to light, *The New Republic* posted the résumé that Wheeler had submitted in his application for an internship there online.

LE AUTHOR

appings, Unmappings, and Remappings – **In progress** ← *2009-2010*

Some of the text in this description closely resembles a Columbia student's dissertation.

ritical work that has attempted to explain the experience of geographical and textual space in modern writing has cused predominantly on the map as an analytical tool of orientation that makes formal writing structures legible. My ssertation, however, articulates a positive and generative potential in the experience of getting lost. Disorientation, en, allows us to come to terms with the difficulty of modernist literature from the ground level—to view these works ot as an abstraction seen from the "God's eye" perspective that is implicit in most maps, nor a teleological outcome of e Enlightenment seen from retrospect. By restoring the experience of disorientation, I argue that getting lost becomes radical discourse that reflects back to us how we orient ourselves—what we pay attention to as we move through ysical space and how we construe meaning as we move through a text from page to page.

he Mapping of an Ideological Demesne – **Under review with Harvard University Press** *2008*

ne massive proliferation, from the fifteenth through the seventeenth century, of technologies for measuring, projecting, d organizing geographical and social space produced in the European cultural imaginary an intense and widespread terest in visualizing this world and alternative worlds. As the new century and the Stuart era developed, poets and ramatists mediated this transformation in the form of spatial tropes and models of the nation. I examine the ographical tropes by which Tudor and Stuart writers created poetic landscapes as a mode of engagement with the ructures of power, kingship, property, and the market. Accordingly, each of the texts that I examine betrays an vareness of writing as a spatial activity and space as a scripted category. The critical topographies that these writers eated are maps of ideology, figural territories within which social conflict and political antagonism are put into play.

-AUTHOR

Representatives at the Univ. of Illinois Press and McGill-Queen's Univ. Press have never heard of Wheeler. The latter press said that Wheeler's name is not listed on the contract for the project.

he Last Class | with Marc Shell | **Under contract with McGill-Queen's University Press** ←

rand Manan; or, A Short History of North America | with Marc Shell | **Under review with McGill-Queen's UP**

ampum and the Origins of American Money | with Marc Shell | **Under contract with University of Illinois Press**

alking the Walk and Walking the Talk | with Marc Shell | **Under contract with Princeton University Press** ←

NIVERSITY SERVICE

Princeton Univ. Press stated on its blog that it has no contract with Wheeler.

eveloped pilot courses for General Education and evaluated their success through student enrollment and course sessments from faculty and students | Conducted rigorous analysis of application and enrollment data, by course, to ntify priority areas where shortage of seats in arts courses is most acute | Formed a faculty committee to solicit ut from Harvard faculty and students, as well as from external experts, on how best to integrate graduate training in s-practice into the existing curricular structure of the university | Developed programs for fellows in the arts

udent-Faculty Advisory Board for Arts and Humanities | Harvard Undergraduate Council *2008-2010*
dent-Faculty Committee on General Education | Harvard Undergraduate Council *2008-2010*
riting Tutor | **Harvard Extension School Writing Center** ← *2009-2010*
dergraduate Committee | Harvard Humanities Center *2008-2010*
ckland House Liaison | Student Advisory Committee | Department of English *2008-2010*
er Tutor | Bureau of Study Council | Department of English *2009-2010*
riting Tutor | **Department of East Asian Languages and Civilizations** *2008-2010*
dent Consultation | Task Force on the Arts *2008*
holar-in-Residence | **MIT Actors' Shakespeare Project** ← *2008-2009*

Wheeler never worked as a writing tutor at the Extension School Writing Center, according to Director Jeannine Johnson.

The position of writing tutor does not even exist in the EALC department, according to chair Wilt Idema.

NGUAGES

Wheeler never worked or interned for ASP, according to Marketing Manager Laura Sullivan.

ench | Old English | Classical Armenian | Old Persian

Soon after Wheeler's arraignment, reporters at *The Harvard Crimson* used it to annotate and publish the résumé seen on these two pages. It shows all the lies that they could verify at that point.

year. But he thought Wheeler's application was "pretty darn weird," and he was not sure it would be a good choice to admit Wheeler. "I can't see him fitting in here," Carlton opined. "Hoopes Prize, Karman Fellowship, getting admitted to Oxford graduate school . . . doing a study on periwinkle feeding on the rocky shore?"

Nonetheless, Wheeler was invited to Mystic for an interview. He came, bringing his girlfriend Sua along with him for the trip. (Even now that he was living at home in Delaware rather than down the road from her in Massachusetts, he had been visiting her regularly and keeping in touch via video chat.) They toured the seaside campus and chatted about the residential facilities and sailing opportunities with officials from the program. Then Wheeler met with Carlton for a half-hour interview. Carlton found him articulate and mild-mannered. The only time he noticed that the student grew flustered was the moment that Carlton asked him why his letters of recommendation seemed to be endorsing him for a Yale graduate program rather than a semester in the great outdoors.

Wheeler offered to ask his professors for new letters, but Carlton said it was not necessary. Program officials decided to let Wheeler in. From the wording of their emails to him, they clearly expected him to come. One day before the deadline to submit various sign-up forms, Wheeler wrote to say he had accepted a publishing internship instead. He acknowledged the concerns that Carlton had had about him, saying that the internship he was pursuing "might be more explicitly connected to my concentration work."

Wheeler had no publishing internship, though. He was finishing his applications to Brown and Yale.

Yale, like Williams at first, did not buy what Wheeler said. Whether something looked suspicious, or whether it was just routine protocol to occasionally call an applicant's previous schools, someone at Yale called Caesar Rodney High School. Kevin Fitzgerald, now the school district superintendent, answered the call. It was the first he had heard about Adam Wheeler in years, since before Wheeler had moved on from Bowdoin to Harvard. His first reaction was that this must be a case of identity theft and Wheeler must be the victim. Surely the unassuming 2005 graduate he remembered could not have made up the claims he was seeing on the Yale application. Courses that were not offered at Caesar Rodney, activities Wheeler had never participated in, honors he had never won, not to mention a graduation year that was two years off—it was all hard to believe. The superintendent told the Yale officer exactly what was and what was not true.

After Fitzgerald hung up, he made a phone call of his own. Richard Wheeler was no longer a Caesar Rodney teacher; he had retired from the school district. Fitzgerald wanted to tell him what he had just heard about his son.

"Yale did what it should have done and checked into its applicants," Richard Wheeler said. He and his wife had been paying the application fees for Adam's many transfer applications. They had not looked at Adam's application when he transferred to Harvard a few years earlier, nor had they asked to see what he was working on now. It did not seem appropriate to ask a child in his 20s to let his parents look over his work. Once they learned from Fitzgerald that there was a problem, though, "We did what any parents would have done," Richard said. He confronted his son and told him to inform Yale of the fibs in his application.

It was under parental pressure, then, that Adam Wheeler sent this email to Yale:

> *I am writing in reference to my transfer application to Yale for the Fall 2010. I must cancel my candidacy, since I submitted falsified documents as part of my application. . . . [I] have been expelled from Harvard. I am very sorry for having put the committee through this.*

Another institution likewise did its due diligence. The employee who first picked up Wheeler's application for the internship at

McLean Hospital, the psychiatric treatment facility affiliated with Harvard, skimmed it and was immediately impressed. "I was completely blown away," she recalled. "It's pretty insane—which maybe should have raised red flags, but as a Harvard undergrad, you think, well, I don't know. I have never seen an actual résumé of a Harvard undergrad. You just kind of hear." While a résumé like Wheeler's might have been a stretch, some members of the student body do enjoy remarkable distinctions. She was not inclined to question Wheeler.

She exchanged some emails with him, telling him about the project he would be working on if he got the job. His response to the description was characteristic Wheeler:

Thank you for sending the excellent precis of your work. I've read your words with special enthusiasm. The project itself is fascinating, timely, very significant in range and consequence. Many aligned issues involved here, and I am excited by the topic. Your conceptual demarche operates on a brilliant set of abstractions which feel seriously grounded in the matters at hand. I have a deeply felt interest in a research assistant position. . . . Please let me know when we can meet at our mutual leisure and pleasure!

With all keen thoughts and best wishes, and in gratitude,

Adam

"This isn't even English," she thought when she read that email, turning to a dictionary to look up *précis* and *démarche*. But she was still gung-ho about Wheeler's candidacy. Someone over in human resources told her to get some references from Wheeler before hiring him for the position. She asked, and he sent her two names but said that his recommenders had requested that he keep their contact information private. What was the point of giving out references if you tell employers that they cannot call them? she wondered. Pick different references.

So she went to the Internet to find them both. These were not the heavy-hitting professors Wheeler had been giving as references on his other applications. Using those people was okay when he was submitting complete letters because the references would not be called. But for this application, he was sending names alone. He probably considered it too risky to put down anyone who knew anything about him. Knowing that the McLean employee might contact the people he named, he reached into more obscure corners to find recommenders.

The first was a Chinese language teacher at Harvard. Apparently Wheeler had tutored her in English at some point. She wrote to the McLean employee, "Adam wheeler [*sic*] was the English teacher of mine for the first few months when I arrived in the US. He is a very nice guy and very easy going. He is also quite knowledgeable. I think you will enjoy working with him."

The other reference, David Evett, took her more effort to find. She tried calling Cleveland State University, where she learned from a Google search he had once been employed, but no one there could tell her his current contact information. Eventually, she tracked him down on Facebook. It turned out that he was in the Boston area and had worked with Wheeler for a short time during his sophomore year. One of Wheeler's professors had recommended that he study more Shakespeare outside of class with Evett. The partnership only lasted for about a month.

The letter that Evett sent to the McLean employee seemed complimentary. "I found him energetic and enthusiastic; he came to our meetings on time and well prepared, and generally did the things I asked him to do with commendable energy, and was articulate and imaginative in his responses. Indeed, enthusiasm was his dominant quality." All lovely. But then the letter went downhill. This part Wheeler certainly would not have written in one of the recommendations he crafted for himself: "My demands were not deeply onerous . . . I have no idea whether he can take on and complete jobs that require patience and devotion over long periods."

For a student with such an outstanding résumé, Wheeler was not drawing the reviews the McLean evaluator had expected. "Supposedly he's published with all these professors, and he can only give me two names of people who can barely vouch for him?" she thought.

Walking out of the office one evening, she stopped at her boss's door. "Have you had a chance to look at the résumé I told you about?" she asked.

"Yeah, it's really impressive," he responded.

Then she mentioned that she would have preferred more enthusiastic references.

"Have you talked to anyone at Harvard?" her boss asked. "Did you call his house master?"

That night, she looked up where Wheeler had lived at Harvard. She wrote to the masters, a writing tutor, and the resident dean. She was surprised to get a phone call from a top administrator the next day. All she had been looking for were some words about what Wheeler was like as a student and house resident. Instead, a dean filled her in on Wheeler's story, and she was floored. She looked back through her correspondence with Wheeler and noticed that his Harvard email address was still working and that he had first heard about the McLean job through a Harvard student employment page that requires a university ID. Harvard might want to remove Wheeler's access to those services, she suggested, since Wheeler had been officially ousted from the university months ago.

Needless to say, Wheeler did not get the spot at McLean. But that did not stop him from sending Yale a recommendation in that McLean employee's name, offering her "complete and unwavering support" of her research assistant Adam Wheeler in a letter that was two single-spaced pages long.

As the lies piled up, they were becoming predictable to Smith. He forwarded the McLean employee's initial email, just the latest evidence of Wheeler's behavior, to Ellison with a virtual chuckle in his message: "Well, well, well . . . thoughts?"

CHAPTER EIGHT

It is conceivable that the story might have ended there. Having ferreted out most of Adam Wheeler's lies at Harvard and having wiped all record of him from the university's official history, administrators might have considered the case closed. Aside from a handful of deans, the members of the Rhodes evaluation committee, and the English department, no one ever would have known what had transpired. And Wheeler, for his part, would have quietly enrolled at Stanford and tried once again to complete an undergraduate degree, this time in sunny Palo Alto.

Instead, Harvard administrators took what they had learned about Wheeler, even though they had already rescinded his admission, and presented it to the police. To their credit, regardless of the unflattering publicity that would result, they wanted to press charges. Rather than covering up a scandal, Harvard made the admirable decision to speak to the law enforcement authorities.

Harvard has its own police force, the Harvard University Police Department, with a criminal investigations team and employees who are sworn state police officers. Two detectives from the HUPD, Kevin Healy and Brian Spellman, took over the Wheeler case. Their investigation took them even further than Jay Ellison and David Smith's. They secured written confirmation from Andover and MIT that Wheeler had never been a student there. With the help of detectives from the county district attorney's office, who soon became involved in the investigation too, they met with a host of people whose names turned up in Wheeler's thick file of academic paperwork. They talked to Harvard English professors, to the McLean Hospital employee who had brought Wheeler's application to Smith's attention, to everyone whose names Wheeler had signed on letters of recommendation in his Harvard application—even though that meant driving two and a half hours up to Bowdoin to obtain some of their statements. Months went by and their investigation grew still broader; by the end of April, they had collected Wheeler's application materials from Brown and Yale.

In early May, a prosecutor by the name of John Verner from the Middlesex County District Attorney's Office in Massachusetts who had been appointed to the case told a grand jury that he felt there was enough evidence to charge Wheeler with 20 criminal counts. Forging professors' signatures, fabricating an Andover transcript, and, most seriously, winning an $8,000 grant, $6,000 in prizes, and what Verner calculated as $31,806 in financial aid from Harvard—all of that was not just academic dishonesty. As he saw it, it was fraud.

There was plenty of precedent for treating cheating in college admissions as a criminal matter.

In 2008, a woman named Ester Reed made the United States Secret Service's list of the 10 most wanted fugitives in the nation—for academic fraud. Reed, convicted of theft as a young woman, reinvented herself after a stint in prison as an outstanding student with gifts for debate and chess. She assumed the identities of three other women in order to study at Cal State Fullerton, Columbia, and Harvard before she was caught by investigators. Charged with aggravated identity theft, falsification of identification documents, and mail and wire fraud for the $100,000 in student loans that she obtained over the course of her university years, she was sentenced to more than four years in prison for her deceitful pursuit of an education under other people's names.

Back in 1988, a man calling himself Alexi Indris-Santana applied to a handful of Ivy League schools with a remarkable story to tell: He had not been to school since kindergarten; instead, he had been working on a ranch and sleeping outside. But he had learned enough to score a 730 and a 680 on the two 800-point sections of the SAT; he had developed a superb affinity for running track; and he wanted to go to college.

A Brown administrator told *The New York Times* that when the university's dean of admissions perused Indris-Santana's application, he said, "There's something wrong with this file. I can't put my finger on it, so I guess we ought to take him." The student, though, did not take Brown's offer. He took Princeton's.

Midway through his career as a track star at Princeton, he was exposed as a 31-year-old parolee, wanted as a fugitive from Utah, whose name was actually James Hogue. Like Reed, he too served prison time for his collegiate heist, a nine-month sentence that came along with restitution of over $20,000 for the financial aid Princeton had given him. But after he was released from prison, he headed to the Ivy League once more—to Harvard this time. Under another false identity, he found a job as a security guard in a Harvard museum. Months into his new occupation, he was caught stealing over $50,000 worth of gemstones from the museum.

The list goes on. Just weeks before Lon T. Grammer was set to graduate from Yale in 1995, university officials learned that the political science student had forged the A-plus transcript and positive recommendations from his junior college in California that had led to his admission as a transfer student. On the day that Grammer pleaded guilty to avoid a larceny trial, another defendant pleaded not guilty to the same crime of cheating her way into Yale. A graduate student in neuroscience, Tonica Jenkins had lasted only a few months at Yale before her forged transcripts from two community colleges and fake recommendations were uncovered by the university.

Some did not see why Jenkins ought to be punished by the criminal justice system for snookering the admissions office. "Oh my god, this poor underprivileged African-American girl stole an education," commented Glenn Conway, an attorney who represented yet another student charged with conning his way into Yale. "Why can't we deal with that in a noncriminal context?" Jenkins walked away from that arrest without receiving jail time. But two years later, she missed a scheduled court appearance. She told the judge she had been raped on her way to court; he did not believe her and put her in jail. She got out after pleading guilty to larceny, forgery, and bribery of a prison guard. But a month later, she was arrested once more, along with her mother, for attempting to buy 22 pounds of cocaine from drug dealers who turned out to be undercover cops. As her trial on the drug charges approached, Jenkins and her cousin kidnapped a woman with the intent of murdering her and then passing the dead body off as her own so that she could start her life over under a new identity. Instead, she was found out and eventually found guilty not only of the drug charges but also of attempted murder.

Right around the time that Harvard decided to admit Wheeler, Yale authorities were yet again tracing the path of a fraudster in their midst. Akash Maharaj, it turned out, had forged a straight-A transcript from Columbia and submitted a letter of recommendation from a professor who said he never wrote it. In a story that sounded awfully like the one that Verner was now prosecuting, Maharaj had spent two semesters as a transfer student at Yale, displayed an exuberant interest in pursuing a PhD in English literature, and even won a writing prize. Yale rescinded his admission and wiped the record of his attendance from its annals, just as Harvard had already done to Wheeler. Then the penalty for Maharaj went further: He was prosecuted in a Connecticut court. After he pleaded guilty, a judge gave him five years to pay back more than $31,000 of financial aid that he received from Yale or else face a three-year prison sentence.

When Maharaj's story broke, a writer for the student newspaper likened him to some of the figures the con man might have studied in his literature classes—a Horatio Alger character, bent on pulling himself up the socioeconomic ladder by his own ingenuity, or a Jay Gatsby, who turns to trickery to achieve the status he pines for. "His is a startlingly common story: A student who, swept up in an admissions frenzy, resorts to bending the rules to secure a spot among the elite," the *Yale Daily News* reporter wrote. "He wanted to make something of himself. So he made himself someone else."

Unsettlingly, one Yale undergraduate whom the student reporter quoted in his article found the news of Maharaj's forgery and larceny charges mundane. The student said, "Didn't we all exaggerate on our applications to some extent?"

As Maharaj's lawyer reflected, it was attitudes like that which Yale hoped to combat by pressing charges against his client. Sure, he acknowledged, in some cases a university might be able to avoid the embarrassment of admitting that it was duped by a 20-something-year-old by quietly expelling the student. A college could choose not to make an admissions matter into a criminal matter, and the press would likely never find out. But colleges have an incentive to go public, even if that means drawing unwanted attention. They hope to dissuade the spread of attitudes toward dishonest applications, like the view expressed to the *Yale Daily News*, that are blasé at best or unscrupulous at worst. "If you want to discourage people from doing it to your university, you prosecute," Conway said. "We'll take on some short-term embarrassment to keep it from happening 10, 20 years from now. Once you see someone exposed to $40,000 in restitution and a felony conviction, that's got to have a pretty good deterrent effect."

That preference for pressing charges seems to have popped up in the last 25 years. Before that, at least one con man who artfully snuck into Yale was treated as a prankster rather than a felon. His name was Patrick McDermit, and he was a 21-year-old who decided in 1976 that he would like to go to college. He set his sights on Yale since, as a high school senior with a lackluster record, he had been told by a recruiter that he had no prayer of getting in. Since then, he had held a grudge against the New Haven school, he later told the *Yale Daily News*. He wanted to outsmart the people who had told him he was not good enough.

He set up a post office box in the name of a fake university and had his high school mail his transcript to that box so that he could use the transcript as a template for his own forged version. He wrote recommendation letters and an essay that told an extraordinary story: He had supported himself since age 10 by making a small fortune in the silver trade, printing greeting cards, collecting precious stones in the desert, and repairing cars. As coeditor of his high school newspaper, he exposed a scandal in the administration—meaning he had to resign not only his editorship (he started his own newspaper afterward) but also his student government presidency. Around the same time, his invention of a new kind of prosthetic limb made him "a young Thomas Edison" in the purported words of the *Los Angeles Times*. Then he spent some time opening a hugely profitable hotel in Alaska and a nightclub in Rio de Janeiro. He founded a school for Brazilian children. And he decided to apply to Yale.

Throughout his first semester in New Haven, he dressed the part of a young millionaire and spoke on the phone in a blend of French and Spanish that he claimed was his native Shumash Indian dialect. His peers and professors were convinced that he really was Andreas Stephan Alrea, the remarkable young man he had invented. But as the semester drew to an end, he decided to end the charade. Fearing that the prank would become "outright fraud" if he earned real Yale credits, according to the *Yale Daily News*, he turned himself in. He was kicked out of Yale but not punished further, though the press had a field day with the kooky story. McDermit found himself flooded with phone calls from strangers, congratulated by professors, and even applauded by a roomful of his peers on one of his last days in a college dining hall.

Responses to such heists, nowadays, tend to be more likely to come in the courtroom. In 2006, Rice University pressed charges against David Vanegas, a young man who had never applied for admission but who hung around campus for a year telling others he was a student. He was charged with theft—the college wanted him to pay back about $3,700, the value of all the food he ate in the dining hall.

A similar story made headlines at Stanford the next year. A young woman named Azia Kim had persuaded one roomful of freshman girls and then a second that she was a student but her housing had fallen through. The girls agreed to let Kim stay in their rooms and to leave their windows open (clearly, this particular con could only work with California weather) so that Kim, who did not have a key, could climb in. For nearly a year, Kim pored over her textbooks in the dorm common room despite the fact that she was not enrolled in any classes and even participated in Reserve Officer Training Corps classes and drills with Stanford students at nearby Santa Clara University. Several newspapers attributed her behavior to pressure so great that she could not bear to tell her parents and her community that she had not been admitted. She just had to go to Stanford, even without an acceptance letter.

"I think the preoccupation with elite institutions and what people will do to get into them is almost a national tragedy," said Norman Pattis, an attorney who represented both Grammer and Jenkins after they were exposed at Yale. "Status and power are a drug in this society. The perceived Yale or Harvard degree is so high that some people will do just about anything to get it. I mean, look at parents who are breaking their necks to get their kids into the right competitive nursery school so that they'll have a shot. There's just something fundamentally wrong with this picture."

"I suspect there are far more than we realize," Pattis continued. "It would not surprise me to see a little bit of fraud in every class. Some of them are just more inventive than others."

The prevalence of academic fraud cases, Pattis said, points to a widespread sense of anxiety over college admissions that affects honest applicants as well. The most egregious cases, in his opinion, serve to illuminate "the depths of the problem."

"Why are we so persuaded that some institutions carry such cachet that we'll do anything to put their names after ours?" he asked.

Conway sees the pure thrill of the feat as part of the allure. These young people are looking for a rush, he says, not just a ticket up the socioeconomic ladder. "It's narcissism. It's something in their psychological makeup that they are driven to do this. They probably get away with it on a much smaller scale as they move along, and then they think, I wonder if I can pull the big one. Harvard, Yale—how cool would that be?" Conway theorized. "There's got to be a tremendous satisfaction in pulling it off."

And the fact is that some of these fraudsters genuinely want to experience an Ivy League education. "Nobody wishes that they had a job that paid a million bucks. You gonna wish? Wish for the million bucks," Barmak Nassirian pointed out. Admissions fraud does not work that way. "If you're going to commit fraud, you know, why not go all the way and just fraudulently give yourself the degree?" Buying or forging a fake diploma, though, would not let someone who loves academia immerse himself in the environment of a university.

At any rate, as the members of the grand jury listened to a case that sounded similar to all those other stories—Wheeler's case this time—they did not need to know his motive. They were convinced that Verner's evidence showed that Wheeler had cheated Harvard out of tens of thousands of dollars and unfairly used the names of his teachers time and again. They indicted him on 20 misdemeanor and felony charges. And because the court feared that he might run away from the government just like he had run away from Harvard when he found out he was under suspicion, they sealed the indictment. That meant that when police arrived at his house in Delaware with an arrest warrant in May, he was caught completely unaware.

He spent a week in jail in his home state before Harvard University police officers made the drive down to Delaware to retrieve him. While they drove, the Middlesex District Attorney's Office convened a press conference to make the news public for the first time: A suspect had been arrested on the charge that he had duped Harvard.

On May 17, 2010, District Attorney Gerard Leone stood next to an easel with a blown-up mug shot on a thick foam posterboard. The photo showed a young man staring intently at the camera, his head tilted to one side and his light blue eyes wide open. It was an image none of the reporters had ever seen before that moment, but it was one that was about to appear on websites, TV screens, and newspaper pages across the country over the next few days.

The man in that photo, Leone told the small crowd, was named Adam Wheeler. He was 23 years old, and he had been admitted to Harvard three years earlier under false pretenses. He had forged a number of people's names to letters they did not write. He had made up phony transcripts saying he had attended MIT and Andover. He had also, from the law's perspective, stolen more than $45,000.

These actions translated into several state crimes:

- Eight counts of identity fraud for the eight people whose names he had signed to letters of recommendation
- Seven counts of falsifying an endorsement or approval, a similar charge that the state can level when the person whose identity is being misappropriated is associated with a college or university (thus one of the eight forged letters that supposedly came from a college counselor at Andover, a secondary school, did not count for that crime)
- One count of pretending to hold a degree, a little-known crime, for telling the Harvard admissions office that he was a graduate of Andover

- Four counts of larceny over $250: one for the Hoopes Prize ($4,000), one for the Sargent Prize ($2,000), one for the Rockefeller grant ($8,000), and one for a year's worth of Harvard financial aid ($31,806)

All together, the maximum penalties for the 20 counts with which Wheeler was charged added up to anywhere from 28 to 36 years in prison, with a fine that could reach as high as $48,000 to $148,000, not to mention the restitution he might be ordered to pay to Harvard.

The DA, a Harvard alum himself, articulated a clear message when he shared Wheeler's story with the world that day: The tricks Wheeler had played were not just pranks a student had pulled on Harvard. They were crimes.

"This defendant seriously undermined the integrity of the competitive admissions process," Leone said from the podium at that press conference, "compromised the reputation of some of the finest educators and educational institutions in the country, and cheated those who competed honestly for what he fraudulently received." The victims, Leone said, were the people who played it straight and lost out to Wheeler.

Within hours, word of Wheeler's crimes was being reported on news websites, starting with local ones like *The Boston Globe* and *The Harvard Crimson* and fanning out from there. That afternoon, as Wheeler's indictment became public information, his old Harvard friends started hearing the news.

It was the kind of surprise that stamps locational details onto people's memories. When asked about their reactions to the news that Wheeler was allegedly a con artist, they mention where they were when they heard it. One was on the golf course. One was hanging out at Wellesley. One was sitting in Kirkland courtyard with other seniors celebrating the end of their last set of college exams.

"My reaction was definitely a lot of expletives chained together," one friend said. "No one in the room had a clue," his ex-girlfriend said about his roommates, who were still her close friends. "We were so shell-shocked when we found out."

Over and over, friends expressed the same sentiment. They were not just stunned that Wheeler had allegedly committed a crime or that he had faked the academic credentials that all of them—elite university students—had worked so hard to attain. It cut deeper than that. It was profoundly unsettling, they said, to learn that someone they had known closely and had spent so much time with was not, as they put it, who he said he was.

Marcel Moran, who had been on the orientation hiking trip with Wheeler, expressed his emotions about the story in an editorial in *The Crimson* several days after he learned about Wheeler's fraud. "When the news of his story start[ed] spreading rapidly, I looked back at the pictures of Adam and me in the woods and tried to call up any memory I had of him," Moran wrote. "With the veracity of his history under fire, it's now hard for me to tell which conversations I had with Wheeler were real, and which were false. I spent a sizeable amount of time with this man, and yet I cannot say who he is."

Max Storto, another friend from the FOP hiking trip, had a similar take on it. "On my FOP experience, my goal was to get oriented to Harvard and see what the student body was like," he said. He was disturbed to learn that one of the seven students he had met was not a good indication of what real Harvard students were like after all. "It was sad that it cheapened that experience a little bit."

He felt far worse, he added, for Wheeler himself. After one night incarcerated in Massachusetts, Wheeler was taken to court in handcuffs the next morning. By that point, word had circulated among most of his friends, and it was quickly rippling out to a much broader audience as well. At the bus station near Cambridge where spectators could depart for the court where Wheeler was being arraigned, a man stood passing out free *Metro* tabloids to the morning commuters rushing past. Wheeler's face covered the entire front page of every copy that hurried passersby absentmindedly grabbed. Soon, the bus station was littered with discarded full-size photos of this wide-eyed man nobody had seen before, with "Real-Life Catch Me If You Can" emblazoned on each sheet.

The Middlesex Superior Court is not often a bustling place. Since it moved 14 miles outside of busy Cambridge to suburban Woburn in 2008, reporters and curious spectators have been a little less likely to stop by for a trial. When they pour into the six-story concrete building that shares its parking lot with Applebee's, Giant supermarket, and other commercial outlets, then something big must be afoot. The morning of May 18, 2010, witnessed just such a stir.

Wheeler was being arraigned that morning, meaning he would hear the crimes he had been charged with and enter his pleas—guilty or not guilty. The wooden benches of the courtroom filled up with reporters before the hearing started. They crisscrossed the room quietly, trading contact information and exchanging tidbits about the case. What are the parents' names? Do you know how long he was at Harvard? Who's the prosecutor? Wait, how do you spell that?

Wheeler's parents and his girlfriend Sua quietly slipped in. They sat together toward the back, Richard Wheeler's arm over his wife Lee's shoulder, all three frowning stiffly throughout the proceedings.

Then Wheeler himself was led into a special cell on the side of the room with one window looking onto the courtroom. After a week in jail, he looked harrowed and scruffy. His long-sleeved blue denim shirt, a button-down garment that he wore open over a gray T-shirt, hung loosely over his frame unlike his normally fitting clothes. He had not shaved in a few days. He kept his head down, his shoulders hunched, and his arms crossed low in front of his body. It was difficult for spectators on the other side of the glass to realize that his posture was not just nerves or shame but the practical effect of wearing handcuffs. In fact, from the left side of the courtroom where his parents were sitting, it was hard to see much of him in his box at all.

"All rise," the magistrate called tersely, and the buzzing cohort of reporters came to their feet. As soon as they were seated, a court official read out the list of 20 charges against Wheeler rapidly and asked, "How do you plead?" In an almost inaudible voice, with his lawyer standing on the other side of the glass pane that separated him from the courtroom, Wheeler said, "Not guilty."

Verner, the prosecutor, stepped up to a podium facing the judge in the center of the room. He cut right to the chase.

"Your Honor," he addressed the judge, "the Commonwealth is asking for a $10,000 cash bail on Mr. Wheeler."

To explain why, he had to tell a story. "In September of 2009, Adam Wheeler, the defendant before you, was a senior at Harvard University," he began. He told the judge—and the many other listeners in the room—a narrative: that Wheeler had been applying for the Rhodes and Fulbright Scholarships when professors noticed that something was fishy about what Verner termed his "quote-unquote 'original' essay." That Wheeler was told about that problem and claimed he had just made a mistake, then decided to leave Harvard when his resident dean made it clear that Harvard was not backing down so easily. That his "abrupt departure" surprised the faculty enough that they started investigating further. That what they turned up was evidence of much more wrongdoing—forged transcripts from Harvard, Andover, and MIT; fake SAT scores on what looked like official documents; signatures affixed to letters their supposed writers never penned; and brazen attempts to defraud institution after institution, even after he had already been caught once.

Verner broke down the numbers pertaining to each theft charge against the defendant. "Mr. Wheeler, in essence, stole $4,000 for the Hoopes Prize, $2,000 for the Sargent Prize, $8,000 for a Rockefeller research grant," he ticked off aloud, "all of which he never would have received if he, one, was never at Harvard or, two, submitted appropriate applications."

Including the total financial aid that Wheeler received, which Verner also enumerated component by component, he summed up, "That comes to about $45,000 that Mr. Wheeler, through his scheme, stole from Harvard University."

Verner's story sounded convincing, and the reporters were jotting down every word. But this moment was not really about persuading anyone of the defendant's guilt. That would come later, before a jury, if Wheeler actually kept up his assertion that he was not guilty. For the moment, the main question was what would happen to him in the meantime while he awaited trial.

Verner asked the judge to keep Wheeler in jail as he had been for the past week and to set the bail required for his release at $10,000. He wanted it to be a high sum, he explained, to make sure that Wheeler, if he paid it, would have a compelling reason to show up for his trial date. Without a lot of money on the line, he was not too sure that would happen.

His lack of confidence, he explained, sprung not from the crimes that Wheeler was formally charged with—his fraudulent applications to Harvard and a variety of Harvard-based prizes—but from the defendant's behavior after those acts, which in his view established him as a serial liar. When Wheeler knew he had been caught at Harvard, he had not learned any lesson from that. Instead, he had fired off untruthful applications to more Ivy League schools. He only sent Yale an email confessing that his transfer application contained false information, Verner said, when his parents made him do it. A man who continues his offenses even after he has been caught, Verner reasoned, is not a man who should be let out of jail too easily.

"It is the Commonwealth's opinion in support of bail," he said, "that Mr. Wheeler's life of deceit would not have stopped if it was not for his parents." They sat there listening, silent and grim. "That's the only reason, in the Commonwealth's opinion, that Mr. Wheeler stopped his scheme."

Wheeler had hired a Cambridge attorney named Steven Sussman, who stood up now to argue that his client was not actually likely to try evading his next court date and that his bail ought to be lower.

"Since his arrest, he has been fully cooperative with the Delaware State Police," Sussman noted. His biggest bragging point on behalf of his client was Wheeler's behavior when the police came to his house to arrest him. He had given up his computer without making the police get a warrant, and he had cooperated by waiving extradition so that Massachusetts would not have to go through formal legal motions to get him out of Delaware. Moreover, Sussman said, Wheeler did not have the money to pay $10,000. He suggested that $1,000 or $2,000 might be more appropriate.

The judge chose $5,000, right in the middle.

A court officer brought some paperwork to Wheeler to sign. Watching their son's clumsy actions as he maneuvered the pen with handcuffs around his wrists, Richard wrapped his arm more tightly around Lee's shoulders. Then the arraignment was over. Wheeler was led out of the windowed room by an officer, and reporters swarmed around his parents and the attorneys as they headed out of the courtroom.

"He's not convicted of anything," Sussman reminded the reporters as they pressed around him. "He's a kid. He's never been in trouble before."

Though the germs of Wheeler fever had been planted the day before when the indictment was revealed, the bug really caught after Wheeler entered his not-guilty plea. Over that day and the several days that followed, Adam Wheeler's name and staring headshot blazed from media across the nation.

Reporters questioned what the story revealed about college admissions and mused about Verner's characterization of Wheeler as a "pathological" liar. Readers sneered in the comments sections of websites that Harvard had been duped by a 20-year-old. TV journalists descended on Harvard Square, interviewing a few students who happened to have been in a class with Wheeler and a number who did not have anything to do with the case other than sharing a campus with the man. At Kirkland House, a security guard angrily turned away reporters who walked into the peaceful communal courtyard. At *The Crimson*, where undergraduate journalists were eagerly producing as much content as they could about the biggest story involving Harvard that term, the writers were surprised to find someone from NBC's *Today* show knocking on their door to ask for information about the case.

"Harvard hoax"—the catchphrase that caught on to describe the case in the blogosphere—briefly became common parlance on the Internet. On the day after the arraignment, Google Trends conferred a "hotness" level of "Volcanic" on the moniker. It was the number 12 search that day, beat out only by such pressing queries as "sammy sosa" and "how old is justin bieber."

Groups popped up on Facebook with names like "Free Adam Wheeler!" and "Adam Wheeler is a Genius." Wheeler's new online supporters suggested actors to portray him in a movie. Commenters at first proposed 37-year-old Adrien Brody but seemed to come to a consensus that 29-year-old Jake Gyllenhaal of *Brokeback Mountain* fame would be best, posting a strikingly blue-eyed and unsmiling picture of the actor to prove it.

The blog Edudemic kept up that theme with a list of "10 Reasons Adam Wheeler's Harvard Hoax Will Become a Movie."

"Harvard sells," the blog declared.

"The media has been gorging itself on every last detail about this case," it observed. "No one died so they can whip the local news viewing audience into a fervor with catchy titles like 'Harvard Hoax' without seeming too crass or impersonal."

The writer posited other features of the story that movie studios might find attractive—the lucrative high school and college audience, the emotional appeal of his parents' involvement, the complexity and sheer number of lies that would keep audiences interested through a full-length film. Then he noted the social benefit of keeping Wheeler's story in the national spotlight beyond the 15 minutes of fame it was enjoying at that moment. "The conversations can continue over how to better serve students and identify those slipping through the cracks," he said.

Some who became involved in the Wheeler frenzy were not quite so focused on the broader social implications. They just wanted to make a profit.

A pair of Harvard seniors capitalized on the story by making T-shirts to sell to their classmates. On the front, the shirts said "Free Adam Wheeler!" over a black-and-white photo of his face. His absurdly inflated résumé, the version he had submitted to *The New Republic* internship a few months earlier (which the magazine had posted publicly on its website amidst the Wheeler fracas), was ironed onto the back.

From the seniors whiling away the hot empty days between their last final exams and graduation, to the reporters and admissions counselors and psychologists opining live around coffee tables in TV studios, to the high school students nationwide who told their friends about somebody who had just faked it all instead of going through the SAT/essay/recommendations rigmarole that they were enduring, it seemed like everyone was talking about Wheeler. Everyone, that is, except Wheeler himself.

The public heard wisps of his high school and college friends' recollections of Wheeler, they heard the claims that he had made on a résumé he had sent to a potential employer, and they heard the litany of lies that the government said he had told. But Wheeler himself, who was imprisoned in a Cambridge jail, did not voice his side of the story.

After one month, Richard posted the $5,000 bail that the judge had set. At that point, in June, Wheeler was free once again but required to remain in the state of Massachusetts until his trial date arrived.

Over the course of that summer and into the fall, the college admissions community felt the sting of the scandal. Columnists snickered that Harvard had been fooled. "Wheeler managed to hoist Harvard on its own pompous petard," Peter Gelzinis wrote in the *Boston Herald*. "He embarrassed the grand pooh-bahs of the Ivy League."

A *Boston Globe* writer who got ahold of Wheeler's Harvard application pointed out flaws that she thought Harvard could have noticed. She said that Wheeler's claim to have taken 16 AP courses was too "improbable" to be believed, and she spotted numerous tiny discrepancies that hinted at the falsity of Wheeler's application, like the fact that he listed AP art history as a one-term course at Andover while the school's online course catalog says it lasts for a full year. She called his essay "inscrutable" and "rambling." Though she quoted from it as well as from the Andover letter of recommendation and his writing sample about his parents' separation (all three plagiarized), she apparently did not Google the phrases she was quoting. If she had, she would have learned that the words in the essay that she was criticizing were not Wheeler's but those of a Harvard history professor.

In light of all that attention, admissions offices looked for ways to avoid similar incidents in the future. "Most people had to take stock internally to figure out if their processes were susceptible," said David Hawkins of the National Association for College Admission Counseling.

The case was a boon for business at TurnItIn.com, which saw interest in its admissions essay verification system spike among elite universities.

"A lot of what we've found with the real top-tier schools is that they're not usually early adopters," Jeff Lorton of TurnItIn for Admissions said. "Given the caliber of their students, there's the potential that they don't think they have as big a problem as maybe other schools. But we've seen that tide really shift as cases like [Wheeler's] happen. This is an issue that really touches upon every demographic in higher education."

The Wheeler case reminded schools of the problem of fraud, but it was not at all clear how to fix it. "For all of its high visibility in the popular press, we do not really know what happened here," Nassirian pointed out. "It's not obvious how he did it. It's not like, you know how sometimes people were telling how these high-end Kryptonite locks that people were buying for their bikes could be opened with a Bic ballpoint pen? It's not like he opened some giant security back door that nobody knew about."

Even if the weak point in security was not obvious, the colleges hit by Wheeler tried to fortify their defenses. Stanford announced that it would begin conducting random audits, intensive fact checks of a portion of the applications that it receives each year. Its undergraduate newspaper drew a connection between that decision and the embarrassing revelation in June that Stanford, not just Harvard, had accepted Wheeler. For its own part, Harvard administrators all the way up to the university's president told reporters that the college was putting more procedures in place to help detect fraud. Officials would not say what those new practices were. To reveal them to the press, they said, would make them less effective. But whatever the specific outcome, it was clear that Wheeler had made his mark.

CHAPTER NINE

After his release from jail pending trial, Adam Wheeler started putting a new life together for himself. He found a part-time job as a researcher for a nonprofit organization that paid minimum wage. He searched for an apartment.

Once, he went to meet two young women who had advertised on Craigslist that they needed one more person to fill their Cambridge apartment. He told them that he was a recent Bowdoin graduate. He introduced himself just as Adam.

He asked the women what their favorite books were. They chatted in a Cambridge coffee shop about literature, and they found him charming. Of the seven people they interviewed, at least one of the women was sure that the sensitive young man who seemed like just a bit of a nerd was her first choice for her new roommate.

Then, talking to a friend who happened to have attended Bowdoin, the young woman asked, Do you know a guy named Adam? He went to Bowdoin with you. He's into literature, and he's in Cambridge now. He might be living with me.

Her friend could not think of anyone who met that description—at first. Then a little while later, something clicked. Her friend emailed her a link to a newspaper article. The email said, Do you mean this guy?

She picked a different roommate.

But Wheeler did find a place to live. It was in Somerville, the town just north of Cambridge. It was within walking distance of Harvard. From the commercial intersection off of his residential street, it was easy on a clear day to see the soaring brick tower of Memorial Hall, one of the most photographed landmarks of Harvard. Even if he was not allowed to set foot on campus, Harvard was still a defining feature of the skyline he looked at every day.

His name had faded from the headlines, and he filled his days with new and unobtrusive pursuits. He went to work. He went running through Cambridge and Boston. He frequented the Cambridge Public Library, which was also within walking distance of his apartment. He started seeing a psychotherapist. He volunteered at a soup kitchen. But all along, the threat of his impending trial loomed in front of him.

His lawyer had been talking on his behalf to the prosecutor on his case. The district attorney's office wanted to offer him a plea agreement in which he would change his plea to guilty to avoid a trial. The government would be spared lots of time and expense, and he would be spared the agony of sitting in front of a jury and probably a courtroom full of reporters who would listen as every bit of evidence against him was brought forth. He would even get a lesser sentence—and there the talks broke down. They could not agree on a punishment.

In December, almost six months to the day since he had pleaded not guilty, he was back in Middlesex Superior Court to change that plea nonetheless. As the judge heard brief other matters on the docket first, Wheeler sat with one of his parents on each side of him.

When she reached his case, Judge Diane Kottmyer read off the list of crimes he had been charged with. Then she asked him how he pleaded. This time, he whispered, "Guilty."

She directed him to sit in the elevated box where witnesses sit during jury trials. Kottmyer ran through a rapid list of questions to make sure that Wheeler was competent to decide to plead guilty. It was her duty to confirm that he understood what he was relinquishing by waiving his right to a trial. Had he taken any drugs in the past week? Any alcohol in the past 12 hours? Was he on any prescription medication? Did he think any mental illness or anything else was interfering with his ability to think clearly?

To every question, Wheeler said no. Kottmyer ascertained that he grasped just how grave the consequences could be for him. If he were placed on probation and broke any of the conditions that he would be compelled to obey, he could be sent to prison and ordered to pay staggering fines, she told him. The maximum sentence was two and a half years in prison and a $5,000 fine for each identity fraud charge (there were eight) and five years and $25,000 for every larceny count (four of them).

"Those maximum sentences would apply to each of the counts that you're pleading guilty to," Kottmyer said. "Do you understand that?" She continued, "If it were alleged that you had violated any condition of your probation, you would be brought before a court hearing. You could be sentenced to up to the maximum sentence on each of the charges—you would not have the right to have a trial. You're giving up that right today. The judge would simply make a decision. . . . On the larceny offense alone, with a maximum of five years, on those alone you would have hanging over your head while you're on probation a sentence of 20 years, plus the maximum sentence on each of the other counts."

Asked if he understood, again and again his answer was yes.

Once, Kottmyer posed a more open-ended question. "Can you tell me in your own words what's happening today?" she asked.

He responded in a near-whisper like before. "Yes," he said.

There was a pause before Kottmyer prompted him for more. He waited awhile before saying slowly, "I'm entering a guilty plea."

Kottmyer's job at the end of the hearing would be to impose a sentence, a punishment for the crimes that Wheeler was confessing to that day. It would not be nearly as harsh as the maximum that she had determined Wheeler was cognizant of, but a sentence was a sentence, and none were easy to hand down. She asked prosecutor John Verner for his recommendation as to what Wheeler's should be.

Verner said that, in the opinion of the Commonwealth, Wheeler should be placed on probation for 10 years. He should not have to go back to jail, but if he broke any of the conditions placed on convicted felons on probation, including specific ones that the judge would dictate for him based on his crimes, then he should face prison time of up to two and a half years. While on probation, Verner said, he should be required to pay all $45,806 that he had received in financial aid and prizes back to Harvard.

Verner ran through a condensed, compelling version of the crimes Wheeler was charged with. He crafted a narrative arc, telling once again of Wheeler's bid for the Rhodes and Fulbright, of the first clues of his fraud, of the gradual unraveling of all his lies by Harvard officials and then by the police. A pack of reporters who had converged on Woburn once again from *The Boston Globe*, *Boston Herald*, ABC, Associated Press, *The New York Times*, and more all scribbled notes on Verner's every word.

Once Verner finished, Kottmyer questioned Wheeler to make sure he understood that by pleading guilty, he was agreeing to the veracity of Verner's story. She went through the tale, mentioning every detail that had led to a criminal count. "You committed identity fraud by writing a false recommendation in Lawrence Simon's name," she started. "Did you in fact do that? Did you in fact create a false letter of recommendation, affix Mr. Simon's name to it, and submit it to Harvard University in an effort to secure admission to Harvard University?"

"Yes."

She repeated the same interrogation word for word, simply changing the name of the identity fraud victim, and received a yes each time. They walked through the larceny charges, too. There was no doubt: Wheeler was admitting to the crimes. The question was how he should be made to pay for them.

Verner had the first chance to justify his sentencing recommendation. "The length and depth and duration of the defendant's crimes," the prosecutor said, made a long probation period appropriate. "This was not a one-time mistake," he said. "From April 2007 to well after he was expelled from Harvard University, he continued to commit these crimes."

He emphasized that Wheeler kept aiming for greater rewards rather than contenting himself with what he had already fraudulently achieved. "Once he got into Harvard, that apparently was not enough for Mr. Wheeler," Verner said. "Instead of just going to Harvard and just simply graduating, he forged documents, plagiarized documents—and won the Hoopes, the Sargent, and the Rockefeller."

And he told the judge that Wheeler had taken advantage of innocent people along the way. "He wrote himself letters of recommendation from good, hard-working professors," he said. "He used their names and their reputations for his own personal gain, to get himself into Harvard."

Worse than that, Verner continued, "He took opportunities from the number two person, who could have taken the $8,000 from the Rockefeller research program and done good with that money. That person doesn't get to say he or she went to Harvard, doesn't have a Harvard diploma."

He read a short statement from Harvard that said that not only had Harvard been the victim of Wheeler's crimes, but public faith in institutions of higher education everywhere had been shaken by his actions.

"Mr. Wheeler's acts of deception and fraud not only harmed Harvard University directly but also undermined the public perception of integrity in higher education nationally and around the world," the statement said. If Wheeler did not receive a long probation term, Verner read, "all of higher education would continue to be negatively impacted."

In fact, Verner noted, Harvard's own lawyers had asked him to demand more than 10 years of probation for Wheeler, though he himself thought that 10 was enough. Harvard wanted full restitution from Wheeler, too. In the university's statement, it claimed the money "can be put to use to support deserving Harvard students."

Steven Sussman, Wheeler's attorney, pointed out that Wheeler's ability to pay back the money to Harvard was questionable at best. "Mr. Wheeler would like to do what he can to make restitution," Sussman said. "But his financial circumstances at this time are obviously minimal. His employment is part-time and minimum wage. He does receive financial assistance from his family for living expenses."

Moreover, regardless of whether Wheeler could afford it, Sussman thought that $45,806 was too much to ask. He pointed out that the bulk of that money was not in the form of checks handed over to Wheeler. He only directly received the prizes and grants: $2,000 for the Sargent, $4,000 for the Hoopes, and $8,000 for the Rockefeller. All the rest was in the form of Harvard financial aid, and Wheeler had never touched that money at all.

Harvard offers no scholarships for academic merit or athletic achievement. Every single student who is admitted to Harvard, the thinking goes, is of sufficient caliber to deserve a scholarship (and indeed, many have turned down full rides from other schools in picking Harvard). So Harvard gives scholarships to anyone who needs assistance, through one of the most flush financial aid programs in the country, which announced its latest and most generous incarnation during Wheeler's first year at Harvard. Under that plan, families with incomes of less than $60,000 per year paid no tuition at all to send their children to Harvard. Any families earning up to $180,000 per year were expected to pay about 10 percent of their annual income, meaning up to $18,000 a year for an education that, according to its sticker price, normally asked upwards of $45,000 a year. The entire amount of the difference is counted as a grant—not a loan—from Harvard.

The student never has to pay the money back, but it never goes into his hands either. To Sussman, the $31,806 in such grants that Wheeler had received were not really funds that he had stolen from Harvard at all. Money just went from one Harvard account to another on his behalf. He never pocketed a dime. Was that larceny that should lead to his paying restitution to Harvard, to refund the university for money that, somewhere in its massive coffers, it might still have? Sussman said no. "It went to another Harvard account," Sussman contended. "It's all the same entity."

"Well, yes and no," countered Kottmyer, who had been keeping up a quick-tongued dialogue with both lawyers as they argued their points. "That money was not available to another student who was legitimately at Harvard. It may be that the money would not have been given out that year, but it would remain in the bank, so to speak, for another student."

Sussman argued as well that 10 years was an inappropriately long period of probation. Four or five, he said, should be adequate.

Kottmyer jumped in. "Having been discovered," she recalled, "the defendant went on to engage in exactly the same type of behavior, in circumstances in which the risk of discovery was, to say the least, enhanced. That suggests to me an element of compulsion, and in my view, that is best addressed by a lengthy period of probation—the 10 years that has been proposed by the Commonwealth."

Verner put forth one more reason that Wheeler needed more time on probation than Sussman urged. The prosecutor wanted a special clause to prohibit Wheeler from profiting from the story of his crimes—selling his story to a movie production company, writing a tell-all memoir about how he tricked Harvard, accepting money to do a talk show interview. To make that clause an effective punishment, he said, it had to have a long duration.

"I would hate to see four years from now Adam Wheeler being able to write a book about this and to gain a profit," he said. "I don't think three or four years is enough time for memory to pass."

He read words from Harvard's statement which backed that up: "We also feel strongly that Mr. Wheeler should be prohibited from profiting from his fraudulent schemes for as long a period as the court has power to impose."

At last, Wheeler had a chance to speak on his own behalf. His statement was brief and almost inaudible at times. He apologized to all the people whose trust he said he had abused: his professors, his friends, his parents. "I'm deeply sorry that my actions deprived others of the opportunity they rightfully deserved. I've been shamed and embarrassed by what I've done," he said. "I'm sorry for the attendant financial loss I caused the university." He spoke about the psychotherapy that he had started, too. It was helping him, he said, to understand the "compulsive quality" behind his actions and to "ensure that this will never happen again."

He was hopeful that he could put his crimes behind him and move on to a new life, which he would spend "possibly contributing to the well-being of the less fortunate in our community." He asked the judge to trust him that he could attain that goal and to help him reach it by giving him a lighter sentence. "I ask you to give me the opportunity to prove that, despite having erred," he pleaded.

As soon as he finished, Kottmyer pronounced her decision. She would impose the sentence recommended by Verner—10 years of probation; $45,806 in restitution to Harvard; and bans on representing himself as a Harvard, MIT, or Andover student or alumnus, setting foot on any of their campuses, or profiting from the story of his crimes. She had one additional restriction for Wheeler of her own: By law, he would be required to continue psychological counseling.

It was over. He had avoided more jail time, but he would have the threat of it—two and a half years of it, Kottmyer decided—hanging over his head for 10 long years. Sussman asked for just one bit of leniency for his client. Massachusetts probationers are not typically allowed to leave the state. Sussman asked that Wheeler be given permission to travel home to Delaware at will to see his family. Kottmyer agreed, subject to the condition that he notify his probation officer before he left and as soon as he returned. It was clear that the young man would be restricted by the strong fist of the law until he was well into his 30s. He was free to live his life outside of the prison that had once threatened him, but he would be in the shadow of the court for a very long time.

As he left with his parents, he waved off the reporters who followed him from the courtroom and the television cameras that had gathered outside in the biting air of Massachusetts in December to await his exit. He would not speak to them, though Sussman said on his behalf that he was "shamed and sorry." From the moment he was indicted, he never gave an interview, declining many requests from the author of this book and others to tell his side of the story. Now, his ordeal was slowly beginning to end.

❧

Or at least that was what was supposed to happen. That December day in 2010 was supposed to be the conclusion of Adam Wheeler's story, at least as far as the media was concerned. He was supposed to quietly check in with his probation officer month after month, rebuild his life in whatever way he chose, and become just one more offbeat news item most people barely remembered. His case made *Saturday Night Live* the weekend after he pleaded guilty. That should have been the peak before a rapid descent into yesterday's news.

For many months, that seemed to be working. He got his job at the nonprofit organization bumped up to full time. But then in July, he lost his job. As he submitted application after application to find another one, he grew increasingly worried about meeting his payments on his apartment and his restitution. In his search for employment, one internship caught his eye.

It was with a company based in Cambridge called U.S. Green Data, Inc. The company's purpose was to process information about energy policies in the United States and create graphic representations of that information for government leaders and environmental activists. The intern would work about five hours per week throughout the school year as one of the company's policy analysts. He would also receive training on many aspects of founding a start-up company, from guidance on hitting up a venture capital firm for funding to advice on legal issues to tips on the psychology of dressing for meetings.

The internship was a volunteer position, and he still needed to find a paying job. But it sounded compelling enough that he sent in a cover letter and résumé by email. The person who opened that email just happened to be a Harvard alumnus—a former resident of Kirkland House just like Wheeler. He had read the press coverage when Wheeler's crimes had first splashed into the news. That was more than a year ago at this point, but the name Adam Wheeler still sounded familiar. Familiar enough that when he saw on the résumé in front of him that Wheeler claimed to have been a graduate student in English at Harvard from 2007 to 2009 and to have won a Rockefeller grant from Harvard, he knew there might be a problem.

He forwarded the application to Harvard, and Harvard started talking to law enforcement officials all over again about Wheeler.

In early November 2011, after a long, unsuccessful search for a job that would fulfill his intellectual appetite, Wheeler resigned himself to a less engaging occupation. He started work in a factory. But one week later, he was summoned back to court.

The same cast was back before Judge Kottmyer—Verner, Sussman, Wheeler, and his parents. This time there was a new face in the courtroom as well: Angelo Gomez Jr., Wheeler's probation officer. Gomez told Kottmyer the reason for the hearing: By stating on a résumé that he had been a Harvard student, Wheeler had broken one of the conditions of his probation.

Kottmyer scheduled a hearing for the next week when she would rule on whether Wheeler had indeed broken his probation. In the meantime, Gomez and Verner said they wanted Wheeler behind bars.

Sussman argued against it. His client was "very fragile emotionally" right now, he said, noting that he was still seeing a psychologist. He was not up to another harrowing stint in jail. Moreover, he might lose the factory job he had so recently started if he were incarcerated for the next week.

"My druthers would be not to hold him," Kottmyer said at first. She was disinclined to put him in jail for an entirely different reason than Sussman offered. Her first thought was that the Cambridge jail was overcrowded. But as she listened to Gomez and Verner's arguments, she became convinced that they were right to see Wheeler as a flight risk if he were released that day. He now faced the threat of a two-and-a-half-year prison sentence if he were found responsible for the violation. This could be the moment that would lead him to flee, Verner argued. As he put it, "The gravity of the situation for Mr. Wheeler is greater today than there ever was." And Wheeler's mental state, Kottmyer said, just made her all the more nervous that he might not show up. She settled on a week in jail.

He left court in handcuffs that day and returned to Kottmyer's courtroom eight days later in a government van. This time, she once again had the power to send him away for years rather than days.

Sussman did not present any evidence on Wheeler's behalf, and just minutes after the hearing began, Kottmyer ruled that Wheeler had violated his probation. Gomez wanted him sentenced to the full two and a half years in prison right away. Sussman said that he should not be given any more time, just a more stringent psychotherapy requirement.

Kottmyer's decision, this time, was not what either side had requested. She knew the facts of the case. Wheeler had risked detection over and over again to commit almost identical deceptions. This time, he had gambled his freedom for an unpaid five-hour-a-week internship. She did not see how anyone in his right mind, quite literally, could do what he had done.

"It does appear that Mr. Wheeler suffers from a mental illness, and the conduct for which he stands convicted is a product, at least in part, of that mental illness," she opined. "There is an element of compulsivity in these offenses."

Thus, she said, she would not be sending Wheeler to jail that day. She was sending him to a mental hospital. For 40 days, he would be locked in Bridgewater State Hospital for a comprehensive evaluation. She would await the hospital's report before making up her mind at one more hearing.

A quick calculation revealed that 40 days meant the hearing would fall the day before Christmas Eve, a Friday. Someone started to suggest a different date, but Kottmyer did not blink an eye. She would resentence Wheeler on December 23. When that date rolled around, Middlesex Superior Court was even quieter than usual. The Associated Press and *The Boston Globe*, which had been sending reporters to cover Wheeler's hearings up until now, were not in the courtroom. Many people, undoubtedly, were taking the day to string Christmas lights and buy last-minute presents. The defendants whose cases Kottmyer heard before Wheeler's that day were probationers who wanted special permission to travel that weekend so that they could be with their families on the holiday. One wanted to tell his family in person that he had been charged with embezzling over a million dollars—quite a Christmas message. Kottmyer granted them permission.

When Wheeler's turn came, the courtroom was nearly empty aside from the legal players and his parents. The discussion this time had nothing to do with the holiday. Wheeler's physical presence was a reminder of just what he had been through in the past few weeks. In the 40 days that he had spent inside the mental hospital, he had grown a dark beard. The focus that day was on what the doctor who had evaluated Wheeler during that time had to say about what was inside his head.

The doctor at Bridgewater knew all the facts of Wheeler's repeated academic frauds. He had interviewed Wheeler. According to Lee Wheeler, the doctor had also heard about the head trauma that Wheeler suffered as an eight-month-old baby, when she left him under a friend's care for the first time and came back to find that her friend had severely shaken and slapped her child. That injury sent the infant back to the mental state of a newborn, Lee said, forcing him to relearn the myriad vital skills that babies acquire in their first few months of life, and kept him visiting a pediatric neurologist for years. As he grew up, when his parents noticed what they identified as reclusive and obsessive tendencies in their younger son, they blamed them on that old attack. But Lee was grateful that by his previous doctors' accounts, Wheeler had, remarkably, made a full recovery many years ago. And most of the time, the Wheelers had only seen that terrifying experience from Adam's babyhood as one more reason to be so deeply proud of all that their son achieved academically. They knew what he had overcome.

Now an adult, Wheeler had just been through a battery of tests at Bridgewater, a state-owned facility that serves as both a hospital and a prison for mentally unstable convicts and suspects. The doctor found again and again that there was nothing wrong at all.

When Kottmyer read Dr. David Holtzen's report and discussed it with Verner and Sussman, Holtzen's conclusion seemed clear: Wheeler had no mental illness. He was just a liar. In the courtroom, Verner said that Holtzen believed Wheeler had even tried to mislead him during their interviews. The doctor also suspected that Wheeler had feigned symptoms of mental illness in hopes of reducing his sentence. And for all the lies Wheeler had told, according to Verner, Holtzen could not see that he felt any "actual remorse."

In light of this report, Verner said, "Mr. Wheeler is not going to stop doing what he's doing unless he's sentenced. He has to be punished." Sussman countered that there was still room for doubt. Two doctors before this one had opined, to the contrary, that Wheeler did need psychological help. But Kottmyer retorted that one of those doctors had met Wheeler only briefly and the other held a doctorate in education, not medicine. The Bridgewater doctor's report, she said, was "persuasive."

"It appears that the defendant does not suffer from any mental illness," she said. "Thus, I cannot see that returning him to probation with treatment is going to do anything to prevent reoffending."

"There are two ways to look at this," she said. "The way I was originally looking at it was that the defendant suffers from a mental illness. There was a compulsivity to it. The violation of probation was a product of that compulsive need, one that could hopefully be addressed with treatment."

She continued, "The other way of looking at it is that the defendant simply has a character flaw that makes him dishonest and that, in effect, he was thumbing his nose at the system by performing exactly the same conduct as before, and that sending him to treatment which he doesn't need and doesn't perceive himself to need . . . is basically feeding his sense of himself as a person who can do these things and get away with them without repercussions."

She announced that she was sentencing Wheeler to one year in prison. After his release, he would be back on probation, with the condition that he continue mental health treatment.

It was two days before Christmas, and Wheeler's parents had just seen their son ordered to prison. After leaving the courtroom, Richard Wheeler scornfully questioned Kottmyer's judgment in ruling that his son was not mentally ill yet must seek psychological counseling following his prison sentence.

"If it smells like a duck, it walks like a duck, and it quacks like a duck, then it is probably a duck," Wheeler's father said. "In this case, that duck, she says, is 'no mental illness.' So why does she say he suddenly needs treatment for a mental illness 12 months later?"

His wife turned to him. "We have to trust her," she said. "He got himself into the system."

As Verner walked past, she wished him a good holiday. "I would wish you the same," he said. "Have a happy holiday, if you can."

Each of them had words of reassurance for the other: "You're doing your job," Lee said to the prosecutor.

And he said what every mother wants to hear. He praised her son.

"Adam's a very, very smart, talented kid."

Academia in America has its foundation in trust. Ideas flow freely in classrooms in which teachers and students all contribute honestly to the intellectual discussion. If a teacher feels compelled to verify that every piece of work a student submits is legitimate, the relationship between them becomes one of watchman and suspect rather than guide and apprentice, a transition that no educator wants to witness.

Society at large proudly rests on the same bedrock expectation of honesty. When citizens see diplomas on the walls of doctors' offices, they trust and assume that the practitioners legitimately earned the degrees that qualify them to diagnose, treat, and operate. So it is for many other fields that rely on the authenticity of credentials attained in the classroom.

A breakdown of this vitally important honor system would leave citizens fearful, mistrustful, and vulnerable. Thus, every time an academic fraudster succeeds in undermining that foundation, the crime has manifold victims. Everyone—from the admissions office, to the university community, to the student denied a spot, to the members of the public who interact with the cheater in his eventual career—is harmed.

The temptation for students worldwide to inflate résumés or buy fake transcripts or paste other people's words into their papers brings us dangerously close to a collapse of the time-honored trust that governs our schools and workplaces. Though it is a rare student who goes to the lengths that Wheeler did, many in the high-pressure world of college admissions cross the line into the moral middle ground. To varying extents, countless applicants seek desperately to gain an edge through some form of cheating.

Harvard may seem to stand for smarts or ambition or achievement. When a pretender tries to sneak into the hallowed halls, he might presume that those are the values that he can attach to his name. But the university recognizes that although its students and faculty may attain dizzying levels of success in all manner of pursuits, merely to succeed is not the aim at the core of the Harvard community.

The motto of Harvard is just one word: *Veritas.* Translated from Latin, it means truth. Harvard does not stand solely for accomplishment, fame, fortune, or even intelligence. When the university proclaims its own highest value, it embraces truth. Harvard understands, as the con artist never will, that without honesty, a degree is meaningless. One cannot lie in pursuit of veritas.

ACKNOWLEDGMENTS

First and foremost, I am grateful to every person interviewed for this book, named and unnamed. Your time and your trust were immensely valuable to this narrative.

Xi Yu poured countless hours into the reporting behind this book. I appreciate her research, edits, and ideas—and above all her friendship.

I am also grateful to the many people at *The Harvard Crimson* who first gave me the opportunity to cover this story and who aided me along the way. In particular, without Esther Yi's intent supervision—even rapping on her desk if Xi and I turned away from the story for so much as a momentary distraction in the early days—we never would have covered Wheeler's story as thoroughly as we did at the very beginning. Her strong guidance made this all possible.

Julian Bouma, George Fournier, Athena Jiang, Lauren Kiel, Jake McAuley, Keren Rohe, Zane Wruble, and Peter Zhu all pitched in when the Wheeler story first broke. Their efforts supported our articles then and our subsequent work on this book. Elias Groll, Eric Newcomer, and Noah Rayman lent us their warm encouragement from the earliest days that we talked about writing a book, and Ben Samuels, Naveen Srivatsa, Sebastian Garcia, and Martin Ye all worked with us to ensure that the book would appropriately benefit *The Crimson*.

So many friends, especially Hana Rouse, George Fournier, Stephanie Garlock, David LeBoeuf, Chelsea Link, Laura Mirviss, Monika Robbins, and Julia Ryan, have been patient listeners and incredible cheerleaders as this project progressed. To my entire amazing *Crimson* family—thank you for introducing me to the calling of journalism and for providing more exhilarating experiences at Harvard than I ever could have imagined. Thanks as well for learning what the word *aposiopesis* means—and Tara Merrigan, thank you for already knowing. See? I got it into the book.

For the chance to bring this story to press, I am grateful to Jeff and Deborah Herman and to everyone at Lyons Press: Holly Rubino, Meredith Dias, Jennifer Blackwell-Yale, Mary Ballachino, Justin Marciano, Josh Rosenberg, and Wendy Allex.

The generous hospitality of Mariya Ilyas at Bowdoin and the Buehler family in Woburn made our research trips possible—and made them fun. Nell Hawley, James Holt, Ethan Solomon, and Zoe Weinberg all kindly offered access to useful information.

The Pforzheimer House community has been a wonderful home away from home. I was not sure if a book ought to be written at 3 a.m. in the dining hall, but I learned with the help of friends and mentors there that it can indeed be done. My roommates in Pfoho and the foyer—Nancy Chen, Heather Hawkes, Isamar Vega, and Dominique Zeier—gave me unbelievable support and sympathy when frustrations arose, much-appreciated writing breaks, understanding when I did not have time for breaks, and space to spread out binders full of documents. The same held true for Xi's roommates, Sasha Mironov and Cassandra Rasmussen.

Countless others have offered advice, assistance, inspiration, and warmth that fueled the process of researching and writing this book. If you are not listed here, please know that I truly appreciate your varied and meaningful contributions to this project.

Now and always, I am unbelievably lucky to enjoy the love and encouragement of my brilliant, caring, and creative family. MiMi has set an example for me in her enthusiasm for language. Ben and Emily provided the wise advice and cheerful camaraderie that I can always expect from my two best friends. Mom inspires me with tremendous thoughtfulness, integrity, and literary talent that I can only hope to emulate. And Dad sparked my interest in legal journalism and suggested that Adam Wheeler's story might make a good book in the first place.

ENDNOTES

Page

Introduction

vii   14 percent of essays are plagiarized: Jeff Lorton, "Countrywide Similarity Report Results," iParadigms, LLC, January 2010.

vii   50 percent of transcripts are faked, and 90 percent of recommendation letters are forged: Tom Melcher, "White Paper No. 4," Zinch Inc., May 2010.

Prologue

x   "I must have made a mistake": John Verner, Commonwealth of Massachusetts v. Adam Wheeler, May 18, 2010.

x   Wheeler had no intention: David Smith, letter to Evelynn Hammonds, September 27, 2009.

Chapter One

1   During the most recent cycle: Elizabeth S. Auritt, "Harvard Accepts Record Low 5.9 Percent to the Class of 2016," *The Harvard Crimson*, March 29, 2012, www.thecrimson.com/article/2012/3/29/admissions-harvard-rate-2016.

4   In a 2010 survey: "2010 Report Card on the Ethics of American Youth," Josephson Institute, 2011, http://charactercounts.org/pdf/reportcard/2010/ReportCard2010_data-tables.pdf.

4   Another survey: Maura J. Casey, "Digging Out Roots of Cheating in High School," *The New York Times*, October 12, 2008, www.nytimes.com/2008/10/13/opinion/13mon4.html.

4   More than half the teenagers: "Hi-Tech Cheating," CommonSense Media, www.commonsensemedia.org/sites/default/files/CSM_hitech_cheating.pdf.

5   Every year, about 75 to 90 percent . . . national average: "Rodney (Caesar) High School—School Profiles," Delaware Department of Education, 2011.

197

Page

6   "We just want to provide": Kevin Fitzgerald, interview by Xi Yu
     and Julie Zauzmer, October 28, 2011.

6   Wheeler came to school: Tracy Jan and Milton Valencia, "This
     Can't Be Our Adam Wheeler," *The Boston Globe*, May 30, 2010.

6   He even took: Transcript of Adam B. Wheeler, Caesar Rodney
     High School.

7   lowercase letters: Jan and Valencia.

7   "He was frustrated": Richard Pieshala, interview by Julie
     Zauzmer, October 24, 2011.

7   "He had a quiet disgust": Jan and Valencia.

7   Pieshala noticed: Pieshala.

7   He came home most days, When it came time: Lee and Rich-
     ard Wheeler, conversation with Julie Zauzmer, December 23,
     2011.

8   financial aid from whatever college: Adam B. Wheeler, Bow-
     doin College application file, 2005.

8   In 2005, the year that Wheeler graduated: "National Liberal
     Arts College Rankings," *U.S. News & World Report*, August 29,
     2005.

8   Bowdoin was not Wheeler's first choice: Lee and Richard
     Wheeler.

9   averaged $37.64: Ryan Lytle, "Top 10 Highest Col-
     lege Application Fees," *U.S. News & World Report*,
     September 14, 2011, www.usnews.com/education/
     best-colleges/the-short-list-college/articles/2011/09/14/
     top-10-highest-college-application-fees.

10   One website promises: College Admissions Services Inc, "Get
     Your Chances of Admission," http://go4college.com.

10   "you can hardly afford": Amazon, "How to Write a Win-
     ning College Application Essay, Revised 4th Edition," www
     .amazon.com/Write-Winning-College-Application-Revised/
     dp/0761524266/ref=sr_1_1?ie=UTF8&qid=1326962329
     &sr=8-1.

11   Out of the 500,000 essays, Most of those students: Jeff Lorton,
     "Countrywide Similarity Report Results," iParadigms, LLC,
     January 2010.

Page

11 He filled out the first few pages: Wheeler, Bowdoin College application file.

11 *50 Successful Harvard Application Essays*: Staff of *The Harvard Crimson, 50 Successful Harvard Application Essays*. New York: St. Martin's Griffin, 1999.

11–12 Wheeler was not applying to Harvard: Lee and Richard Wheeler.

14 Farschman found Wheeler: William Farschman, interview by Julie Zauzmer, October 25, 2011.

Chapter Two

16 quirky. . . . Cutting-edge: Raymond Miller, interview by Xi Yu and Julie Zauzmer, December 8, 2011.

16 The college started: Bowdoin College, "History," www.bowdoin .edu/about/history.

16 The college touts, More than 40 percent, Nowadays: "Bowdoin at a Glance" (handout, Bowdoin College).

17 The average low temperature: The Weather Channel, "Average Weather for Brunswick, ME," www.weather.com/weather/ wxclimatology/monthly/graph/04011.

17 At the outset, In a survey for entering students: Adam B. Wheeler, Academic Advising Questionnaire, Bowdoin College, June 13, 2005.

18 The two lofty sentences: Staff of *The Harvard Crimson, 50 Successful Harvard Application Essays*. New York: St. Martin's Griffin, 1999.

19 He selected courses, He earned a C: Adam B. Wheeler, Academic Record, Bowdoin College.

19 "It seems to me": Interview with Bowdoin English professor by Xi Yu and Julie Zauzmer, December 9, 2011.

19 "He had real interest": Interview with Bowdoin religion professor by Xi Yu and Julie Zauzmer, December 9, 2011.

20 Dogfish Head: Interview with Bowdoin student by Xi Yu and Julie Zauzmer for *The Harvard Crimson*, May 19, 2010.

20 Every Friday afternoon: Bowdoin English professor.

Page

20   Wheeler played alongside guys: Conor Williams, "Fris-
      bee Team Ultimately Awesome," *The Bowdoin Orient*,
      April 29, 2005, http://orient.bowdoin.edu/orient/article.
      php?date=2005-04-29&section=5&id=5.

20   After Wheeler dove into a puddle: Maureen O'Connor,
      "The Talented Mr. Wheeler: Meet the Kid Who Faked His
      Way Into Harvard," Gawker, May 18, 2010, http://gawker.
      com/5541765/the-talented-mr-wheeler-meet-the-kid-who-
      faked-his-way-into-harvard.

20   its inspired lines: Raffi, "Bananaphone," *Bananaphone*, 1996,
      Rounder/Umgd.

20   An annual Bowdoin naked party: Kelsey Abbruzzese,
      "Naked parties: an expose," *The Bowdoin Orient*, Decem-
      ber 1, 2006, http://orient.bowdoin.edu/orient/article.
      php?section=3&date=2006-12-01&id=5.

20   "He was not athletic," He sometimes sat in: Bowdoin student.

21   One of Wheeler's English professors read it: Bowdoin English
      professor.

21   Paul Muldoon: Robert Potts. "A New Direction for
      the *New Yorker*," *The Guardian*, September 25, 2007,
      www.guardian.co.uk/books/booksblog/2007/sep/25/
      anewdirectionforthenewyo.

21   "he was hard to shut up": Bowdoin English professor.

22   "Everybody knew him": Bowdoin student.

22   a lengthy form: Bowdoin College, "College House Application,"
      www.bowdoin.edu/reslife/colhouse/documents/college-house-
      application.shtml.

23   Most of them nodded: Howell House resident, conversation
      with Julie Zauzmer, December 9, 2011.

23   The once-skinny teenager: Tracy Jan and Milton Valen-
      cia, "This Can't Be Our Adam Wheeler," *The Boston Globe*,
      May 30, 2010, www.boston.com/news/local/massachusetts/
      articles/2010/05/30/this_cant_be_our_adam_wheeler

24   "He was not the kind": Bowdoin student.

24   he stuck entirely: Wheeler, Academic Record.

Page

24   he started the semester: Miller, Bowdoin religion professor.

24   After two semesters: Wheeler, Academic Record.

24   the syllabus included: Scott Sehon, syllabus for Philosophy 241:
        "Philosophy of Law," Bowdoin College, spring 2006–07.

24   As Scott Sehon: Scott Sehon, letter to Bowdoin College Judi-
        cial Board, February 27, 2007.

25   It warned against: The Bowdoin College Academic Honor
        Code.

26   "They're not quite so gullible": John Turner, interview by Julie
        Zauzmer, December 20, 2011.

26   "suspension is likely": Bowdoin College, "2006 Judicial Board
        Letter to the Community," www.bowdoin.edu/studentaffairs/
        judicial-board/community-letters/judicial-board-community-
        letter-2006.pdf.

26   On the first day: Sehon, letter to Bowdoin College Judicial
        Board.

26   He knew the field: Scott Sehon, interview with Xi Yu and Julie
        Zauzmer, December 8, 2011.

26, 27 His purpose in discussing, he plagiarized from sources: Sehon,
        letter to Bowdoin College Judicial Board.

Chapter Three

28   resulted in scores: *Commonwealth of Massachusetts v. Adam
        Wheeler,* Middlesex Superior Court, Indictment No. 2010-460.
        Statement of the Case, p. 4.

28   Bowdoin's median range: "National Liberal Arts College Rank-
        ings," *U.S. News & World Report,* August 29, 2005.

29   close to 23,000: Aditi Balakrishna. "Class of 2011
        Admits Beat Lowest Odds," *The Harvard Crimson,*
        April 2, 2007, www.thecrimson.com/article/2007/4/2/
        class-of-2011-admits-beat-lowest.

29   In 2012, just five years later: Elizabeth S. Auritt, "Harvard
        Accepts Record Low 5.9 Percent to the Class of 2016," *The
        Harvard Crimson,* March 29, 2012, www.thecrimson.com/
        article/2012/3/29/admissions-harvard-rate-2016.

Page

29   James Engell: James Engell, Gurney Professor of English Literature and Professor of Comparative Literature, "Publications," http://scholar.harvard.edu/jengell/publications.

30   Wheeler's statement to Harvard: Adam B. Wheeler, Harvard College application file, 2007.

30   "The internal orientation": James Engell, "Only This: Connect." In *Essays on General Education in Harvard College*, by Harvard University Faculty of Arts and Sciences, 16–28, 2004.

30   That professor, Stephen Greenblatt: Stephen J. Greenblatt, "Cultural Mobility." In *Essays on General Education in Harvard College*, by Harvard University Faculty of Arts and Sciences, 76–78, 2004.

30   "I don't know anybody": Lois E. Beckett, "Greenblatt To Be Next 'Keeper of the Canon'," *The Harvard Crimson*, January 11, 2006, www.thecrimson.com/article/2006/1/11/greenblatt-to-be-next-keeper-of.

30   written by George Whitesides: George Whitesides, "Undergraduate Education at Harvard." In *Essays on General Education in Harvard College*, by Harvard University Faculty of Arts and Sciences, 109–19, 2004.

30   some by Jorge Domínguez: Jorge Domínguez, "Liberal Education at Harvard in this New Century." In *Essays on General Education in Harvard College*, by Harvard University Faculty of Arts and Sciences, 10–15, 2004.

30   served as a vice provost: Weatherhead Center for International Affairs, "Jorge I. Domínguez," www.people.fas.harvard.edu/~jidoming/cvs/index.htm.

30   entire paragraph from Charles Maier: Charles S. Maier, "'Only Connect': Changing Aspirations for General Education." In *Essays on General Education in Harvard College*, by Harvard University Faculty of Arts and Sciences, 86–88, 2004.

30   had been teaching: Harvard University Department of History, "Charles S. Maier," http://history.fas.harvard.edu/people/faculty/maier.php.

31   The next essay prompt asked: Wheeler, Harvard College application file.

Page

31   came from Helen Vendler: Helen Vendler, "On a Harvard Education for the Future." In *Essays on General Education in Harvard College*, by Harvard University Faculty of Arts and Sciences, 104–8, 2004.

31   the words of Peter Galison: Peter Galison, "If Wishes Were Horses: A Thoroughly Impractical Proposal or Two." In *Essays on General Education in Harvard College*, by Harvard University Faculty of Arts and Sciences, 29–31, 2004.

31   plagiarized Julie Buckler: Julie A. Buckler, "Towards A New Model of General Education at Harvard College." In *Essays on General Education in Harvard College*, by Harvard University Faculty of Arts and Sciences, 7–9, 2004.

32   he did not say this outright: Wheeler, Harvard College application file.

32   the words of Stanford professor Roland Greene: Roland Greene, "New World Studies and the Limits of National Literatures," *Stanford Humanities Review* 6.1 (1998), www.stanford.edu/group/SHR/6-1/html/greene.html.

32   passage from a memoir: James Merrill, *A Different Person*. New York: Alfred A. Knopf, 1993.

32   Wheeler's essay ended up, Wheeler checked off: Wheeler, Harvard College application file.

33   The last time he applied: Adam B. Wheeler, Bowdoin College application file, 2005.

33   After almost two years: Adam B. Wheeler, Academic Record, Bowdoin College.

33   Throughout high school: Wheeler, Bowdoin College application file.

34   he gave himself flawless 800s: Wheeler, Harvard College application file.

34   Less than 1 percent: College Board, "SAT Percentile Ranks," www.collegeboard.com/prod_downloads/highered/ra/sat/SAT-PercentileRanks.pdf.

34   In the year Wheeler applied: College Board, "SAT Subject Test Percentile Ranks," www.collegeboard.com/prod_downloads/highered/ra/sat/SubjTestPercentileRanks.pdf.

Page

35   via snail mail: Kathleen F. Steinberg, email to Julie Zauzmer, January 2, 2012.

35   That seemingly official document, he said he had taken 16 AP tests: Wheeler, Harvard College application file.

36   In the year Wheeler graduated: College Board, "Summary Reports: 2005," www.collegeboard.com/student/testing/ap/exgrd_sum/2005.html.

36   polled college admissions offices: Valerie Strauss, "AP Courses: How Many Do Colleges Want?", *The Washington Post*, January 29, 2010, http://voices.washingtonpost.com/answer-sheet/college-admissions/ap-courses-how-many-do-college.html.

36   Between 2008 and 2011: College Board, "Number of AP Examinations Per Student," http://professionals.collegeboard.com/profdownload/AP-Number-of-Exams-per-Student-2011.pdf.

37   meticulously forged score report: Wheeler, Harvard College application file.

37   It was founded: Britannica, "Phillips Academy," www.britannica.com/EBchecked/topic/456592/Phillips-Academy.

37   George Washington: BookScan Station, "Phillips Academy Oliver Wendell Holmes Library," www.bookscanstation.com/phillips-academy-oliver-wendell-holmes-library.html.

37   Today, it boasts: Phillips Academy, www.andover.edu.

37   The transcript that he printed out: Wheeler, Harvard College application file.

41   He broke a few rules: Betsy Korn, letter to Kevin Healy, November 18, 2009.

41   his real high school printed: Wheeler, Bowdoin College application file.

41   Wheeler forged a letter: Wheeler, Harvard College application file.

42   "Your college counselor": Katherine Cohen, *The Truth About Getting In: A Top College Advisor Tells You Everything You Need to Know*. New York: Hyperion, 2002.

43   contained in another book: Katherine Cohen, *Rock Hard Apps: How To Write a Killer College Application*. New York: Hyperion, 2003.

Page

44 less than 4 percent: Massachusetts Institute of Technology, "Enrollments 2011–2012," http://web.mit.edu/facts/enrollment.html.

44 the 12 areas: Massachusetts Institute of Technology, "School of Humanities, Arts, and Social Sciences," http://shass.mit.edu/undergraduate/majors.

45 he checked off no: Wheeler, Harvard College application file.

45 he had not applied: Lee and Richard Wheeler, conversation with Julie Zauzmer, December 23, 2011.

45, 46 fake MIT transcript, For letters of recommendation: Wheeler, Harvard College application file.

49 testimonials section: Tracy Quantum, "Testimonials," www.tracyquantum.com/about/testimonials.

49 list of accolades: Wheeler, Harvard College application file.

50 National Merit Scholarship: National Merit Scholarship Corporation, www.nationalmerit.org.

50 When he applied to Bowdoin: Wheeler, Bowdoin College application file.

50 he sent nine pages: Wheeler, Harvard College application file.

50–51 He took the poems: Richard Kenney, *The Evolution of the Flightless Bird*. New Haven: Yale University Press, 1984.

51 its foreword: James Merrill, foreword to *The Evolution of the Flightless Bird* by Richard Kenney, ix–xii. New Haven: Yale University Press, 1984.

Chapter Four

52 submitting his finished Harvard application: Adam B. Wheeler, Harvard College application file, 2007.

52 group email: Scott Sehon, email to Philosophy 241 students, February 19, 2007.

52–53 Wheeler had been on Sehon's mind ... discussed with his students: Scott Sehon, letter to Bowdoin College Judicial Board, February 27, 2007.

54 Two days later: Wheeler, Harvard College application file.

54 "You have been charged: Laura Kim Lee, letter to Adam Wheeler, March 2, 2007.

Page

54   Now, on the very day: Bowdoin College record of Adam
      Wheeler.

54   He already knew that Sehon had noticed: Sehon, letter to Bow-
      doin College Judicial Board.

54   He had had his brush: Bowdoin College record of Adam
      Wheeler.

54   less than a week: Lee.

55   Less than four hours: Peter Igoe, email to Tim Foster, March 8,
      2007.

56   Wheeler received a letter: Timothy W. Foster, letter to Adam
      Wheeler, March 9, 2007.

56   Wheeler heard from Harvard, an urgent request: Sage Suorsa,
      email to Rob Brooks, April 27, 2007.

56   the very next day: Summary report on Adam Wheeler's alumni
      interview on April 28, 2007.

56   They advised him to wait: Lee and Richard Wheeler, conversa-
      tion with Julie Zauzmer, December 23, 2011.

56   he brazenly planned, The first question: Summary report on
      Adam Wheeler's alumni interview.

61   takes notes on a sheet of paper, it totaled 50 pages, the officer
      circled, The officer dashed check marks, the second reader inked
      in judgments: Wheeler, Harvard College application file.

64   An officer might also: Matthew Greene, interview with Julie
      Zauzmer, January 6, 2012.

64   a paid service such as TurnItIn.com: Chris Harrick and Jeff
      Lorton, interview by Julie Zauzmer, December 20, 2011.

65   "If you're going to admit": Barmak Nassirian, interview by Julie
      Zauzmer, November 22, 2011.

66   "I suspect a lot of things": Greene.

66   remembers one transfer applicant: Erinn Andrews, interview by
      Julie Zauzmer, January 10, 2012.

67   close to 500 colleges: George Phillips, interview by Julie
      Zauzmer, January 6, 2012.

67   He knows all about watermarks: Richard Isom, interview by
      Julie Zauzmer, January 6, 2012.

Page

68   Anyone intent on forgery: Phillips.

68   student who spent his time at school: DiplomaMakers.com, "Transcripts," http://diplomamakers.com/transcript.html.

68   increase his self-esteem: BuyaFakeDiploma.com, http://buya fakediploma.com.

68   too time-consuming or complicated: Back Alley Press, "10 Reasons to Buy a Fake Diploma," http://backalleypress001 .blogspot.com/2010/10/10-reasons-to-buy-fake-diplomas.html; Diploma Company, "My Diploma Was Destroyed. Document Damaged," http://diplomacompany.com/my-diploma-was-destroyed.-document-damaged..html; PhonyDiploma.com, "Fake Transcripts," www.phonydiploma.com/Transcripts.aspx.

68   might boost him: Back Alley Press; PhonyDiploma.com; Superior Fake Degrees, "Ways to Use Fake Transcripts," www .superiorfakedegrees.com/ways-to-use-fake-transcripts.

69   "A college is really not able": David Hawkins, interview by Julie Zauzmer, November 9, 2011.

69   recommends that colleges check: Nassirian.

70   "We're moving through applications": Andrews.

71   "Transfer applicants are handled": William H. Honan, "Bogus Candidates Sometimes Slip Through the College Admissions Screen," *The New York Times*, April 16, 1995, www.nytimes .com/1995/04/16/us/bogus-candidates-sometimes-slip-through-the-college-admissions-screen.html.

72   "We're on high alert": Andrews.

72   A 2010 survey: Tom Melcher, "White Paper No. 4," Zinch Inc., May 2010.

72   a 2011 study: Yi (Leaf) Zhang and Linda Serra Hagedorn, "Chinese Application with or without Assistance of an Education Agent: Experience of International Chinese Undergraduates in the US," *Journal of College Admission* (Summer 2011): 6–16.

72   have attested to the prevalence: Jiang Xueqin, "Selecting the Right Chinese Students," *The Chronicle of Higher Education*, November 3, 2011, http://chronicle.com/article/ Selecting-the-Right-Chinese/129621.

Page

72   American admissions officers complain: Tom Bartlett and
        Karin Fischer, "The China Conundrum," *The Chronicle of Higher
        Education*, November 3, 2011, http://chronicle.com/article/
        Chinese-Students-Prove-a/129628.

72   backed up by the 2010 survey: Melcher.

72   a problem that Hawkins said: Hawkins.

72   One company: Dan Levin, "Coaching and Much More for
        Chinese Students Looking to U.S," *The New York Times*,
        May 29, 2011, www.nytimes.com/2011/05/30/business/
        global/30college.html.

73   In a tragic incident: Associated Press, "Officials: 1 Killed as
        Prospective Students Stampede at South African University,"
        The Washington Post, January 10, 2012, www.washingtonpost.
        com/world/africa/officials-1-killed-as-prospective-students-
        stampede-at-south-african-university/2012/01/10/gIQAkLc-
        WnP_story.html.

73   a 2011 crackdown: Jenny Anderson and Peter Applebome,
        "Exam Cheating on Long Island Hardly a Secret," *The New York
        Times*, December 1, 2011, www.nytimes.com/2011/12/02/edu-
        cation/on-long-island-sat-cheating-was-hardly-a-secret.html.

73   other high school students: "Pressure and Lack of Repercus-
        sions Are Cited in SAT Cheating," *The New York Times*, Octo-
        ber 12, 2011, www.nytimes.com/schoolbook/2011/10/12/
        pressure-and-lack-of-repercussions-are-cited-in-sat-cheating.

73   poured out tales: Stacy Teicher Khadaroo, "SAT Cheating
        Scandal: Are Stakes Getting Too High for College Admis-
        sion?" *The Christian Science Monitor*, September 28, 2011, www
        .csmonitor.com/USA/Education/2011/0928/SAT-cheating-
        scandal-Are-stakes-getting-too-high-for-college-admission.

74   "Who would claim": Nassirian.

74   "With homeschooled students": Andrews.

74   "There are very few protections": Hawkins.

76   mere 1 percent: Justin C. Worland, "Fifteen Trans-
        fer Students Admitted," *The Harvard Crimson*, August
        31, 2011, www.thecrimson.com/article/2011/8/31/
        students-transfer-harvard-admissions.

Page

Chapter Five

80   once suffered the indignity: Clifford M. Marks, "Winthrop
        Wages War With Waves," *The Harvard Crimson*, Febru-
        ary 14, 2008, www.thecrimson.com/article/2008/2/14/
        winthrop-wages-war-with-waves-adams.

80   "Oh Kirkland": Justin Ide, "A Look Inside: Kirkland House,"
        Harvard Gazette, June 29, 2011, http://news.harvard.edu/
        gazette/story/photo-journal/a-look-inside-kirkland-house-3.

81   Then over the summer: Interview with Adam Wheeler's former
        roommate by Xi Yu, July 8, 2011.

82   "Goodfellae": Adam Wheeler, email to residents of Kirkland
        G-31, August 17, 2007.

83   His new roommates read: Adam Wheeler's former roommate.

84   They get to know each other: William Ball, interview by Xi Yu,
        September 27, 2011; Benjamin Kultgen, interview by Xi Yu,
        October 5, 2011.

84   "To go from here": Raymond Miller, interview by Xi Yu and
        Julie Zauzmer, December 8, 2011.

85   "utter, ridiculous pretentiousness": Kultgen.

85   "legendary": Interview with Harvard graduate by Julie Zauzmer
        for *The Harvard Crimson*, May 18, 2010.

85   "Hi, I'm Adam": Adam Wheeler, email to transfer students list,
        September 1, 2007.

86   "It was kind of hilarious": Harvard graduate.

86   FOP, short for First-Year Outdoor Program: Harvard First-
        Year Outdoor Program, www.fas.harvard.edu/~fop.

86   Wheeler picked the most advanced: Marcel Moran, interview
        by Xi Yu and Julie Zauzmer, September 19, 2011; Max Storto,
        interview by Julie Zauzmer, September 23, 2011; interview with
        2007 FOP participant by Julie Zauzmer, October 18, 2011.

87   hiker asked him once, the group played Mafia: 2007 FOP
        participant.

87   Wheeler's use of the word "pellucid": Storto.

88   "It was nice having": Adam Wheeler's former roommate.

Page

88   "He was going to sort of reform": Joe Resnek, interview by Xi
      Yu, August 18, 2011.

88   he wore a few shirts, "He showed us his driver's license," whis-
      key and bourbon, when the cashier asked him: Adam Wheeler's
      former roommate.

89–90 He went out to a bar: 2007 FOP participant.

90   The Sad Man, "A lot of times": Abel Acuña, interview by Xi Yu,
      August 30, 2011.

91   One member of that group: Adam Wheeler's former room-
      mate; interview with Adam Wheeler's ex-girlfriend by Julie
      Zauzmer, January 16, 2012.

91   "Adam has trouble": Adam Wheeler's former roommate.

91   "it wasn't anything": Adam Wheeler's ex-girlfriend.

92   as students . . . in the late 1990s: Victoria C. Hallett, "From
      Barbecue to Kegerator: Harvard's Party Suites," *The Har-
      vard Crimson*, April 16, 1999, www.thecrimson.com/
      article/1999/4/16/from-barbecue-to-kegerator-harvards-party.

92   *The Crimson* was still listing: Catherine A. Zielinksi, "Where
      the Party At: Harvard's Sweetest Party Suites," *The Har-
      vard Crimson*, March 18, 2009, www.thecrimson.com/
      article/2009/3/18/where-the-party-at-harvards-sweetest.

92   "It was always kind of": Acuña.

93   Wheeler had packed the lightest, he groaned to a roommate,
      But when it came to his computer, "To be honest, we were not":
      Adam Wheeler's former roommate.

94   When Wheeler's girlfriend heard: Adam Wheeler's ex-girlfriend.

94   one friend had even: Adam Wheeler's former roommate.

94   "I didn't think we would break up": Adam Wheeler's ex-girlfriend.

94   Acuña met a lot of women: Acuña.

94   Mather Lather: Rachel Aviv, "Togas? They Are So Last Cen-
      tury," *The New York Times*, January 7, 2007, www.nytimes
      .com/2007/01/07/education/edlife/07partybox.html; Punit
      N. Shah, "Mather Lather Foam Sets Off Fire Alarm," *The
      Harvard Crimson*, April 18, 2010, www.thecrimson.com/
      article/2010/4/18/mather-according-fire-night; Deanna Dong,
      "Lather Suds Rub Partiers Wrong Way," *The Harvard Crimson*,

April 19, 2005, www.thecrimson.com/article/2005/4/19/
lather-suds-rub-partiers-wrong-way.

Page

94   One woman noticed Wheeler: Acuña.

94   "on the prowl": Adam Wheeler's former roommate.

95   Super Mash Bros.: Acuña.

95   The Swamp heard: Adam Wheeler's former roommate.

95   Wheeler finally officially resigned: Adam B. Wheeler, Aca-
        demic Record, Bowdoin College.

95   University of Chicago: Interview with close acquaintance of
        Adam Wheeler by Xi Yu and Julie Zauzmer for *The Harvard
        Crimson*, May 17, 2010; interview with Bowdoin student by Xi
        Yu and Julie Zauzmer for *The Harvard Crimson*, May 19, 2010.

95   "an extremely nice guy": Interview with classmate of Adam
        Wheeler by Julie Zauzmer, September 22, 2011.

96   in his first semester at Harvard: Adam Wheeler, Student
        Record, Harvard College.

96   Harvard declared Wheeler exempt: Charles G. Ruberto, letter
        to Adam Wheeler, February 19, 2008.

96   Wheeler seemed uninterested: Craig Nishimoto, interview by
        Julie Zauzmer, November 14, 2011.

96   When he was confronted: Adam Wheeler, Administrative
        Board Decision, Harvard College, February 19, 2008.

96   "He was really into philosophy": Storto.

97   A problem on the final exam: FAS Final Exams. "Quantitative
        Reasoning 22, Final Examination, Fall Semester, 2004–05,"
        www.fas.harvard.edu/~exams/final2004f/1122.pdf.

97   "He was quite clearly interested": Harvard graduate.

97   courses he selected: Wheeler, Student Record.

97   quantitative courses are harder: Nishimoto.

98   D-plus on his record: Wheeler, Student Record.

98   the administrative board: Wheeler, Administrative Board Decision.

98   in the spring: Wheeler, Student Record.

98   cozy seminar room, "a little exhausted": Stephen Greenblatt,
        interview by Xi Yu, June 22, 2011.

98–99   In another class he took, Wheeler rarely spoke, he seemed
        touched, "He was a master": Classmate of Adam Wheeler.

Page

100 he scored two As: Wheeler, Student Record.

100 he earned his way: Richard Craig Crouch, letter to Adam Wheeler, June 12, 2008.

100 He signed up: Wheeler, Student Record.

100 Only about 20: Rebecca D. Robbins, "Six Classes, One Semester," *The Harvard Crimson*, November 1, 2011, www.thecrimson .com/article/2011/11/1/students-take-six-classes.

100 he received As in five: Wheeler, Student Record.

100 "swooping transcendent meditations": Classmate of Adam Wheeler.

101 he carried a Vladimir Nabokov book: Mohindra Rupram, interview by Julie Zauzmer, September 25, 2011.

101 He took a seminar devoted: Wheeler, Student Record.

101 He started talking about *Lolita*: Adam Wheeler's former roommate.

101 He brought up the idea, "We all thought": Rupram.

101 Wheeler was always quiet at the meetings, he did not want an adviser: Daniel Donoghue, interview by Julie Zauzmer, December 14, 2011.

102 He asked for $500: Adam Wheeler, Common Application for Research and Travel, Harvard University, February 27, 2009.

102 the Middlebury program cost: James Maddox, letter to Adam Wheeler, February 3, 2009.

102 until August 29, On top of a résumé: Wheeler, Common Application for Research and Travel.

104 "Unclear what he is applying for," a committee member's notes: Adam Wheeler, Rockefeller summer award evaluations, 2009.

104 he would get $8,000: Evelynn M. Hammonds and Robert A. Lue, letter to Adam Wheeler, April 6, 2009.

104 The decision to hand out: Paul Bohlmann, interview by Xi Yu and Julie Zauzmer, October 18, 2011.

105 "needlessly ponderous," "strong reservations": Suparna Roychoudhury, Harvard College Tutorial Report for Adam Wheeler, Fall 2008.

105 "pushing the matter too hard": Adam Wheeler, email to Suparna Roychoudhury, December 11, 2008.

Page

105   Six days later: Adam Wheeler, email to Suparna Roychoudhury, December 17, 2008.

106   "He needs to edit himself": Roychoudhury, Harvard College Tutorial Report for Adam Wheeler.

106   prize that the English department gives out: Harvard University Department of English, "Francis James Child Prize for Excellence in Teaching," http://english.fas.harvard.edu/files/jtp.pdf.

107   "The subtle, elegant, and profound": Suparna Roychoudhury, Hoopes Prize Project Evaluation for Adam Wheeler's "The Mapping of an Ideological Demesne," Harvard University, April 23, 2009.

107   it came up for discussion: Donoghue.

108   a doctoral dissertation completed eight years earlier: Daniel G. Brayton, "Critical Topographies: Possession, Place, and Power in the English Renaissance," PhD diss., Cornell University, 2001.

108   his junior paper: Adam Wheeler, "Mapping an Ideological Demesne: *Utopia* and *The Tempest*," Winthrop Sargent Prize submission, Harvard University, 2009.

108   his Hoopes submission: Adam Wheeler, "The Mapping of an Ideological Demesne: Space, Place, and Text from More to Marvell," Hoopes Prize submission, Harvard University, 2009.

108   "That piece of work": Daniel Brayton, interview by Xi Yu, December 14, 2011.

110   A Kirkland student forwarded: Russell Rennie, email to Kirkland list, May 15, 2009.

110   One of Wheeler's roommates quickly replied: Dan Robinson, email to Kirkland list, May 15, 2009.

110   Another Swamp resident replied: James Fish, email to Kirkland list, May 15, 2009.

110   "Just out of curiosity": Patrick Ziemnik, email to Kirkland list, May 15, 2009.

111   "Our junior spring": Adam Wheeler's former roommate.

Page

Chapter Six

113   It depicted him, Wheeler declared: Adam B. Wheeler, Application for Harvard College Endorsement, U.S. Rhodes Scholarship, 2009; Adam B. Wheeler, Application for Study, Research, or Teaching Assistantships 2010–2011, Fulbright, 2009.

115   a published Greenblatt piece: Stephen J. Greenblatt, "Cultural Mobility," In *Essays on General Education in Harvard College*, by Harvard University Faculty of Arts and Sciences, 76–78, 2004.

115   the résumé that Wheeler submitted: Wheeler, Application for Harvard College Endorsement, U.S. Rhodes Scholarship; Wheeler, Application for Study, Research, or Teaching Assistantships 2010–2011, Fulbright.

116   the publishing company denies: Xi Yu and Julie M. Zauzmer, "A Dissection of a Harvard Faker's Fabricated Resume," *The Harvard Crimson,* May 19, 2010, www.thecrimson.com/article/2010/5/19/resume-wheeler-shed-crimsons.

116   whose description he lifted: Catherine Nicholson, "Geographies of English Eloquence," PhD Diss. Abstract, University of Pennsylvania, 2008,ProQuest.

116   Two of the titles: Linda Shu, conversation with Julie Zauzmer, October 24, 2011; Yu and Zauzmer, "A Dissection of a Harvard Faker's Fabricated Resume."

117   that talk was not given: Yu and Zauzmer, "A Dissection of a Harvard Faker's Fabricated Resume."

117   Stauffer made a point: John Stauffer, interview by Xi Yu and Julie Zauzmer, October 21, 2011.

118   writing tutor: Yu and Zauzmer, "A Dissection of a Harvard Faker's Fabricated Resume."

118   summer literature researcher: Robert Mitchell, emails to Xi Yu and Julie Zauzmer, October 25–26, 2011.

118   Center for Electronic Projects: Randy Bass, email to Xi Yu and Julie Zauzmer, October 25, 2011.

118   East Asian Languages: Yu and Zauzmer, "A Dissection of a Harvard Faker's Fabricated Resume."

119   This professor had been impressed: Harvard University English professor, letter in Adam B. Wheeler, Application for Harvard

College Endorsement, U.S. Rhodes Scholarship, 2009; Harvard University English professor in Adam B. Wheeler, Application for Study, Research, or Teaching Assistantships 2010–2011, Fulbright, 2009.

Page

121   by email, While Russell said: James Russell, email to David Smith, September 24, 2009.

121   the version he received in his inbox: Christine Gerrard, email to David Smith, September 25, 2009.

121   He scrapped it entirely: Wheeler, Application for Harvard College Endorsement, U.S. Rhodes Scholarship; Wheeler, Application for Study, Research, or Teaching Assistantships 2010–2011, Fulbright.

122   When one tutor from Lowell House: Susana Mierau, email to Paul Bohlmann, September 9, 2009.

122   "once in a blue moon," goes to about half: Paul Bohlmann, interview by Xi Yu and Julie Zauzmer, October 18, 2011.

123   Before the interview: James Simpson, interview by Julie Zauzmer, September 2, 2011.

124   "It is a truth universally acknowledged": Wheeler, Application for Study, Research, or Teaching Assistantships 2010–2011, Fulbright.

125   printed four years earlier: Harvard University Faculty of Arts and Sciences, *Essays on General Education in Harvard College.* 2004.

125   The byzantine set of requirements: "Core Curriculum," President and Fellows of Harvard University, 2010, http://my.harvard.edu/core.

125   Back in 2002: Jessica E. Vascellaro, "Dean's Curricular Review Kicks Off," *The Harvard Crimson*, October 15, 2002, www.thecrimson.com/article/2002/10/15/deans-curricular-review-kicks-off-the.

125   actually called "radical," "changing undergraduate education": Allison A. Frost, "Core Curriculum Gets a Makeover," *The Harvard Crimson*, June 8, 2005, www.thecrimson.com/article/2005/6/8/core-curriculum-gets-a-makeover-when.

Page

126   Just three minutes: Simpson.

129   Lui headed back: Adonica Lui, interview by Xi Yu and Julie Zauzmer, October 18, 2011.

129   This was his Fulbright: Bohlmann and Lui, interview by Xi Yu and Julie Zauzmer, October 18, 2011.

130   Simpson's first thought: Simpson.

131   sent a two-sentence email: David Smith, email to Adam Wheeler, September 20, 2009.

131   "I must have made a mistake": John Verner, *Commonwealth of Massachusetts v. Adam Wheeler*, May 18, 2010.

131   cosmopolitanism, formal Ad Board hearing, leave of absence: David Smith, letter to Evelynn Hammonds, September 27, 2009.

131   And minutes after: Adam Wheeler, email to David Smith, September 21, 2009.

132   his parents picked him up: Smith, letter to Evelynn Hammonds.

Chapter Seven

133   One of his roommates sent: Interview with Adam Wheeler's ex-girlfriend by Julie Zauzmer, January 16, 2012.

133   One friend picked up hints: Interview with close friend of Adam Wheeler by Xi Yu and Julie Zauzmer for *The Harvard Crimson*, May 17, 2010.

133   Wheeler was studying abroad: Abel Acuña, interview by Xi Yu, August 30, 2011.

133   One roommate told another, "Oh, my brother's just still ill": Interview with Adam Wheeler's former roommate by Xi Yu, July 8, 2011.

134   "I vaguely remembered": Email from resident of Adam Wheeler's entryway to Xi Yu, May 20, 2010.

134   Another friend, unaware: Interview with classmate of Adam Wheeler by Julie Zauzmer, September 22, 2011.

134   His Swamp rooming group: Adam Wheeler's former roommate.

Page

134   his backstory: Adam B. Wheeler, Brown University transfer application file, 2010; Adam B. Wheeler, Maritime Studies Program of Williams College & Mystic Seaport application file, 2009; Adam B. Wheeler, Yale College transfer application file, 2010.

136   one letter: Marlyn E. McGrath, letter to Adam Wheeler, October 2, 2009.

136–38   grew worried . . . could not be correct: David Smith, letter to Evelynn Hammonds, September 27, 2009.

138   James Engell: James Engell, "Only This: Connect." In *Essays on General Education in Harvard College*, by Harvard University Faculty of Arts and Sciences, 16–28, 2004.

138   William Kirby's preface: William C. Kirby, preface to *Essays on General Education in Harvard College*, by Harvard University Faculty of Arts and Sciences, 2004.

139   Slavic languages professor Julie Buckler: Julie A. Buckler, "Towards a New Model of General Education at Harvard College." In *Essays on General Education in Harvard College*, by Harvard University Faculty of Arts and Sciences, 7–9, 2004.

139   "the unity of intellectual frameworks": Edward W. Younkins, "Toward the Unity and Integration of Knowledge: The Study of Political and Economic Philosophy," *Rebirth of Reason*, http://rebirthofreason.com/Articles/Younkins/Toward_the_Unity_and_Integration_of_Knowledge_The_Study_of_Political_and_Economic_Philosophy.shtml.

139   "manifestly topical, thematic": Marjorie Garber, "General Education." In *Essays on General Education in Harvard College*, by Harvard University Faculty of Arts and Sciences, 32–63, 2004.

140   "We all know of": Drew Gilpin Faust, "Letter from President Faust about the Global Economic Crisis," Office of the President, Harvard University, November 10, 2008, www.harvard.edu/president/letter-from-president-faust-about-global-economic-crisis.

140   they had a better understanding: Smith, letter to Evelynn Hammonds.

Page

141–42   "baffling," Russell was especially bothered, "beyond anything one might expect," "Adam has been a superb student," "How could parts": James Russell, emails to David Smith, September 24 and 25, 2009.

142   Ellison and Smith contacted Christine Gerrard: David Smith, email to Christine Gerrard, September 2009.

142–43   She looked at the letter: Christine Gerrard, email to David Smith, September 25, 2009.

145   Smith forwarded: David Smith, email to Jay Ellison, September 25, 2009.

145   They followed that trail, Smith had a hunch: Smith, letter to Evelynn Hammonds.

146   not only gushed for pages: Harvard University English professor, letter in Adam B. Wheeler, Application for Harvard College Endorsement, U.S. Rhodes Scholarship, 2009; Harvard University English professor in Adam B. Wheeler, Application for Study, Research, or Teaching Assistantships 2010–2011, Fulbright, 2009.

146   He included letters: Wheeler, Brown University transfer application file; Wheeler, Maritime Studies Program of Williams College & Mystic Seaport application file; Wheeler, Yale College transfer application file.

146   he had taken two challenging English courses: Adam Wheeler, Student Record, Harvard College.

146   Helen Vendler's entry: Helen Vendler, "On a Harvard Education for the Future." In *Essays on General Education in Harvard College*, by Harvard University Faculty of Arts and Sciences, 104-8, 2004.

146   "I write this letter": Wheeler, Maritime Studies Program of Williams College & Mystic Seaport application file.

148   learned that he had never been: Smith, letter to Evelynn Hammonds.

148   the director of transfer admissions found: Marlene V. Rotner, email to Peter Quesada, September 30, 2009.

148   They checked with the College Board: Dan R. Zupan, email to Marlyn McGrath and Andrea Balian, September 30, 2009.

Page

149 "Occasionally candidates," "To be very clear": McGrath.

150 internship at the magazine *The New Republic*: "Adam Wheeler's Resume," *The New Republic*, May 18, 2010, www.tnr.com/blog/jonathan-chait/75025/adam-wheelers-resume.

150 Stanford, however: *Commonwealth of Massachusetts v. Adam Wheeler*, Middlesex Superior Court, Indictment No. 2010-460. "Commonwealth's 1st Notice of Discovery," June 9, 2010.

150 "as strange an application": James T. Carlton, email to Aislinn Doyle, October 20, 2009.

150 professors wanted to keep: Adam Wheeler, email to Williams-Mystic Admissions Office, October 14, 2009.

150 Private?, "No one writes": Carlton, email to Aislinn Doyle.

151 Is Daniel Brayton: Wheeler, email to Williams-Mystic Admissions Office.

151 he was informed: Aislinn Doyle, email to Adam Wheeler, October 15, 2009.

151 he would mail: Adam Wheeler, email to Aislinn Doyle, October 18, 2009.

151 His best guess: Carlton, email to Aislinn Doyle.

154 He came, bringing his girlfriend: James T. Carlton, interview by Julie Zauzmer, January 10, 2012.

154 visiting her regularly: Adam Wheeler's former roommate; Adam Wheeler's ex-girlfriend.

154 video chat: Adam Wheeler's ex-girlfriend.

154 They toured the seaside campus: Carlton, interview by Julie Zauzmer.

154 expected him to come: Aislinn Doyle, emails to Adam Wheeler, November 5 and 6, 2009.

154 accepted a publishing internship: Adam Wheeler, email to Aislinn Doyle, November 14, 2009.

154–55 It was the first: Kevin Fitzgerald, interview by Xi Yu and Julie Zauzmer, October 28, 2011.

155 "Yale did what it should": Richard Wheeler, conversation with Julie Zauzmer, December 23, 2011.

155 "I am writing": Adam Wheeler, email to Yale transfer admissions program, April 24, 2010.

Page

156 "I was completely": Interview with McLean Hospital employee by Julie Zauzmer, October 11, 2011.

156 "Thank you for sending": Adam Wheeler, email to McLean Hospital employee, January 26, 2010.

156 "This isn't even English": Interview with McLean Hospital employee by Julie Zauzmer.

156 She asked: Email from McLean Hospital employee to Adam Wheeler, February 4, 2010.

156 he sent her two names: Adam Wheeler, email to McLean Hospital employee, February 5, 2010.

157 "Adam wheeler [sic]": Qiuyu Wang, email to McLean Hospital employee, February 9, 2010.

157 took her more effort: Interview with McLean Hospital employee by Julie Zauzmer.

157 he was in the Boston area: David Evett, email to McLean Hospital employee.

158 "Supposedly he's published": Interview with McLean Hospital employee by Julie Zauzmer.

158 noticed that his Harvard email address: Email from McLean Hospital employee to Jay Ellison, February 22, 2010.

159 "Well, well, well": David Smith, email to Jay Ellison, February 20, 2010.

Chapter Eight

160 confirmation from Andover and MIT: Betsy Korn, letter to Kevin Healy, November 18, 2009; Jessie Combs, letter to Brian Spellman, November 5, 2009.

160 county district attorney's office: Cara O'Brien, press release, December 16, 2010.

161 Secret Service's list: U.S. Department of Homeland Security, *United States Secret Service Fiscal Year 2008 Annual Report,* www.secretservice.gov/FY2008_AnnualReport_WM.pdf.

162 "There's something wrong": James Barron with M. A. Farber, "Tracing a Devious Path to the Ivy League," *The New York Times,* March 4, 1991, www.nytimes.com/1991/03/04/nyregion/tracing-a-devious-path-to-the-ivy-league.html.

Page

162 But after he was released: "Top 10 Imposters," *Time,* www.time.com/time/specials/packages/article/ 0,28804,1900621_1900618_1900619,00.html.

162 Lon T. Grammer: Raymond Hernandez, "Yale Says It Sees an Impostor in the Ivy," *The New York Times*, April 21, 1995, www.nytimes.com/1995/04/12/nyregion/yale-says-it-sees-an-impostor-in-the-ivy.html.

162 On the day that Grammer: "Grad Student Held as Impostor," *Yale Alumni Magazine*, February 1998, www.yalealumni magazine.com/issues/98_02/l_v.html.

162 larceny trial: "Impostor Rejects Plea Bargain," *Yale Alumni Magazine*, December 1997, www.yalealumnimagazine.com/ issues/97_12/l_v.html.

162–63 "Oh my god": Glenn Conway, interview by Julie Zauzmer, January 10, 2012.

163 But two years later: Rochelle Steinhaus, "Yale Imposter Stands Trial for Attempted Murder," CNN, February 4, 2003, http://articles.cnn.com/2003-02-04/justice/ctv .jenkins_1_while-jenkins-drug-charges-murder-case.

163 eventually found guilty: William Sullivan, "Tonica Jenkins Convicted of Attempted Murder." *Yale Daily News*, February 12, 2003. www.yaledailynews.com/news/2003/feb/12/ tonica-jenkins-convicted-of-attempted-murder.

164 Akash Maharaj, "His is a startlingly common": Isaac Arnsdorf, "The Man Who Duped the Ivy League," *Yale Daily News*, September 10, 2008, www.yaledailynews.com/news/2008/sep/10/ the-man-who-duped-the-ivy-league.

164 it was attitudes like that: Conway

164–65 he had held a grudge, "outright fraud": Isaac Arnsdorf, "Yale No Stranger to Application Fraud," *Yale Daily News*, April 10, 2008, www.yaledailynews.com/news/2008/apr/10/ yale-no-stranger-to-application-fraud.

165–66 Rice University pressed charges: Ruth Samuelson, "Faking College," *Houston Press*, October 12, 2006, www.houstonpress .com/2006-10-12/news/faking-college/full.

Page

166   "I think the preoccupation": Norman Pattis, interview by Julie Zauzmer, January 11, 2012.

167   "It's narcissism": Conway.

167   "Nobody wishes": Barmak Nassirian, interview by Julie Zauzmer, November 22, 2011.

167   they sealed the indictment: *Commonwealth of Massachusetts v. Adam Wheeler*, Middlesex Superior Court, Indictment No. 2010-460, "Commonwealth's Motion To Seal Indictment."

168   He spent a week: *Commonwealth of Massachusetts v. Adam Wheeler*, Middlesex Superior Court, Indictment No. 2010-460, "Commonwealth's Motion To Unseal Indictment."

169   the maximum penalties: General Laws: Crimes, Punishments, and Proceedings in Criminal Cases: Crimes and Punishments, Commonwealth of Massachusetts, www.malegislature.gov/Laws/GeneralLaws/PartIV/TitleI.

169   "This defendant seriously": Cara O'Brien, press release, May 17, 2010.

169   on the golf course: Joe Resnek, interview by Xi Yu, August 18, 2011.

169   One was hanging out: Abel Acuña, interview by Xi Yu, August 30, 2011.

169   One was sitting: Interview with Adam Wheeler's former roommate by Xi Yu, July 8, 2011.

169   "My reaction": Interview with classmate of Adam Wheeler by Julie Zauzmer, September 22, 2011.

169–70   "No one in the room": Interview with Adam Wheeler's ex-girlfriend by Julie Zauzmer, January 16, 2012.

170   "When the news": Marcel E. Moran, "Why Honesty Matters to Us," *The Harvard Crimson*, May 27, 2010, www.thecrimson.com/article/2010/5/27/harvard-honesty-wheeler-story.

170   "On my FOP experience": Max Storto, interview by Julie Zauzmer, September 23, 2011.

175   At Kirkland House: Adam Wheeler's former roommate.

175   "Harvard sells": Jeff Dunn, "10 Reasons Adam Wheeler's Harvard Hoax Will Become A Movie," Edudemic, May 20, 2010,

http://edudemic.com/2010/05/10-reasons-adam-wheelers-harvard-hoax-will-become-a-movie.

Page

176   A pair of Harvard seniors: Jim McFadden, email to Xi Yu and Julie Zauzmer, October 27, 2011.

176   making T-shirts: H. Zane. B. Wruble, "Get an Adam Wheeler T-Shirt!" *The Harvard Crimson*, May 21, 2010, www.thecrimson .com/article/2010/5/21/wheeler-adam-free-mcfadden.

176   After one month: Xi Yu, "Adam Wheeler Released From Jail Upon Posting Bail," *The Harvard Crimson*, July 3, 2010, www.thecrimson.com/article/2010/7/3/ harvard-wheeler-fraudulent-plagiarized.

177   "Wheeler managed": Peter Gelzinis, "The Price of Making Fools of Harvard," *Boston Herald*, December 17, 2010, www .bostonherald.com/news/columnists/view.bg?articleid-1303772.

177   "improbable": Tracy Jan, "Harvard Missed Signs It Was Being Hoodwinked," *The Boston Globe*, December 28, 2010, www .boston.com/news/education/higher/articles/2010/12/28/ students_rsum_was_full_of_errors_unlikely_claims.

177   a Harvard history professor: Charles S. Maier, "'Only Connect': Changing Aspirations for General Education." In *Essays on General Education in Harvard College*, by Harvard University Faculty of Arts and Sciences, 86–88, 2004.

177   "Most people": David Hawkins, interview by Julie Zauzmer, November 9, 2011.

177   "A lot of what we've found": Jeff Lorton, interview by Julie Zauzmer, December 20, 2011.

178   "For all of its high visibility": Nassirian.

178   Stanford announced: Lauryn Williams, "Admissions Office Moves Forward with Random Audits," *The Stanford Daily*, October 18, 2010, www.stanforddaily.com/2010/10/18/ admission-office-moves-forward-with-random-audits.

178   up to the university's president: Tracy Jan, "Harvard Links ROTC Return to End of 'Don't Ask'," *The Boston Globe*, September 23, 2010, www.boston .com/news/education/higher/articles/2010/09/23/ harvard_links_rotc_return_to_end_of_dont_ask.

Page
Chapter Nine

179 He found a part-time job: Steven Sussman, interview by Julie Zauzmer and others, December 16, 2010.

179 Once, he went to meet: Maia Raber, interview by Julie Zauzmer, October 25, 2011.

179 It was in Somerville: Adam Wheeler, Middlesex Superior Court Disposition Information.

180 He went running: Raber; interview with Bowdoin English professor by Xi Yu and Julie Zauzmer, December 9, 2011.

180 He started seeing: Adam Wheeler, *Commonwealth of Massachusetts v. Adam Wheeler*, December 16, 2010.

187 His case made *Saturday Night Live*: Xi Yu, "*Saturday Night Live* Jokes About Wheeler, Harvard," *The Harvard Crimson*, December 19, 2010, www.thecrimson.com/article/2010/12/19/wheeler_snl_clip.

187 He got his job: Steven Sussman, *Commonwealth of Massachusetts v. Adam Wheeler*, November 9, 2011.

190 the doctor had also heard: Lee Wheeler, conversation with Julie Zauzmer, December 23, 2011.

192 "If it smells like a duck": Richard Wheeler, conversation with Julie Zauzmer, December 23, 2011.

Index

225